RETHINKING VILLAGES

About the Editors

Bhaskar Majumder is at present a Professor in Economics in G.B. Pant Social Science Institute, Allahabad. He got his education in Calcutta and taught in Calcutta for many years. He has published so far eight books, several research papers in journals of national and international repute, many articles in magazines and print media. He has completed several research projects on basic needs, environment, and governance supported by Planning Commission, Government of India, World Bank, and ICSSR, New Delhi. He was a Visiting Fellow in France, and is a Guest Faculty in BHU, Varanasi. He is a member of many professional bodies. In addition to academic research, he is also involved in movements for social change.

Badri Narayan Tiwari, poet, author and social scientist was born in Bhojpur, a village in Bihar, in 1965. He is a faculty member of Social History/Cultural Anthropology, in the Centre for Culture, Power and Change, at G.B. Pant Social Science Institute. He also heads the *Manav Vikas Sanghralaya* and the *Dalit Resource Centre,* at G.B. Pant Social Science Institute, Jhusi, Allahabad.

His two anthologies of poems, *Such suney kai din hue* and *Shabadpadiyam* are well known. Widely read by international and national audience, his poems have been translated into English, French, Dutch, Oriya, Bengali, Gujarati, Marathi and Urdu.

Narayan has been writing on several issues dealing with history, literature and social sciences, in Hindi and English. His poems and write-ups have been published in several literary magazines like *Hans, Alochana, Thadbhav, Kathadesh, Tatha,* etc.

He has recited poems at Leiden (2005), Amsterdam (2005), Cambridge University (2007), Sahitya Akademy, New Delhi, Bharat Bhawan, Bhopal, Madhya Pradesh Sahitya Parishad, Oriya Sahitya Parishad and many other literary organisations of Hindi, Bengali, Oriya, etc. in multilingual poetry meets. He also recited poems on TV channels.

Publications: *Lok Sanskriti mey Rashtravaad* (Research), *Sanskritik Gadya* (Essay), Documenting Dissent (English), Women Heroes and Dalit Assertion in North India, 2006 (English) and Fascinating Hindutva—Saffron Politics and Dalit Mobilisation, 2009 (English).

Literary Awards: He was awarded the Bharat Bhusan Agarwal Award (1991), Banarsi Prasad Bhojpuri Samman (2002) and Kedar Samman (2006).

Rethinking Villages

Edited by
Bhaskar Majumder
B.N. Tiwari

CONCEPT PUBLISHING COMPANY PVT. LTD.
NEW DELHI-110 059

ISBN-13: 978-81-8069-764-7

First Published 2011

Published and Printed by

Concept
Since 1974

Concept Publishing Company Pvt. Ltd.
Regd. Office:
A/15-16, Commercial Block, Mohan Garden
New Delhi-110059 (India)
Phones : 25351460, 25351794, *Fax* : 091-11-25357109
Email : publishing@conceptpub.com,
Website : www.conceptpub.com

Editorial Office:
H-13, Bali Nagar, New Delhi-110 015, India.

Cataloging in Publication Data--*Courtesy*: D.K. Agencies (P) Ltd. <docinfo@dkagencies.com>

Rethinking villages / edited by Bhaskar Majumder, B.N. Tiwari.
p. cm.
Includes bibliographical references and index.
ISBN 9788180697647

1. Villages--India--Uttar Pradesh--Congresses. 2. Rural development--India--Uttar Pradesh--Congresses. 3. Uttar Pradesh (India)--Rural conditions--Congresses. I. Majumder, Bhaskar. II. Nārāyana, Badrī.

DDC 307.141209542 22

Preface

The book 'Rethinking Villages' is an offshoot of a National Seminar on the theme organized by the G.B. Pant Social Science Institute, Allahabad in 2004. The basic purpose was to have an assembly of persons with interest in village studies. We are thankful to all those who took keen interest in the seminar and interacted purposefully to throw light on issues some of which remain bypassed in conventional literature.

Only a few of those who participated in the seminar coordinated by Bhaskar Majumder and B.N. Tiwari could ultimately manage time to send full paper for publication in the form as it stands now. Ramashray Roy had been kind enough to provide support in editing the book. His services deserve immense praise.

We are thankful to Ravi S. Srivastava who had interacted sharply in the Seminar. We are also thankful to the then Director of the Institute, R.C. Tripathi, the present Director Pradeep Bhargava and the faculty members of the Institute. The research scholars and other support staff deserve warm praise for providing unforgettable help for running the Seminar. The assistance in typing by J.K. Chaubey and computer related assistance by S. K. Jaiswal need special mention. The silent support of the present Director of the Institute, Pradeep Bhargava, deserves remarkable acknowledgement.

We strongly believe that the book as a collection of papers contributed by both experienced and young scholars from diversified fields will add to the existing knowledge based on village studies.

Allahabad
20.11.2009

Bhaskar Majumder
B.N. Tiwari

Contents

Preface 5

The Contributors 9

Introduction 11

1. **Importance of Village for Collective Action : A Critical Analysis of Natural Resources Development Programmes in India**
   —Amitabh Pandey 27

2. **Lineage, Clan and Caste as Units in Cooperative and Conflicting Situations**
   —Brij Raj Chauhan 40

3. **Changing Indian Agrarian Village Economy**
   —D.M. Diwakar 53

4. **Villages and Villagers of the Naugarh Region in Chandauli**
   —R.C. Mishra 81

5. **Mapping Cultures : Modernity, Homogenization and Change in Village Shahabpur**
   —B. N. Tiwari 98

6. **Baigapada : A Biography of an Indian Village**
   —Raj Kumar 118

7. **Living Conditions of People in Village Bhaganpur : Some Observations**
   —Bhaskar Majumder 148

8. **Selection of Villages for Understanding Social Sciences**
—*K.N. Bhatt* and *Bhaskar Majumder* 183

9. **Rethinking Village**
—*Ramashray Roy* 199

10. **Globalization and Linguistic Diversity**
—*Yogesh Atal* 231

11. **The Rural Scene**
—*Kripa Shankar* 252

Index 258

The Contributors

Amitabh Pandey is a member of Indian Institute of Forest Management, Bhopal.

B.N. Tiwari is a Reader in G.B. Pant Social Science Institute, Allahabad.

Bhaskar Majumder is Professor in G.B. Pant Social Science Institute, Allahabad.

Brij Raj Chauhan is a former Visiting Fellow at G.B. Pant Social Science Institute, Allahabad.

D.M. Diwakar is Professor of Economics at Giri Institute of Development Studies, Lucknow.

K.N. Bhatt is a Reader in G.B. Pant Social Science Institute, Allahabad.

Kripa Shankar is Honorary Fellow, G.B. Pant Social Science Institute, Allahabad.

Raj Kumar, teaches English at Khalsa College, Delhi.

R.C. Mishra, teaches Psychology in Banaras Hindu University, Varanasi.

Ramashray Roy is a former Visiting Fellow at G.B. Pant Social Science Institute, Allahabad.

Yogesh Atal is a former Principal Director of Social Sciences, UNESCO.

Introduction

The need for rethinking about the village arises because of the intrusion of several factors in recent times to shake, even disturb, the ongoing flow of life in the Indian villages. These factors are of recent origin and have their roots in a perspective entirely different from those that governed life and relations in the Indian villages. Their origin goes back to the seventeenth century when the world saw the rise of new world view that swept the world to rule unhindered if not unchallenged. The centre from which this world-view rose 'sphinx-like' was, of course, Western Europe which also constituted the core of the ecumene whose extension did not go much beyond Europe and its periphery.

It is this centre that radiated certain forceful influences that gradually changed both thought—ways and work—ways of the entire world as we know it today. Two of the influences need special mention since their role in transforming the people and their orientation all over the world has been crucial. The first of these influences is, of course, the radically changed idea of who man is? The other influence pertains to the what Robert Solomon refers as "Universal Ego" shaped by the understanding of the western man of his own civilization as the superior one. It is this understanding that is the genesis of what has come to be known as the "Whiteman's Burden." These twin influences are by no means genetically separate and different from one another; they are organically linked and derive their substance and strength from each other.

So far the first influence is concerned, what the emergent world-view did was to cut-off the idea of man from its grounding in divine entity. Earlier, the idea of man treated man as *homo religious* or *homo credence*. This meant, simply stated, that man was never before the advent of the modern age considered as self-complete and totally reliant on his own resources to do whatever he chose. He was considered to form an integral part of a larger order which included the divine, the human and the natural dimensions of the cosmos. The cosmos itself was treated as a closed one whose apex was occupied by the divine; it is this divine element that was considered the source both of order in the cosmos of human motivation and behaviour and regulatory principles of the phenomenal world.

The divine entity is not only the exemplar of order but also the source of order in the phenomenal world, it is then both transcendent, apart from that which it orders but also immanent in it as order; it is this that lies at the root of the distinction between Being and Becoming. It is this Being that in the course of its procession gets progressively transformed into Becoming. It is in this sense that it is meaningless to say that Being is prior to Becoming; what is more apt to say is that Being does not precede in time; it is eternally present in Becoming. Given this essential truth, what assumes importance is the man's understanding of the relationship between this phenomenal world and the world beyond, the world here and now, and the world unseen but real.

It is not necessary to stress that, materially speaking, the relationship between the phenomenal world and the world beyond is tantamount to visualizing the relationship that physically exists and that which does not physically exist. It is essentially because of this that the relationship between the phenomenal and the non-phenomenal is full of mystery and subject, therefore, to speculation. We gain understanding of this mystery through the primordial insight into the structure that sages and poets acquire. It is not, therefore, surprising that we encounter a plurality of accounts of the relationship between Being and Becoming, between one and the many.

It is these accounts that we know as cosmogony or what Plato calls "the likely story". Cosmogonies perform three vital functions: (a) they refer to certain essential features of the world we live in; (b) we are made aware of the manner we are related to this cosmos and the precise way in which we are an integral part of it; and (c) they underline the need for us to imitate the order prevailing in the cosmos and regulate our interior by it. Thus the cosmos we live in is fully ordered and man is an integral part of this cosmos. This cosmos is considered to be the perfect exemplar or order and at the same time, the cause of all order in particular that define the phenomenal world, which only in degrees can approximate the whole. It should, however, be pointed out, that the totality has no being except through the expression of these components, and the individual particulars have no being except by reason of their mutual relation both with the totality and with other parts that constitute the whole. It does not need any demonstration to suggest that it is this fitting together of different cosmic dements with each other as well as with the whole and of the cosmos with its creator that is the basis of harmony in the world. In this living, breathing and ordered cosmos, man, as an integral part of it, is related to God by virtue of his being the abode of the divine.

What is distinctive about this perspective that is rooted in traditional cultures, in general, and in the Indian tradition, in particular, is that it projects a cosmos that is characterized by God in heaven, man in the world, and the world both as the habitat and support structure for man. What is also distinctive about this perspective is that all these elements—divinity, humanity and the world—represent universal absolutes which are organically linked. It is this organicity of these absolutes as the constitutive principles of the cosmos that go into the making of a world-view, a way of life, which accords superiority to divinity and underlines the need to make the pursuit of material concerns subservient to the demands of the soul as the sensorium of the divine. It is against this background that we can appreciate the quaternarian division of *purushartha* into *kama* (desire), *artha* (resources), *dharma* (religion), and *moksha* (release from the cycle of rebirth) as well as the need of submitting the first two *purasharthas* to the suzerainty to the third, i.e. *dharma*.

It is not necessary that it is the only world-view that can be said to be possible or to have prevailed all over the world. Given the mystery shrouding the relationship between the seen and the unseen, between the phenomenal world and the world beyond, thing and no-thing, there can be and have been as many world-views as civilizational entities. Apart from the diversity of world-views, it is quite possible that even while different world-views recognize the centrality of the divinity in man's existence, the original primordial insight into the structure of order might get, over time, dimmed; the spiritual dimension in man's existence may got diluted and be reduced to lifeless performance of rites and rituals without contributing anything to what the *Rigveda* calls *atmayajna*. Once the primordial insight into the structure of order, the world-view based on it, and the pattern of man's existence imprinted by this insight enter the stream of history, they tend to be corrupted and ultimately changed beyond recognition.

It is also quite possible that a world-view denies completely the notion of divine and projects a world that revolves around the material concerns of human existence. The emergence of such an understanding marks the beginning of what we know as the modern era. The coming of the modern era sounds the death-knell of the transcendent ground of reality that provided the foundation of traditional cultures. This results in the de-divinization of the world and absolutization of the mundane, that is everydayness of man's life in the phenomenal world. As a consequence, reality is conceived in a way that locates mankind at its centre. It also means that the empowerment of mankind to create the order of reality in its own image. At the core of the modern project is, therefore, an attempt to create an image of reality that is capable of sustaining the possibility that mankind itself becomes the source of meaning and order. The modern project makes the natural man the central hero who, completely cut-off from divine ground of reality, makes the quest of felicity (in the Hobbesian sense) his central concern and it is expected that the search for felicity by separate and autonomous individuals would cater to the greatest good of the largest number. What must also be added here is that the organization of society must be such that it supports and subserves the individual need of fulfilling his ordinary life needs involved with the acquisition of wealth, power and prestige.

The purpose of delineating these two distinct paradigms of world-views is not simply heuristic. They are the paradigms which, with their variations, have had pragmatic expression in history. What is important to note here is that the traditional paradigm of the world-view did provide the basis in one way or another of organizing pragmatic affairs of man till the end of the Middle Ages. It was only in the seventeenth century that the traditional world-view with its variants was replaced by the modern world-view which constitutes the dominant, if not the exclusive, basis for deriving the essential impulse for organizing and ordering human existence. With the coming of the modern age, then, divinity has been banished to the remote corner of consciousness and, with this, man emerges as an autonomous entity, who cuts off from all divine connection legislates for himself the term on which his existences must be organized, his life must be lived, and his life activities must be organized and conducted.

The ramifications of this changed perspective on man and his world for the organized existence of man in a community of men are several. In the first place, this change installed the natural man at the centre of the Universe and made him the master of objects on the surface of the earth, under it and over it. As the master of the world, he turns his back to any superior authority, especially divine, and engages in the pursuit of concerns involved with production and reproduction. In essence, then, he turns spiritually blind. In the second place, as a natural man, his passions, his appetites assume a very high significance; consequently, man turns primarily into a desiring being. As a desiring being, he turns into a self-defining subject who finds his purposes in his own nature and uses the external world, both society and nature, as potential means of realizing his purposes. In the third place, to be able to realize self-defined purposes, the natural man must create a social order which not only accords legitimacy to his life purposes but also evolves principles, institutions, and practices that support and facilitate the realization of his purposes.

In the fourth place, the socio-political system that comes into being for enabling man to realize his self-defined purposes, drains society of its significance as an entity that bears the responsibility of transforming the natural man into a social, even a spiritual being, who leads his life according to an ideal vision of life. Drained of its significance, society now turns into a mechanical aggregate of self-defining subjects. In its redefined role, society is reduced to an arena where different individuals and diverse socio-economic interests pursue their private life concerns. In effect, then society turns out to be a vast theatre where different players, endowed with different capacities, resources, and talent, engage usually peacefully, sometimes even violently, in establishing greater control over what McIntyre calls "the goods of effectiveness." As an arena without any significance of its own, society provides the space in which men and groups co-operate and compete with each other for access to and control over societal resources; it loses its capacity as well as authority to integrate these diverse elements into civic unity and wholeness, a wholeness Plato yearned for and dwelt upon it in his *Republic* or one that the *Rigveda* calls "*Sarvata*".

Given the primacy of the need to realize self-defined purposes as the key to what Vico, Hegel and Marx call the process of the self-making of man. This process centres on felicity that signifies not the quest of happiness that spiritual life brings, but pleasure that one gets from satisfying the conditions necessary for ensuring the fulfilment of ordinary life needs involved with production and reproduction. But pleasure is something that cannot be shared with others; only the means which make pleasure possible can be shared. Such means are scarce but access to them is *sine qua non* for ensuring pleasure. This makes competition, even violent competition, among individuals and groups for access to and control over societal resources very intense and pervasive. The need to gain and retain privileged access to societal resources propels men and groups to mobilize power resources through both augmentation of material resources and combinations and alliances based on patronage, negotiated compromises, etc. It is in this process of what Duv Ronen characterizes as the transformation of "I" into "we" against "they" occurs and the politicization of socio-cultural referents of identity formation assumes a serious scale. The traditional socio-cultural referents of identity-formation, which, of course, referred to certain non-political markers of social differentiation now become the markers of political division and the bases of political mobilization essentially for getting access to material resources of society.

It is this politicization of the traditional socio-cultural referents to identify formation that symbolizes the transformation of politics from yielding constitutive principles of society as Plato envisaged into a process of reciprocal resistance focusing on resolving the question of who gets what, when, and how, as Lasswell explicates. As already indicated, politics as a process of reciprocal resistance makes it necessary for aspiring individuals and groups to reinforce and, strengthen their power base in whatever manner possible. In this process, competing groups formed always remain fragile since all such compromises and alliances are temporary, tenuous and shifting insofar as change in the vantage point from which a person perceives his socio-political environment brings in a commensurate change in alliance formation. The overall impact of this is that entirely a different principle of organizing diversity comes into operation in the modern times. Diversity of people, of language, of religion etc. that Prithiwi Sukta of the Atharva Veda speaks of has characterized all complex societies once their size passes a particular limit. However, principle of organizing diversity in traditional society underlined a two-way linkage between the whole and the parts. If the parts were linked with the apex of the system, they were also linked with each other, in contradistinction to this, the principle of organizing diversity in modern times depends on the apex to link and keep them linked in some semblance of unity and cohesion. Since parts are not linked with each other and since there is no such apex that is expressed in each of the parts, an apex has to be artificially created which then functions as the symbol of the unity in diversity.

The two paradigms of how man's world is or should be organized represent two polar ideas about man and his world. The traditional paradigm that governed man's existence and his life activities did, in fact, exist and persisted till the end of the Middle Ages. However, it was replaced in the seventeenth century by the modern world-view which still shows no sign of abetting despite challenges to it. As a matter of fact, industrialism has given it a new lease of life and its centre has decisively shifted to the United States of America; it is from here that vital impulses of thought-ways and work-ways are transmitted all over the world, although Europe still retains the privilege of the propounder as well as the votary of the modern world-view. What is remarkable about this world-view and its capacious vessel, i.e. industrialism, is its capacity to provide a unity to such diverse civilizations as the Chinese, the Indian, etc. It has a spiritual unity insofar as the perspective which wields various civilizations together into one universal society makes then patterns in one set of problems, consists of forms of intellectual behaviour and technique that have their centre in Europe and America and, thus, are at home in the West.

The entire world outside the West is experiencing the second wave of westernization and is being re-westernized insofar as the western standard of living, developed first in the United States, has become the paradigm, the example, for all other parts of the world. All wish to live under such pleasant national conditions as the Americans have—an understandable material desire that can be realized if industrial society is introduced and institutionalized. The first wave of westernization had entirely a different objective; it represented an intent to find suitable space to accommodate the countries of Europe which, released from the shackles of Christian world-view, mobilized their intellectual, economic, and political resources to begin the process of what Polanyi calls "the great transformation", signifying a radical transformation of economic life and relations. Their expansion began with a three pronged objective. These three components of their objective were: colonization for obtaining raw materials for their burgeoning industries and reliable markets for the finished industrial goods, finding converts to Christianity, and teaching the colonized mankind the art of civil administration and instilling in them civic virtue. At the root of all these factors were three basic orientations which defined the western mankind's interaction with the non-western mankind. In the first place, there was a feeling of superiority of the western mankind as compared to that portion of the mankind, which had the misfortune of inhabiting colonized parts of the globe. Since the former had come to be equipped with numerous gadgets, it was felt that those with gadgets had the right to rule over those without gadgets.

In the second place, the western mankind had also come to believe that it was its responsibility as the bearer of a superior civilization to uplift the primitives from their lowly social, cultural and economic conditions to a level, where they could enjoy some degree of cultural elevation, economic betterment and civic polish. This is a continuance in time of the apprehension of the ancient Greeks of being surrounded by a sea of barbarism, which would devour their superior civilization if not suitably transformed either by conquest or by acculturation. The colonial rulers too had harboured this apprehension and in early twentieth century Captain Alfred Mahan also gave expression to it in respect of American civilization. In the last place, the sea of barbarism had to be transformed or tamed in order for the western civilization to survive and rule. This transformation had to be wrought by allowing a free play to what Robert Salomon calls "Universal Ego" or "Universal Pretense", articulated strongly both by Rousseau and Kant. Universal Ego suggests that there is only one way of teaching the barbarians the civilized way of living developed in the West. The non-western people must be converted into one religion, that is Christianity, one way of looking at the world, that is, literalism, and one of governance, that is liberal democracy.

It is these features of the first wave of westernization that affected the socio-political destiny of the countries of the non-western world. The first phase is characterized by political subjugation which provided the means and opportunity of both economic exploitation and cultural transformation. The potent and fateful combination of political, economic and cultural ingredients in the potion of westernization—patented in the name of White Man's Burden—went a long way in introducing far-going changes in the thought-ways and work-ways in a large part of the non-western world. This change affected first the English eduated elite and later, as the colonial era in world history came to its close after the Second World War, the large mass of the common man. After the World War II, comes the second wave of westernization, which differs subtly in many respects from the first wave. The end of colonization put paid to political subjugation but not political dependence; it also saw the emergence of economic factor as the most attractive and effective way of deepening the impact of westernization; and with the shifting of the centre of transmitting western way of life to the United States, the impact of what Eric Voegelin calls a new "world revolution" has deepened and became more pervasive.

It is a revolution that has the goal of bringing the entire world up to a level of civilization—in the material sense of the word—comparable to that found in the West. It seems to be a worldwide movement that cannot be stopped, at least in the foreseeable future, and in which the various civilizational societies intend to maintain their independence and their organization. Other civilizational entities—the Indian, Chinese, Islamic, African and Latin American peoples—want to organize themselves into industrial societies that will make possible for them a standard of living similar to that enjoyed by the United States and Western Europe today. This is tantamount, as Mahatma Gandhi would unhesitatingly say, to selling one's soul for seven days of existence.

India too has been not unaffected by these two subtly different waves of westernization. The presence of the Englishman on its soil for almost two centuries, the first to trade and to grab territories and the second to rule, initiated and consolidated the process of westernization. It is a process that did not cease to operate even after the Englishman left Indian shores in 1947. As a matter of fact, this process has dug its roots deeper helped in this by the concerted effort by the Indian State to transform the country socially, economically and politically. Indians even in remote villages, are increasingly becoming what Mahatma Gandhi would call English without becoming Englishman. The essential instruments of this process have been certain inversions through which the British rulers sought to change Indian consciousness and re-form economic and political institutional arrangement in Indian society. The first of these inversions had the effect of gradually transforming the individual in India from his spiritual orientation to economic motivation. This is a transformation that gradually and, to a large extent, transformed the *homo religiosus* or *homo credens* to *homo economicus*.

The second important inversion aimed at shifting the basis of integration of diverse socio-economic interests into one cohesive whole from society to politics. Earlier, Rabindranath Tagore had emphasized that if the Hindus had not achieved a Universal Empire, it was because they were more concerned to establish a Universal Society pervaded by universally acknowledged religious values and ethos. It was society, then, that provided the framework within which different socio-economic interests and groupings could be woven into a bond of unity. With the coming of the British rule this basis shifted to politico-administrative mechanism as the instrument of forging unity in diversity. Committed as Sir Percival Spear was to the view that it is politics that provided the basis and framework of unity, he could only see that diversity in India has existed from time immemorial, whereas the unity is of recent growth and still takes observers by surprise. The last inversion that must be taken note of pertains to the replacement of *dharma* and convention by law. It is these three inversions that joined together to initiate a process of change in Indian psyche as well as in Indian socio-cultural universe.

This change has now also invaded villages and has successfully broken their isolation from national and international forces making for homogenization. People in the villages have become more receptive to modern thought-ways and work-ways. The image of village republics has effectively been erased and the people in villages are as willing and impatient to take part in the competition of gaining control over goods of effectiveness as their counterparts are in urban areas and urbanized societies. The village as an organized entity has lost its cohesion with the result that all structures of inter-dependence and co-operation are in tatters. The village itself is increasingly emerging as a conflict system where consensus about community affairs becomes the victim of privilege, status, and interest. Co-operation and conflict do occur but their parameters have changed to accommodate interest and power. In short, the Indian village is caught in the whirlpool of change whose substance as well as direction can still not be clearly visualized.

The invasion of change on the long standing isolation and placidity of the Indian villages makes it necessary to have a close look on how villages in India are faring under the pressure of change. It is this necessity that has provided the stimulus for exposing the village as it copes up with the phenomenon of change for a better understanding of what it is becoming and in which direction it is moving. It has never been the belief that this scrutiny will yield a definitive picture of the impact of the process of change on the village. This picture will ever evade as long as the village remains caught up in the process of change. As Hegel emphasizes, Minerva's owl flies at dusk. This signifies that our understanding of any social phenomenon cannot be conclusive as long as it is in process of growth; as such, theory must play the role of witness to history. Be as it may, we may not definitively know where the owl will deposit itself for repose; however, we can, at least, identify some of the markers of the path of the owls' flight and determine the direction of its flight. *Rethinking Village* is simply an attempt to catch even a fleeting glimpse of an entity which is inexorably caught in the process of fast change, like a piece of wood floating in the fast-flowing stream.

Initiating the process of rethinking, Amitabh Pandey refers in "Importance of Village for Collective Action : A Critical Analysis of Natural Resource Development Programmes in India", to the paradigm shift that affects the management and conservation of natural resources in the background of the steps taken towards decentralization. Decentralization makes the community, i.e. the village, the focus of decision-making in this regard. It is, he suggests, therefore, necessary to understand two things: (a) the type and nature of villages that exist in India; and (b) the theory of collective action as a prerequisite of collective action at the village level. Pandey concludes with the observation that there must obtain a suitable match between the type of village and its needs, resource endowment and development plan. With "Lineage, clan and caste as units in co-operative and conflicting situation" by Brij Raj Chauhan, "the process of rethinking focuses upon the importance of social structure for both co-operative and conflicting interactions in the village as a sociological entity. The point of departure for Chauhan is the collectivity with its connection to the individual placed in a multiplex role structure. The link between the individual and the collectivity assumes importance both for the individual and different official and non-official functionaries insofar as the realization of individual purposes and the performance of bureaucratic functions are concerned. In-between the individual and the official stands the middleman who links the two and contributes to either solution of problems or their aggravation. Chauhan explores this nexus of linkages and points out their relevance for both sacred and secular functions.

D.M. Diwakar in his "Changing Indian Agrarian Village Economy", argues that for understanding the process and impact of change in the context of the village, it is necessary to identify and evaluate the process of development consequent upon changes in the form, contexts, and operative mechanism of base and the superstructure along with changing productive forces, which start transforming themselves within existing productive organizations. This mode of analysis of the ongoing process of change in the village must focus on agrarian relations and identify the causative factors impinging on the process of change. Diwakar analyses the usefulness of this mode of analysis by focusing on the historical experience of change in U.P.

The theme that R.C. Mishra pursues in "Villages and Villagers of the Naugarh Region in Chandauli (U.P.)" concerns the process of acculturation as the surrogate of change. With the help of two time-studies at an interval of ten years, Mishra probes into the psychological changes induced by the process of development. Focusing on Kherwar villages in Chandauli district of U.P., Mishra analyses how these changes have affected the psychological life of the people in those villages during the span of a decade.

The impingement of the process of modernization on the village community in Shahabpur, a village in central U.P., is the subject of analysis for B.N. Tiwari. In his "Mapping Cultures : Modernity, Homogenization and change in village Shahabpur", he focuses on changes, mostly visible in respect of dress, ornaments, festivals, etc., he argues that the observed changes intimate the deeper impact of modernization on village life. He concludes that a strong homogenization and death of varieties in the cultural life of the people happen to be a dominant trend.

With Raj Kumar, "Baigapada : A Biography of an Indian Village", the discussion moves into a village, Baigapada, in Kalahandi district of Orissa. Although located in a backward region, the village has not been untouched by the wind of change most noticeable in the relationship between the upper castes and lower castes. The forty-year history of Baigapada after Independence has seen, as Raj Kumar notes, both desirable and undesirable changes which have upset the power relationship, on the one hand, and promoted corruption, on the other. Bhaskar Majumder looks at the village from entirely a different perspective, that is, whether or not the developments taking place since Independence have facilitated the fulfilment of basic needs of the people. Majumder looks at the pattern of ownership of residential and agricultural land and the availability of physical and social infrastructure, two components that have great importance for the central question of the fulfilment of basic needs of the people in Bhaganpur village located in eastern U.P.

Ramashray Roy raises the question of appropriate theoretical perspective to be employed in the case of the village caught in the maelstrom of change whose direction is dim and distant at best. B.N. Tiwari in his paper aims to present cultural data on the eroding multiplicity and emerging homogeneity in the lives of the people of a village, and also record the history of the changes that have appeared in the culture of the village over time. The study was carried out in village Shahabpur in Phaphamau district near Allahabad. Bhaskar Majumder's paper deals with the living condition of people settled in a particular village in Uttar Pradesh. The village is located in the block of Karchhana in the district of Allahabad in Uttar Pradesh. The village is Bhaganpur. The joint paper prepared by K.N. Bhatt and Bhaskar Majumder focuses on the selection of villages for understanding social sciences. They pose the question, 'How can we reach the sections of society that are the most deprived from the changes taking place all around'? Of the various options available, one could be to define certain geographical regions as small units on which such experiments could be conducted. A village serves this purpose as a unit for developmental interventions. Yogesh Atal in his paper opines that Modernity did not kill all the traditions; societies developed a veritable symbiosis of tradition and modernity. Yogesh Atal shows what happens when a society, such as India, is simultaneously experiencing the twin processes of globalization and indigenization. The emerging profile is a changed profile and the twin processes of attrition and accretion are causing change. The interesting part is that change is now recognized as a universal phenomenon, and certain kinds of change brought about by rapid advances in technology, particularly in IT, are simultaneously affecting all societies. The crises created by these changes are making all societies cautious of the danger of degeneration of their cultures, and all are exhibiting concerns to prevent the ill effects of growing consumerism and decline on the intellectual front. Kripa Shankar comments that developmental process has not led to any significant diversification of the economy. No less important is the issue of popular participation, control, transparency and accountability of what is being spent. There are vast leakages as the colonial bureaucracy has absolute power over execution with absolutely no popular control, transparency and accountability.

1

Importance of Village for Collective Action : A Critical Analysis of Natural Resource Development Programmes in India

AMITABH PANDEY

Introduction

In natural resource management, the understanding of village plays a vital role, which is the arena of all the human activities. These activities could range from economic, social and cultural to resource management. In the decade of nineties there was shift in development approach; which can be called bottom-up approach, emphasised planning up and implementation from micro level, i.e. the village. Similarly, all the livelihood related rural development programmes and resource management schemes made, the village the basic unit for programme implementation. The mode of application of development was through institutionalisation process and empowerment. The theory of collective action was made the basis of inducing people to co-operate in the management of natural resources like forest, water, grazing land, etc.

The understanding of village projected in such programmes is very fuzzy. Village, in this understanding, is considered to be a homogeneous unit with nucleated and compact settlement. The social unit of village, i.e. community, is supposed to be cohesive and altruistic in nature. However, in reality the situation prevalent in Indian villages is very different; Indian villages evince diverse characteristics. In the changing context, Indian villages are much more influenced by the market, the press of modernity and the extension of mass media. Therefore, it needs to be understood in a dynamic situation. The insight yielded by such an understanding must, then, influence the framing and implementation of the development programme. This paper critically examines the Indian village in the present context in spatial and temporal extensions. It also discusses the theory of collective action in relation to village settlement and its development.

Village and its Typology

Indian villages can be classified into four prominent types on the basis of settlement and natural resource. They can also be classified in three types on the basis of administrative classification. The village is the smallest composite and self-sustained unit of social, cultural, economic and administrative organization in rural areas of a country. It has clear-cut physical boundary markers demarcated by natural objects like tree, river, stream or hill etc. and a particular type of social composition of the community. A village comprises of resources like land (private agriculture land, common land), water (pond, well, irrigation system, both traditional and/or modern), grassland and forest (community owned or government-owned). Apart from endowment of natural resources, the village also constitutes a unit; as a social unit, it is endowed with population either tribal or differentiated on the basis of caste. In addition, the village also represents a cultural system.

According to the Census definition, a village represents a parcel of land, the boundaries of which are defined and settled by revenue survey. It may, but need not always necessarily be, a single house cluster marking its distinctiveness as a residential locality. The villages of India from the point of view of administrative classification are categorised into three types.

These are: (a) Revenue village, (b) Forest village, and (c) Panchayat village.

Revenue villages are those villages which are under the jurisdiction of revenue department; it is the revenue department that carries out all the administrative and development work in such villages. The Patwari is the government official at the local level who looks after the management of a revenue village. There is a village level worker in the village who works on behalf of the revenue department in the village.

The revenue village need not be a single agglomeration of habitations. However, the revenue village has a definite boundary fixed by survey and each village is a separate administrative unit with separate village accounts. It may have one or more hamlets. The entire revenue village is, however, one unit. Revenue village is referred to in common parlance as representing a parcel of land whose boundaries are settled and defined for revenue purposes. Village with no population is termed as deserted or uninhabited.

Forest villages are those villages, which are under the jurisdiction of Forest department; it is the forest department that carries out all the administrations and development work in such a village. Forest villages were set up during the British regime to supply the labour needs of the forest areas. Villagers were given a small patch of forestland to do agriculture for meeting their livelihood requirements. There are approximately 5,000 forest villages presently in India. The existing forest villages, which are not part of an existing village panchayat, are treated as a village panchayat.

Panchayat village is the entity where the primary unit at the local level of the Panchayti Raj Institutions (PRI) becomes operational in India. A village or a group of villages with a population not less than 500 is declared as a Panchayat village. Every Panchayat village has a Gram Panchayat duly notified by the Government. The Government can however, relax the condition pertaining to the required minimum population if it so wishes. However, the reason(s) for introducing change in the condition must be duly recorded in writing.

Forms of Village on the Basis of Settlement Pattern

There are about four forms of villages usually found in India classified on the basis of settlement set up. They are : (a) Nucleated village, (b) Clustered village, (c) Linear village, and (d) Isolated homestead village (Desai 1978).

Nucleated village or single settlement village is that in which the community shares a common and compact settlement site. The nucleated village has a central settlement as the nucleus around which there are a number of smaller satellite settlements. Its houses, located in close proximity in the settlement area and habitation, are clearly defined from surrounding cultivated fields. These villages are found to exist in river basin plains and high plateaus of Deccan.

While habitation areas are well marked, in such villages, the boundaries of the village together with its fields are never clearly demarcated. Fields owned by one village merge into those owned by another except where a hillock or a stream or a highway forms the boundary. The utilization of productive land in river basin is one of the reasons for nucleated form of the settlement.

These villages are spread out and a number of clusters form on the basis of kin groups. The houses are situated in their own fields in clusters of two or three huts all belonging to a close single kinship group. They are either the huts of a father and grown-up sons or brothers and their wives. The next cluster of huts may be a furlong or two away depending on how big the holding of each cluster is. Such villages are found in hilly areas and plains.

The second factor in the formation of a cluster settlement pertains to occupation. This type of cluster bespeaks of the requirement of the community for more space that permits social exclusion or separation of the community from the main settlement. For example, the pastoral community or service caste community, like *Kumhar* (Potter), needs more space for its activities. Such communities, therefore, live in a separate cluster from the main settlement. Settlement of communities like *Mushar* is usually located in clusters that is far removed from the main settlement due to social separation or exclusion by other communities. The village boundaries are many a time not demarcated by streams or hillocks because the houses belonging to one village are situated on different locations.

These villages may be of two types: (i) massive cluster or (ii) dispersed type. Dispersed type is so-called because dispersed settlements are in far-off areas due to ecological reasons. In Himalayan zones habitations and mountain regions of other parts of India, dispersed settlement are commonly found. The boundaries of the village are difficult to mark out due to extensive dispersal of settlements. Sometimes, a village may be an assemblage of more than ten dispersed settlements on different hilltops of comparatively small size. Such villages are mainly formed for the protection of agricultural crops against raids of wild animals and raiding tribes (for example in Northeast states). Another reason that prompts the formation of such villages is the paucity of water resources.

Such villages are usually settled length-wise on the two sides of a road. These are mostly found in coastal areas of the country. The houses stand in their own compounds with their fruit and coconut gardens and are fenced on all sides. Usually numerous streams that ultimately join the sea and natural obstacles separate one village from the other. Where these streams are absent, one village merges into another and it is difficult to distinguish them. Such villages exploit land resources in two ways: horticulture and agriculture. The orchards of coconuts, areca nuts, plantain, jack fruits and cashew nuts are planted near the house and fenced, while some rice fields may lie a little distance away from the houses. In contrast, these two types of settlements are homestead villages. These villages are formed of isolated homesteads located near agricultural fields and new houses belonging to a family are built away from the original house. The village is dispersed and spread out in a large area. Such villages are found to exist in Satpura ranges and semi-arid region of north-west India.

Village Classification on the Basis of Society

In the anthropological literature two types of villages are mentioned on the basis of society found in existence. They are rural village and tribal village. Rural villages comprise mostly caste groups living in them. They have their own social structure and set up. However, the tribal village differs from the Rural village in that it is located in the ecological setting of forest and hills. Such villages are marked with tribal economy, display culture-bound features, and are associated institution of secular and religious heads of the village, as well as traditional Panchayat, etc. (Vidyarthi and Rai, 1978). The settlement pattern of tribal villages in India is distinct and is mostly of one type; it is best described as i.e., hamlets with a few exceptions of other, a rather general type, i.e., compact. The hamleted village is usually scattered over a large area sometimes covering even 25 sq.km. Sometimes, the distance between these hamlets may be three to five kilometres. Generally, the satellite settlements are scattered over the fields or forests or hills of the village. This type of village can usually be found in almost all parts of tribal India, especially in middle and southern India (Vidyarthi and Rai, 1978).

Theory of Collective Action

Collective action is action directed towards the achievement of a common purpose that cannot be obtained by acting individually. Underlying the debate about collective actions are particular views of the ways in which communities interact, the role of the individual within the community and the nature of institutions. Blaikie (1997) has pointed out that 'It is said that economists see nothing but choice, whereas sociologists see no possible role for choice'. Economists typically consider human action as decision-making under constraints, whilst sociologists quite often see action as constrained by structure.

The debate about collective action in the management of common property resources is based on the work of Hardin (1968), 'Tragedy of the commons', with its assumptions on free riding; he is driven on to argue that communities cannot regulate resource use. Individuals are believed to operate on the principle of rational choice and institutions are viewed as 'working rules' that are the base-line of an organisation which is expected to reduce transaction costs. These assumptions have been challenged from a number of perspectives. Bromley (1991) noted that, 'The real tragedy of the commons is the process by which indigenous property rights structures have been undermined and delegitimised'. Efficiency argument suggests that provided that rules and regulations for monitoring and enforcement exist, common property regimes are efficient because they allow for economics of scale and access and control of ecologically sensitive management. Access to the commons, whether open access or common property, is especially crucial for members as it is the only resource that is 'unmediated by dependency relationships and provides a safety net.'

Oakerson (1986) in his model for collective action gives importance to physical and technical attributes of physical resources. He lays emphasis on gaining a clear understanding of the physical and technical nature of common resource. Along with decision-making arrangement (organisation and rules) that govern relationships among users, the pattern of interaction among decision-makers also shapes the outcomes or consequences. According to him, for an effective and efficient management of common property resources, all the four attributes have to be fulfilled and optimally achieved.

Ostrom (1990) in her design incorporates certain principles that especially give emphasis to physical and social boundary of the common resource. According to her, common assembly as a general rule is one that creates a constitution, defines, modifies and enforces hierarchically layered sets of rules; appoints officers, monitors resource sustainability, collects and disburses money for improvements, adjusts the allocation of benefits, defends the resources from encroachment and theft and deals with external agencies on behalf of its members. If above rules are efficiently, and effectively implemented, institutions will function vibrantly. The component of collective action like social capital, the type of village settlement and composition of village affect reciprocity, trust and solidarity etc. The theories of collective action give importance on the physical and social nature of user groups or community.

Collective Action and Village

Collective action emphasizes the centrality of incentives to individual decision-makers to make co-operation attractive. The perceived benefits from co-operation are usually communal on clearly defined grounds pertaining to resources and rights that are socially recognized and which can be monitored. It has been suggested that collective action is most likely if the resource and the user group are small. Common property regimes are promoted as an institutional answer to forest management for reasons of efficiency, equity and welfare. The element of physical unit is an important element dealt in theory of collective action. The physical unit is generally embedded in the village system. The social unit of the village designs the management system of these physical resources. The types of village highlighted above have different designs of collective action depending on the type of village and nature of social composition.

Natural Resource Management in India

For development of rural society and natural resources, the Government of India implements a number of natural resource management schemes. These are Joint Forest Management (JFM), Eco-development Programme, National Afforestation Programme in Forest areas, Wasteland Development and Watershed Management Programme in watershed zones, participatory irrigation management for irrigation management system, drinking and water supply programme at village level.

In the decade of 1990, all these programmes were implemented in participatory mode. This means collaborative interaction between government and community at micro level.

Guidelines were prepared for each programme that delineated the process of interaction, in the context of the village considered as the micro unit of implementation and participation.

Misunderstanding of Village and Community (Social Unit) in Natural Resources Management

Geographical location in relation to resource is a major determinant of preferences in management and these may be difficult to reconcile with those of a differently located user group, even when both have the same property rights and are related through ties of kinship. In fact, the attempt to simplify the relation to natural resources by using the concept of User Groups only served to add further questions concerning the matter that should be at the centre of policies for decentralised natural resource management. In the Indian context, this complexity is due to ambiguous understanding of village; this can be seen in the criteria set up for development of common user group in development process for natural resources management.

The criteria for selection of village for implementation of JFM activities differ from state to state. In Andhra Pradesh, JFM is constituted out of the hamlets/village/clusters of villages in which all the adults of the hamlets/village/clusters of villages can participate. In Madhya Pradesh village forest committee is formed of residents of village/group of villages within the Panchayat area adjoining degraded forest area. In Arunachal Pradesh the committee is constituted of one adult member from each family of all the villages located within or adjacent to the selected JFM area.

Bihar State has a provision of holding a General Body Meeting in the selected village or group of villages in which all adult residents may participate. In Himachal Pradesh, area selection criteria is that there shall be only one Village Forest Development Committee (VFDC) in each tikka/village. In Karnataka, Village Forest Committee is formed of persons belonging to village or selected group of villages and interested in Forest Development and Conservation. In Rajasthan, all residents of the revenue village adjacent to the forestland made available to the society/institution for development/ conservation, could be included, if it is so desired, in the society. In Orissa, all adults living in the selected village constitute of a Vana Samrakshana Samiti (VSS) of the village by the Gram Panchayat. It has a Samiti for a group of hamlets or villages if these are all located adjacent to the forest area to be regenerated.

Similarly, in Watershed Development programmes, all members of the village whose land is situated in the watershed area constitute the User Group (UG) and all those members who derive sustenance from the watershed area are characterized as Self-Help Group (SHG). At the micro-watershed (villages) level, Watershed Committees (WCs) are constituted; they have elected members and presidents and have the sanction of the village (Gram Sabha).

The community as a concept is marked with complexity, and heterogeneity. Constant transformation in it makes it difficult to define it but its centrality to everyday life makes it difficult to dismiss it. Insofar as discussions about natural resources are concerned, the community has a physical anchor against which it can be defined. However, this relation has not, led in practice to any clarification about the name of the community. The connotation of community in the context of the debate over decentralized natural resource management is insignificant. Territorially bound units are those villages in which people have repeated face-to-face interactions. Some observers consider that communities are, in general, harmonious with internal mechanisms for fairly equitable conflict resolution; others place more emphasis on heterogeneity and conflict within the community.

Agarwal (1999) makes a useful distinction between two different meanings attributed to the community in natural resource management. 'Community as shared understanding' is an organic unit, in which members have common ties, interests and beliefs, and thereby there exists a propensity to act collectively; it is this propensity that dispels alienation. 'Community as social organization' refers to a different set of attributes; a common and stable territorial location with stable membership and regular interaction over a range of issues. Agarwal argues that these concepts have become linked because of the implicit belief that by participating in the community as social organization, members can gain a new understanding of their collective interests. It will, as a result, align divergent interests, beliefs and identities based on caste, class, gender and religion. He points out that development interventions can only hope to influence the second concept of community by setting up regular meetings, rules for interaction etc.

Communities are far from homogenous. While they are usually conflict ridden, they are also comprised of individuals who themselves are caught up in overlapping circles of relationships. These may be external linkages for work, electoral politics that provide regional alliances, the impact of targeted programmes or relations based on caste, marital and religious circles, etc. In fact, these links can serve to break oppressive place-based relationships and build new forms of social capital.

Community is conceived of as settled but excluding migrants, pastoralists and shifting cultivators and any links that settled villagers have to these categories. The term 'user group' or stakeholders is often employed to simplify the definition of these relations and enable programme implementation. In contrast to the assumptions made about the community, the term stakeholder implies a 'society made up of free floating actors, each with different interests which they pursue by bargaining with each other in international space.' This tends to lose sight of the appreciation that various actors are already part of a system in which there are uneven bargaining powers. Allowing the community to define itself will probably mean that the definition of the more powerful will prevail.

Need to Define Village in Rural Development

Seen from the above complexities of village and its understanding in the natural resource management, village social unit plays a vital role in collective action and outcome of the collaborative activities. However, as mentioned above, in natural resource management programmes implemented in India, there is lack of clarity about the entity, village. Different states have set up different criteria. Secondly, the implementing agencies lack understanding of the village. This creates confusion in the constitution of common groups. Mostly, common user groups are constituted on the basis of interaction pattern evident at ground level with the resources. However, at village system level, the understanding of the resources in different, social organisation is done accordingly. This can be clearly understood with the help of the distinction between institutions of sacred and non-sacred bio-resources at village level. For example, sacred groves of tribal villages have an exclusive person in the form of village priest to manage it. Similarly, to manage water distribution from the tank irrigation systems, a separate individual is appointed on hereditary pattern. If the crafted institution is more in tune with rational choice theory, the village system is also governed by the cultural patterns of the village. The village identity and solidarity are more important as they are based on reciprocity and trust founded in the process of a long term interaction.

The need of the time is cultural understanding of village in different geo-spatial and cultural set-up and then plan for crafting an institutional structure. Secondly, for co-management equity in resources utilization plays an important role. In case of village dispersed over a large area equity factor becomes difficult to implement. Take, for example, the tribal village in Bastar region Malakot, which is spread over a distance of 11 km. and has 11 hamlets. To constitute a management committee in such a village does not fulfil the clear criteria of social boundary. Therefore, the creation of social and physical unit needs to be based on the congruity criterion if objective collective action is to be met.

Conclusion

Village is an important component when communities undertake management for effective and efficient conservation and utilization of natural resources. In this collective action becomes an effective tool. In such a case, a clearer understanding of village is *sine qua non.* The understanding of village is full of ambiguities at planning level. There are classifications of village on administrative, spatial, settlement and society type. This diversity of village type is needed to be understood and utilised for collective action in conservation and management of natural resources. Therefore, it is necessary that more research and village study in changing context of development are carried out. The development tool like Participatory Rural Appraisal (PRA) needs to be improved in order to catch the complexity of village in planning process.

REFERENCES

Agarwal, B. (1999) *The Gender and Environment Debate: Lessons from India,* in Menon, N. (Ed.) Gender and Politics in India, Delhi: OUP.

Bromley (1991) *Environment and Economy: Property Rights and Public Policy.* Oxford: Basil Blackwell.

Hardin, G. (1968) *The Tragedy of the Commons, Science, No. 162.*

Oakerson, R.J. (1986) *A Model for the Analysis of Common Property Problems, Proceedings of the Conference on Common Property Management.* Washington D.C. National Research Council, National Academy Press.

Ostrom, E. (1990) *Governing the Commons: The Evolution of Institutions for Collective Action.* Cambridge: Cambridge University Press.

2

Lineage, Clan and Caste as Units in Cooperative and Conflicting Situations

BRIJ RAJ CHAUHAN

Interrelations among the individual and society can be assayed from two vantage points: (1) The individual as the starting point begins defining every successive link in the chain until he reaches the climax; and (2) the collectivity, like the state, or any other, tries to reach from the top to the bottom through a set of intermediaries. In the first case, the discovery of the primary group and its enunciation by Charles H. Cooley provided a conceptual breakthrough even as he was wondering on the nature of a modern society. While discussing the material on primitive societies, the idea of segmental units had entered the classical literature wherein a person got successively incorporated into ever widening structural arrangements. In these cases, the primordial ties became the starting point, and the process of knowing and interacting with the wider world followed what can be conveniently called moving from the familiar to the unfamiliar. It is contended here the same approach in reverse is followed as we take into account the collectivity as the starting point, and trace its connections for reaching the end of the chain variously described as a taxpayer, a beneficiary or the 'common man'.

For the individual in the rural setting, the starting point in wider communications is the primary group, the family age sets of one's own clan as well as the intergenerational linkages, then the caste and the village folk, and it is through them that the villager contacts urban centres, administrative and political authorities. In the process he builds up a series of networks and action sets, occasionally using earlier confidence in the capacity of the patrons to deliver goods to the clients. It is through these channels that the wider world gets connected. Certain political and social workers or the NGOs too get into the act. On the part of the social institutions of the wider society, the people at the grass roots level have to be approached through a set of officials of various cadres. In case of the state though the district and block or tehsil level functionaries down to the village level called by various designations like the Collector, Tehsildar, Patwari on the revenue side, others like the District Magistrate, subordinate judiciary, the police officials from the Superintendent or the Inspector General to the constable; in case of Political Parties the state, district, block and ward units; and the market has its own mechanism of dealers and contractors from retail to the wholesale operations. The central point being brought forward here is that from both of these starting points there is a sort of a negotiating process at work, that initially both the ends need to be informed of each others' needs and desires, and the initial difference in their idiom and style of functioning are different. Thereby each approaches the other and uses the connecting links for the purpose. These links are couched in terms of primary relations for one set and the secondary relations for the other and problems in communication are intrinsically built in the process. The middlemen, the brokers, facilitators, extension agents arise as 'Interpreters between us and the millions we govern' to borrow a phrase from Macaulay and contribute to either solutions of problems or their aggravation. These aspects of social interaction through the ties of clan, caste and lineage are probed further in the context of the material available on rural Uttar Pradesh, which may be supplemented with notes from Rajasthan with which the author is familiar.

An individual first acquires the membership of the family and immediately gets connected to the two lineages, that of the father and the mother. In the north Indian setting the patrilineal links put him in the company of brothers and cousins of his generation, and in the culture of a joint family with a group of the father and his brothers all treated as uncles or *chacha* and classificatory system of kinship terminology allows him to negotiate with other preceding generations. Links with the mother connects the child to a host of her relations in the village of her original residence, her brothers and sisters who too get into a relationship of care and affection for various ritual purposes. For purposes of day-to-day life, however, relatives on the mother's side are less significant, and for the child male members of the joint family and the connected *kunba* or *khandan* become the important members of the playgroup or the peer group. In a society where birth is a significant contributor of status, and in the rural society where generations of people continue to live together, the question of the extent of relations based on generation depth becomes important and members define themselves as belonging to the line of some recognizable ancestor. Where every link can be so traced, the concept of Lineage becomes a social unit for defining one's status. Pauline Kolenda mentions that in the village, called in sociological literature by the name of 'Khala Pur', the lowest of the social groups, the *chuhra,* can count their connections up to four ascending generations and *kunba* could designate the unit; and their lineage to even six or eight generations; whereas the Rajput claimed to back to sixteen or twenty generations (1983) and the local term *Khandan* could designate the generation depth for social purposes. Then as a further exercise, connections are tried to be traced to some ancestor of antiquity who had been a great figure from whom the lineage had once 'branched off'. It is normally called the clan and treated as an exogamous unit and members constitute a sort of brotherhood. In terms of territorial spread, normally *khandan* is found in one village, and the clan in a number of contiguous or nearby villages thereby providing inter-village links where nearness is felt, but marriages do not take place, though on occasion of a death of a member common mourning ceremonies get organized. Adrian Mayer had used the phrase 'kindred of recognition' for this group and 'kindred of cooperation' (1960) for the one referred to earlier as *khandan.* Raheja has been able to trace the ancestry of *Gujar* families of Pahansu village in Saharanpur district to five generations; and then to the connections purported to include 13 generations up to a legendary figure of Phule Singh whose seven sons are 'said to be ancestors of all the *Khubars* in the *chaurasi* ("eighty four" villages)'(1988). The *Khubar* are a clan among the *Gujar*. Among the *Jat* in the Meerut region two clans of the *Baliyan* and *Malik* have likewise been identified spread over a number of villages (1991) by Stig Toft Madsen. In his study of education among the *Rajputs* for the same region, Raghuvanshi refers to *satha* or the group of sixty. Such references are available for other parts of Uttar Pradesh in Baden Powell's work—The Indian Village Community (1896) and earlier writings.

Lineage as units for organizing political boundaries for estate-like formations have been significant enough to be noted by various historians dealing with the period of medieval and early modern periods in India. Examining the evidence for the period 800-1200 A.D. historian Romila Thapar suggests that the Pratihar rulers had divided groups of villages into 84-84 units, a practice which later tended to become a territorial governing unit for a prince or a feudal chief by the tenth century; whereas in other areas units of 12 or their multiples could make up the sum of 84 or the *chaurasi* unit (1975, 2006 : 221). For the eastern U.P. Bernard S. Cohn records how the *Thakur* of Senapur trace their descent from one Ganesh Rai, a Raghuvanshi *Rajput* who in the sixteenth century (had) migrated to Jaunpur district where there are well over 20,000 of them living in the local area (taluka) (1987: 91).

Marriage alliances normally occur outside one's clan and the village in the north Indian setting. These specialities had been taken note of by Karve (1953) and gone into details by Marriott who has further noted directional hypergamy in getting daughters of a village married to spouses towards the north-west (1955). Thus a village gets linked to a hundred others even in the conduct of marital ties as a feature of traditional arrangements. The obligations of a family towards a daughter continue after her marriage; every return visit is an occasion for giving gifts to her and for her children and in-laws. On all ritual occasions, the obligations are well defined and reminded through folk songs. In the event of a person having daughters only and no son, the son-in-law gets invited as a *ghar jamai* to take charge of the household, and his son accepted as the legitimate heir ; whereas in the event of the death of the daughter's husband, she and her children could be taken care of by the parental family should that be necessary. Under normal business of day-to-day life, however, the practice of a girl passing most of her time in the husband's village is the norm. The higher castes do not permit widow remarriages, but the lower castes allow the practice as a normal course. Among the Jat, the practice of levirate is also found. At times, disputes arise in regard to breach of some norms and caste councils come into play. Madsen has looked into the case where two clans among the Jat living in the same village got caught up in a debate whether one of them could marry the other one from another village. This involved lot of consultations among the *sarva khap* and efforts at mutual agreement kept on going into several rounds of group meetings (1991, 96: 402-412). And a solution was till then not in sight, as the consensus had not been struck. For the lower groups, however, Kolenda has worked out the norms for levirate and other forms of unions of widows in case of the *Chuhra* of Khalapur (1982, 87: 289-354). The role of caste *sabhas* for various purposes has begun to receive attention in the life of the people, particularly in the context of introducing reforms or developing of pressure groups in modern polity.

From the individual's point of view, the lineage then provides the channel through which socialization takes place, marriage relations defined and life thereafter regulated along with provision for such contingencies as might arise in case of breakdowns and in the conduct of ritual obligations. A reference to a Rajasthan case would be pertinent here. A boy from *Ranawaton ki Sadri* had to be married to a girl in a village where the Chundawat were the main Thakur group. This was mentioned to a Rathore boy who too had been married to a girl there. Promptly he said 'This must be a case of a boy marrying a Jhala girl'. The investigator was surprised at such a depth of knowledge, and the explanations are the following: The Ranawat and Chundawat both trace their descent from the royal family of Mewar and are therefore exogamous units so a marriage cannot take place among them. However, among the Rajput there is another clan that of the Jhala living in the village from which a girl can be taken; but the manner in which the Jhala were being referred was such as to convey a sense of second class citizenship. Here the explanation was that they were not the "Thakur" in the sense of owners of the village. Various clans trace their descent from a remarkable ancestor who gains a near legendary status. In the royal lineage of Mewar, a young prince Chunda got an offer for marriage along with the traditional custom, but his father said that it was only proper that youngsters should get such an offer, not the elders like himself. This was considered insulting and the prince declined the offer saying let the elder get the offer. He was deprived of the right of succession, but left the court instantly and carved out a space for himself away from the capital. His descendants became lords of the first order and call themselves Chundawat. There are four such *jagirs* in Mewar. Then the historic figure of Maharana Pratap had two brothers, one Shakti Singh who had gone over to the Mughal emperor Akbar's court, but returned to the rescue of his brother at the end of the battle of Haldighati. The descendants of Shakti Singh call themselves Shaktawat. The other brother happened to be one Pura ji, and his descendants style themselves as Purawat. The manner in which the different clans get concerned with their privileges is best illustrated by a competitive bid by the Chundawat and the Shaktawat for the right to be in the forefront of the battle formations. The king told them whoever enters the fort of Unthala held by the enemy first will have the right. Both of the groups marched towards the destination. An elephant was used to attempt the breakthrough, but on seeing the spikes there, it got afraid. The Shaktawat leader put his body on the spikes and ordered the elephant rider to press on. That was done and the gate crashed. Meanwhile the Chundawat leader had sensed the urgency, and requested his followers to cut his head and throw the same inside the wall of the fort. The head reached the fort earlier than the gate crash and the Chundawat won the prestigious position. The sacrifice of the two leaders for the prestige of their respective clans or lineages is remembered by the posterity. Events such as these again help identifying links with the great names and promoting a sense of heightened glory. Yet the more important point is that the two lineages belong to the same stock, are therefore brotherly insofar as retaining exogamous relations are concerned. A few joking relations also help in consolidating the respective identities. The investigator was reminded of another episode during an election to a local body where the voters belonging to the Rajput said 'we ought to know the place and the lineage to which a candidate belongs' to form a proper judgment of his status. In determining the proper appreciation of a person in the inter-village setting among the Rajput in Rajasthan, a mention of name of the village and clan are almost sufficient to locate the relevant and expected relationship.

Meerut region has a special significance in the study of lineages and castes in relation to political events that have been variously interpreted as mutiny and First War of Independence of 1857. First a look at the caste formations in the traditional setting: Among the first settlers in the region the Taga or the Tyagi claim their mythological links with king Janmejaya and the serpent sacrifice for which their Brahmanical or priestly role was sought. Later they are said to have given up some of the functions and taken to agriculture. They occupied a large part of the district from which the Jat and the Gujar groups pushed them into the central eastern direction sometime in the 12th century. Among the Rajput clans, the Tomar are said to be the earliest of the occupants who had ruled over an area as extensive as Gwalior to Delhi and included portions of Meerut region in their realm in the 8th century. For some time, the Gurjar Pratihar of Ujjain ruled over the territory with *Raja* Bhoj being the most outstanding among them (836-882). This connection has led to two interpretations; the first that the rulers of Kannauj claimed themselves to be the Kshatriya of the Pratihar clan, connecting themselves to a Rajput lineage that had moved from Malwa to west Rajasthan, driven away or stopped the advance of Arabs in Sindh in the early 8th century and then moved eastwards to claim Ujjain. They were at one time subordinates to the Rashtrakut but later became autonomous. They dropped the prefix Gurjar and got the word Pratihar meaning as a doorkeeper, linked to the role that Laxman had played to the legendary Rama, thereby claiming a royal mythological connection. The second influence is among the Gujars who claim *Raja* Bhoj as their historical hero from whom marital traditions can be claimed. The Gujar chieftains in the Meerut region in the 18th century had established important fort like formations in Parichitgarh in Meerut district and Landhaura in Saharanpur. At a more popular and administrative level, however, the Gujar have been known as a pastoral group living mostly in the ravines of the Yamuna and the Ganga, specializing in cattle trading and animal husbandry and occasionally also indulging in cattle transfers in a non-formal manner. The opening of canals towards the middle of the 19th century attracted the group to intensive cultivation as well, and it is in this and an earlier process in the reopening of the eastern Yamuna canal (early 19th century) that the Gujar began converting themselves from pastoral group to a settled agricultural one. In the process they came into conflict with the earlier occupants, mainly the Taga and the Jat. The Gujar are the principal caste group in Saharanpur rural area and have a strong presence in Meerut region along the banks of the Yamuna and south of Ghaziabad with some villages in the north-eastern part of the district along the Ganga.

About the middle of the 10th century Chauhan king of Shakambhari in Saharanpur district came into conflict with the Tomar; and the Dor clan from Baran (Bulandshahr) took advantage of the situation, established the fort at Meerut and the town of Hapur around 983, named after the chief Haradatta, first called Harapur, then shortened to Hapur. The 12th century saw the consolidation of the Chauhan power in Delhi and Ajmer with the legendary Prithvi Raj being declared as an emperor of a sort and a court poet Chandbardai composing the *Prithvi Raj Raso* which became an exaggerated heroic account with some historical relevance as well. The story of his conflict with the king of Kannauj and the romantic escape with his daughter are well-known. The period was also marked by his downfall at the hands of Muhammad of Ghor in the second battle at Tarain which led to the rise of what is known later as the Sultanate of Delhi under various lineages like the Ghulam, the Khilji, Tughlak followed by the Saiyid and then the Lodhi kings. The period is marked by invasions, but also by some regulation of the agrarian structure by Allauddin Khilji, and frequent tussles among the central and regional powers.

The Mughal rule commencing in 1526 is connected with the establishment of a few Islamic structures in the region, viz. mosques in Saharanpur, Meerut and centres of learning in Saharanpur and Deoband. The region had also been connected with demolition of temples, a few looting of treasures, taxation of *Jazia* on the peasants and traders, and conversion of a large number of artisans and quite a few members of upper groups to Islamic faith.

In terms of organizing rural structures the region was a part of the *suba* of Delhi and the northern districts were put under the control of Saharanpur. The *Ain-e-Akbari* mentions the amount of land revenue that had to be collected from various Mahals as also the contribution expected of them in terms of soldiers and horses, but more important from the point of the presentation at hand is the distribution of major caste groups from among the peasants responsible for paying the land revenue. For tehsil Baghpat the Brahman and the Rajput; and for the mahals of Jalalpur Baraut, Chaprauli, Tanda Phugana and Kotana the Jat had been identified; for Ghaziabad tehsil Jalalabad was with the Jat and Dasna with Gahlot Rajput who were believed to have come to that region in the 12th century from Chittorgarh in Rajasthan. The tehsil of Hapur had Tomar Rajput in Puth mahal, other Rajput in Garh Mukteshwar, and the Taga in Hapur as well as Hastinapur mahal. Meerut mahal was a mixed settlement, prominent being the Taga and the Chandal and two converted groups the Kamboh and the Rangar. The Shiekhzada were in charge of Barnawa, whereas the Taga and Ahir were significant groups in Sardhana. The Jat continue to be an important group and set the pattern of life for the rest of the cultivators of the region. They trace their descent from 'one Jaswant Singh, and according to one tradition came from Jaisalmer (in Rajasthan) about 1200 years ago' (District Gazetteer 1963:32). The fall of the Mughal empire is connected with a number of peasant uprisings among which historian Irfan Habib specifically mentions the 'Revolts in the Agra Region, and the Jats' (1990-398) with the official sources of the period treating the participants as 'ganwar' or rustic, though also rated as par excellence a peasant caste. The active role of three leaders in succession has been recalled and facts like those of a Jat Zamindar having sway over 25 villages also mentioned. The Jat expended their habitation in parts of western Uttar Pradesh, particularly the Brij area. The declining years of the Mughal rule were accompanied by peasant unrests that in some measure got reflected also in the events of 1857 which need special attention in terms of the role of different castes and clans involved in various degrees and the manner in which the British administration dealt with them.

Castes and Clans in the First War of Independence or the Mutiny of 1857

From the point of view of the British administration three principal castes in the Meerut region played significant part in the events of 1857. The Gujar were considered to be the most troublesome, the Jat defined at first as friendly and the Tyagi or the Taga as helpful. The mutiny itself had started in Meerut on May 10 and the first after effects appeared in the form of looting of urban property in Meerut city itself. The principal participants in the proceedings were identified as the Gujars of the neighbouring villages who were aided by such of the link men who had entered the services of chowkidars and policemen. It is through them that the relevant intelligence used to pass onto the countryside where the 'tribal caste' fellows lived and 'urban crime had become a secondary occupation'. In the open looting the local Muslim population of lower groups too found scope for their own share. These groups generally came from the butchers, and converts from lower groups of the Hindus. By that time the Mughal kings nominally at least ruled Delhi, and in general the Muslims favoured the king against the British rulers. The Banias of Meerut were the victims. In the rural setting the Taga and the Jat were defined as 'loyal' and their historical enmity with the Gujar was a part of the administrative intelligence resource.

The overall understanding got disturbed on two counts. Among the Jat a local leader had arisen and his lineage went against the British establishment and it took time to realize that not caste but lineages were playing the organizing role. On the other hand, the absence of a leader among the peasantry was assumed as per the theory of their being like a sack of potatoes. The Jat leader and subsequently his son carried on the struggle. Meanwhile, the Gujar revolt had spread wide and supported by a deputy commander of the Mughal emperor. In the northern parts, however, the Gujar chieftain of Landhaura in Saharanpur district had been recognized by the British and this chieftain remained loyal to his patrons. The mutiny and the peasant rebellion have been analyzed by Eric Stokes in details, the connections among castes and lineages and their perception or lack of proper understanding of the roles of lineages within caste structures in administrative cognition at that point of time highlight the need for better appreciation of the units of traditional structures in their roles in conflicting situations.

History of inter-caste relations and their differential exposure to levels of agricultural growth continue to be relevant to events as they happen toward the end of the twentieth or the beginning of the twenty first. Meerut region got a name for itself through the organized efforts at peasant movements led by Mahendra Singh Tikait and the outfit named as a Kisan Union. A number of demonstrations regarding adequate pricing of sugarcane and of facilities needed by the peasants have been organized for over a deacde. A Satyanarayana has gone into details regarding differential participation of peasants in what is popularly called the *'Jail Bharo Andolan'*. A scrutiny of police records shows that the participation was more active where the Jat population in village sway concentrated, and comparatively weaker where the Gujar dominated. Again within the Jat, the question of leadership of the lineage was an important factor; and in the traditional Jat conclave, the peasant leader was given a secondary importance. Where political leadership among the Jat was concerned, it tried to take necessary steps to see that its hold was not diluted, whereas the peasant leadership tried to steer clear of the political conflicts. The interplay among traditional units of social organization, the political parties and the state have produced their own dynamics that need to be grasped to come to a better understanding of the phenomenon of what goes on today by the name of a peasant movement. The different units become significant at different stages of a movement like attending a meeting, organizing a demonstration or going to jail, and questions relating to the degrees of participation get discussed in group meetings or private conversations.

Introduction of the Panhayati Raj at the village level in the first phase led to the consolidation of existing sources of traditional power in the new set-up and castes by and large maintained the power structure with minor replacements within their lineages. With the Constitutional amendment on reservation of seats becoming effective, every village got obliged to elect its representatives from particular categories, and the extension of political parties to rural levels, either openly or covertly, created competitive atmosphere in which members of a caste or a group got pitted against one another. Here to begin with, the lineage or a group of linked families became important and the qualities of the candidate also came into play. At the wider level, in case of multi-village constituencies, horizontal ties of castes acquired a new political role. These steps ensure creation of a committed section of support, which usually needs support of other groups; but, what is important here is the finding in a Muzaffarnagar village among the Jat that the internal divisions within a village for local elections could get glossed over for mobilizing support for a wider constituency at the state or national election. In terms of the relevance of particular social units for political mobilization, the area over which they are effective has to be assessed with caution ; and care taken to see that given assets always present a challenge to the mobilizing or leadership qualities and rise of unforeseen situations.

REFERENCES

Chauhan, Brij Raj, 1999, *A Rajasthan Village, Udaipur,* A.C. Brothers.

Cohn, Bernard S. 1987, *An Anthropologist among the Historians and Other Essays,* Delhi, Oxford University Press.

Gazetteer of India Uttar Pradesh Meerut 1965, Lucknow, Department of District Gazetteers, U.P.

Habib, Irfan, 1999, *The Agrarian System of Mughal India 1556-1707,* Second Revised Edition, New Delhi, Oxford University Press.

Karve, Irawati, 1963, *Kinship Organization in India* (3rd edition) Bombay, Asia Publishing House.

Kolenda, Pauline, 1987, *Regional Differences in Family Structures in India,* Jaipur, Rawat Publications.

Madsen, Stig Toft, 1991, *Clan, Kinship and Panchayat Justice among the Jats of Western Uttar Pradesh* in Anthropos vol. 86, excerpted in Social Conflict (ed.) N. Jayaram and Satish Saberwal, New Delhi, Oxford University Press.

Mayer, Adrian C. 1960 (1986). *Caste and Kin in Central India—A village and Its Region,* First Indian Reprint, Delhi, Universal Book Depot.

Minturn, L. and Hitchcock L.T. 1963, *The Rajputs of Khalapur'* in Whiting, Beatruce (ed.) Six Cultures in Child Rearing Practices, New York, John Wiley & Sons.

Thapar, Roomila, 2002, *The Penguin History of Early India from the Origins to AD 1300,* New Delhi, Penguin Books, India (Pr. Ltd.).

.... 2006, *Bharat ka Itihas* (12th revised ed.), New Delhi, Raj Kamal Prakashan (Pvt. Ltd.).

Stokes, Eric, 1978, *The Peasant and the Raj: Studies in Agrarian Society and Peasant Rebellions in Colonial India,* Cambridge, Cambridge University Press.

Whitcombe, Elizabeth, 1971, *Agrarian Conditions in Northern India,* New Delhi, Thomson Press, University of California.

3

Changing Indian Agrarian Village Economy

D.M. DIWAKAR

Village usually refers to a consolidated agricultural community (Geertz, 1972) isolated from or interconnected with the world. Studies on villages attracted broadly three approaches—(i) Microcosmic—looking from micro unit to world, an anthropological approach, (ii) Historical—a general view from the top through historical development of a society with respect to time and space, and (iii) Complex societies—a mix of the two. Redfield began with microcosmic villages and folk culture (1930; 1941), and borrowed "part societies" from Kroeber while dealing with compound peasant society and culture (1956) where he analysed "great" and "little" traditions, "parochialization" and "universalization". Steward (1956) dealt with complex societies dividing into vertical and horizontal segments and formal institutions. Eric Wolf (1955) analysed Latin American communities with closed or corporate and open categories. This was further extended to open corporate, centripetal and centrifugal framework of analysis of peasants' community. Economists have been concerned with structural changes and distributional aspects of resources and growth with time series, cross-sectional, and longitudinal analyses. These analyses basically covered isolated and interlinked villages with their identities and institutions of livelihood, control over resources and distributional structure. Technological changes and participation of direct producers remain in the centre while discussing above dimensions. Approaches to see the changes may differ but the elements in process of changes are broadly common to be dealt with. This paper intends to deal with process of change with economic indicators spread over four parts. Part I dwells into trends and debates in process of changes and class formation. Part II locates the debates of agrarian structure in villages of Uttar Pradesh. Part III analyses with indicators of growth performance and Part IV consolidates the analysis focussing on emerging relations.

I. Trends and Debates in Process of Change

Process of changes for the development of a society may broadly have two aspects: (a) Basis of changes, and (b) Superstructure. Later may have two dimensions. First, changes in institutions—may be socio-economic, political, etc., at a given stage of productive organisation and development and second, technological progress with its impact on these institutions in the corresponding time and space. An exercise is required to identify and evaluate the process of development consequent upon changes in its forms, contents, and operative mechanism of base and superstructures along with changing productive forces, which start transforming themselves within existing productive organizations. We learn from history that so long as these factors are compatible among themselves process of changes may continue smoothly. Incompatibility, on the contrary, among these factors creates contradictions, challenges the continuity of outmoded institutions and replaces the outdated technology in the historical process of social change.

There could *inter alia* be three main dimensions of agrarian questions for change. One is nature of State and its intervention as an agent of development which may be seen in terms of various policy measures for agrarian changes for instance, regarding land size and productivity, technological progress, mechanisation and labour absorption, peasant capitalism (i.e. capitalism from below) or landlord capitalism (i.e. capitalism from above), etc. (Byres, 1995; 508). Two, internal dynamics of agrarian changes is required to be examined in terms of changing class relations, emergence of new classes and their hegemonic role in this context. In other words, one of the most important tasks towards this end is to identify emerging contradictions in the context of changes that are taking place in production relations and productive forces for the development of agriculture and rural economy at large. And third dimension of agrarian questions is related to the external dynamics and linkages of rural changes. There could be "three main linkages, i.e., the flow of agricultural surplus for the accumulations of industrial capital, absorption of proletarianized peasantry as wage labour in industry and the creation of home market for industrial products in farm production and farm households with specialisation and division of labour between agriculture and manufacturing" (Breman and Mundle, 1991; xxi).

In this context of changes, internal dynamics of class relations in production and appropriation of surpluses and external dynamics of accumulation and formation of capital decide the course of changes and development. 'When we speak of production, we always have in mind production at a definite stage of social development, production by individuals in a society, i.e., various phases in the historical process of development. All stages of production, however, have certain common features, elements and categories without which production is inconceivable. For example, no production is possible without an instrument of production (simplest form may be hand), without past accumulated and materialised labour (may be the skill acquired by repeated practice and concentrated in the hand of savage). Thus, capital is a universal and eternal relation, which turns the instrument of production or accumulated labour into capital. Production is always appropriation of nature by individual within and with the help of a definite social organisation' (Marx, 1970, 189-90). It is worth mentioning here that "total product of a community is a social product. One portion serves as fresh means of production and remains social. But another portion is consumed by the members as means of subsistence. A distribution of this portion amongst them is consequently necessary. The mode of this distribution will vary with the productive organisation of the community and the degree of historical development attained by the producers" (Marx, 1986; 83). Thus, epochs of development are so much associated with the institutional and structural set up that any analysis of changes in isolation from modes of production is an exercise in futility (Prasad, 1986; 3). Because "it is not the articles made, but how they are made and by what instrument that enables us to distinguish different economic epochs" (Marx, 1975; 175). Thus, historical process of movement of a society, from one mode of production to another, makes a course of changes of a society.

Mode of production consists of two aspects—production relations and productive forces. Production relation explains the relations between individuals, i.e., those who are involved in the process of production, exchange, distribution and consumption, and productive forces explains the relationship between human beings and nature and consists of means of production created by society and acquired labour skill. Human being exists in nature and transforms it. Human being makes over nature into an expression of itself and, in the process becomes human being, i.e., he or she transforms himself or herself while transforming nature with means of labour. Means of labour and objects of labour together constitute means of production. The instruments created by society are means of labour, which help the labourers to modify the objects of labour. Objects of labour are the objects found in nature on which labour is applied to modify them, for the requirement of man. To be more precise, productive forces reflect the development of technology through which man tries to dominate over nature and production relations explain the nature of ownership and control of means of production by man. Thus, the relation of human beings with the means of production determine their position and place in production and the mode of distribution of the products of labour. Therefore, identification of the modes of production helps in understanding the process of changes of a society and the nature and course of development (Nadkarni, 1991; 100).

Agrarian change in India has its root in institutional arrangements for revenue collection from farming through tax and tributary mode during Mughal India. Revenue farming was not only the root of inequality and poverty but also the seed of the growth of the Zamindar class. This mechanism of revenue collection through tax was further elaborated from tax to rent and reinforced by the British East India Company Government in India, which entered into agreement with Zamindars (Tandon, *et al.*, 1936: 2-3). The British worked out broadly three types of settlement: Permanent Settlement, Ryotbari and Mahalbari, as organised exploitative revenue structure. In this process, peasants were subjected to rack renting and exploitation, which led to ejection of large section of small peasantry who lost their right of ownership on land and forced them to be subordinated as tenants at will to Zamindars. However, peasant resistance forced the British Indian government to introduce many reforms measures in tenancy relations. Independent India also witnessed many reforms in agrarian institutions, structure and technology. A few initiatives such as abolition of zamindari and intermediaries, imposition of ceiling, acquisition of ceiling surplus land and redistribution of land to the land poor, and now new institutional arrangement—contract and corporate farming—have changed agrarian structure significantly. Introduction of new technology: irrigation, fertilizer, high yielding varieties of seeds, known as green revolution, besides providing other infrastructure—electricity, credit facility, road, etc.; as well as poverty alleviation, employment generation and other development programmes for empowerment to uplift weaker sections of the society to transform their standard of living and thereby rural lives, economy and society as a whole.

Debates on Agrarian Changes

Debates on changes in agriculture were necessarily focused around modes of production. Identifying modes of production in the context of Indian agriculture spread over a period from 1969 onwards till 1981 (Patnaik, 1990) and concentrated thematically, on three broad issues: (i) Identifying the process of capitalist production: (Rudra, 1969, 1971; Rudra *et al*. 1969, 1970; Rao, 1970; Patnaik 1971, 1972; Chattopadhyay, 1972; Frank, 1973; Sau, 1973) (ii) Colonial mode of production: (Banaji, 1972; Alvi, 1975, 1981; Rudra 1975; Omvet, 1975); and (iii) Problems of class formation and analysis: (Rudra, 1978, Rudra *et al*., 1976; Patnaik 1976; Prasad, 1974, 1988; Banaji 1977).

Identification of Capitalist Mode of Production

It is argued that when capitalism tends to become the dominant mode of production, it replaces the pre-capitalist modes and is expected to be accompanied by increasing trends in: (a) Production more for sale than for own use, (b) Use of hired labour, (c) Increasing monetisation, and (d) Generation of surplus over costs and consequently accumulation of capital. Being historically an advanced mode over pre-capitalist one, capitalism takes the economy including agriculture to a higher level of development. The central point of the debate was whether such a progressive, if not egalitarian mode was in operation in India particularly in agriculture and if not what constrained it. Rudra took a sample of big farmers from Punjab and after setting capitalist criteria, the findings of his study could not establish the association among these variables. If there were indeed a category of capitalist farmers and if capitalist farmers do have: (a) Higher rate of cash expenditure on wage payments; (b) A greater intensity of utilisation of modern capital goods per unit of cultivable land; (c) A greater market orientation; and (d) A higher rate of profit per unit of farm land than non-capitalist farmers; then one would expect strong association between pairs of variables. Rudra's data, however, failed to indicate any strong association. What they conclude is that capitalist development to the extent it took place had not led to a clear polarisation into two classes of capitalists and proletarians in Punjab agriculture (Rudra, 1969) to which Utsa Patnaik also agreed. However, her thesis of the process of limited capitalist development in some pockets could not be denied despite the fact that the rate at which it was occurring varied widely and thus lacks strength of generalisation. However, she was clear in her observation when she maintained: "To expect a farmer landlord or peasant to display all the characteristics of the pure capitalist would be to abstract him from his class background." This observation was based on sample study of 66 big landowners distributed over various districts of India. She found that landlord and dominant farmers usually tied destitute labour with combined productive capital investment with money lending and combined intensive capitalist production on a part of their land with leasing at high rents on other parts of their land (Patnaik, 1971:3-19). Now reverse tenancy with contract farming has changed the relation of production in agriculture where small and marginal farmers have gradually been alienated from the market and agriculture and medium and large farms have been trapped in a usury network of exploitation (Sukhpal Singh, 2005).

Banaji maintained that capitalist development took place at the cost of the colony, the burden of which could not be eased even after the transfer of power from the British to Indian ruling class. This was the major factor limiting the process of change (Banaji, 1972). However, Rudra did not agree to consider the circuit of draining surplus as mode of production (Rudra, 1990: 14). Frank attacks the tendency of escaping from the reality of capitalism and capitalist underdevelopment of the erstwhile colonies in a world dominated by capitalism (Frank, 1973). Patnaik, however, called it an extremist approach as it denies any breakthrough after 1947 (Patnaik, 1990). Explaining the other side of the limited capitalist development, Prasad emphasises the reactionary role of usurer's capital and role of semi-feudal or pre-capitalist forces within economy (Prasad, 1989; 37-43, 95-106). With usurer's and merchant capital bringing more returns, economically productive lines of real accumulation suffered which explains the stagnation, non-viability and non-development syndrome in agriculture. Declining public investment in agriculture and inefficient public credit institutions and then neglect of agriculture reinforced the private money-lending (usury) network wider and stronger than ever before. Farmers of diversified and developed agriculture of Punjab, cash crop growing area of Maharashtra, Andhra Paradesh and Karnataka depend badly on moneylenders for credit support. Even small farmers are badly trapped. Emergence of contract farming mainly tied with big farmers initially appeared as facilitating network for them but later denying buy back contract and successive failure of seeds supplied by multi-national companies, and absence of proper public support system, brought farmers to debt and death traps. Micro-finance through self-help group approach came in a big way to rescue agriculture, which in fact is serving the purposes of moping out rural savings for speculative markets and metropolitan cities and have successfully been depriving the investment possibilities in rural areas for its agricultural and industrial development.

Problems of Class Formation

There might be another way of looking into the problems in terms of class formation, for example, on the basis of land owned and operated, labour use, family and hired labour or net labour use, family female labour participation, gross and net sale of agricultural produce, etc. An agrarian structure in terms of four classes was forwarded to landlord (feudal and capitalist), rich peasant, poor peasant and full-time labour (Patnaik, 1990). Another classification considered only two groups: feudal landlords leasing out land from a single class with rich capitalist farmers and tenants and labour combined. Others, who were out, did not come under analytical class frame (Rudra, 1969).

Yet another approach to understand the society and to capture the key characteristics of this social formation could be on the basis of generation of surplus value in agriculture and its appropriation through labour process (Prasad and Rodger, 1983). Among the households, which supply physical labour in agriculture on other people's land in return for some payments either in cash or kind, these households are directly exploited and command the lowest status in agricultural community, may be put in the block of agricultural labour. Further break-up of agricultural labour may improve the precision, for example, attached non-cultivating, not attached non-cultivating, not attached cultivating, and attached cultivating. The households in which neither the labour is hired out nor hired in and agricultural activities are conducted with hundred per cent participation of family labour with an exception of the exchange labour may be categorised as poor middle peasant. Some of the agricultural households from which family male and female both work in agricultural activity and also hire labour, may be classified as middle peasant. Those households, which consider allowing female members of the households to work physically even in their own field below their dignity, may be kept as big peasant. And the last category is of the landlords who are distinctly different from others in the way that who lease out some amount of land and cultivate remaining lands with hired labour. Here, the term landlord may appear a little misleading, since many of those concerned may not have large landholdings and cannot be regarded as lords. However, this terminology is more familiar even though it sounds traditional and thus has been used as it is, to avoid confusion.

This classification of agrarian structure does not depend directly on area owned and operated but on the way the households utilise labour and land. However, even in this classification anomaly remains. For example, those who are leasing out their land due to old age or illness will be treated as landlord. Even the middle peasant households without female workers will not come under its own category. Undoubtedly, further break-up may improve the precision but to maintain the simplicity of limited numbers of categories this formation broadly captures the main features of the social system. Moreover, illness, widowhood and old age generally may not have many numbers to influence the basic feature of this classification in general. Thus, these may be treated as an aberration. In order to capture the ground reality of the society and to identify the process of rural changes, applying this framework of analytical classification a few studies (e.g. Prasad and Rodger, 1983; Diwakar, 1996; 1998; 2000) have been conducted and found useful. Like these there may be many other ways of looking into the agrarian system. This debate has in fact raised more questions and opened many more dimensions to understand the problems than the answers. However, complexity of agrarian structure and the diversity of its nature across regions defy any particular given framework of analysis and thus pose challenges to social scientists and demands concrete contents and hard empirical analysis of ground realities with a broader base.

II. Agrarian Structure in Uttar Pradesh

Agrarian structure includes production relations among people engaged in production, exchange, distribution and consumption and productive forces, i.e., technology and labour. In order to understand these relations therefore, we need to go in details of *inter alia* land and labour market, technology, production and consumption pattern. But to do all these exercises in one go may be a difficult reading, which I do not intend to and therefore, this section confines itself to a brief discussion focused on distribution of land, tenancy reforms and relations and growth performance in agriculture.

Land Distribution

Land has been the basis of productive organisation and rural assets. Forms of agrarian structure are reflected in distribution of operational holdings. Persisting inequality in distribution of which reflects the existing relations in an agrarian society. Studies provide a basis to argue that in the Fifties distribution of land ownership holdings in Uttar Pradesh was highly inequitable (Singh, 1964; Shrimali, 2005; Mishra and Diwakar, 2005; Diwakar, 2000; 2006). Persisting inequality in distribuiton of land reflects the existing relations. The Sen Committee Report categorically underlined skewed distribution of land as one of the major constraints for agrarian changes (RBI, 1984; 76-84, 384-393). After abolition of Zamindari system two generations have elapsed. Although land reform was implemented and partly it contributed also in narrowing down the inequality in distribution of land, it remained incomplete and neglected in absence of effective implementation and sincere commitment and strong political will (Mishra & Diwakar, 2005). Even medium-cum-big farm holdings could manage land allotment reflecting procedural lapses of the scheme. A sizeable number of non-deserving beneficiary households were selected at the cost of genuine potential households, because of lapses in procedure, bribery, lack of awareness and sensitive implementing agencies, etc.

Sub-division and fragmentation of landholdings was witnessed in the process of natural attrition caused by division of family consequent upon growing population. As a result, landholding size in fifty years has decreased and therefore it is also argued that inequality in distribution of landholdings has lost its relevance to some extent. Latest data available so far on distribution of operational holdings indicate (Table 3.1) that about 75.6 per cent marginal holdings have possessed only 34.1 per cent of the land area whereas top ten per cent of the households possessed about 43 per cent. Data suggest that only 0.2 per cent of the landholders owning above 25 acres of land have about 3.2 per cent of the total operational area in their possession. If we add the households above ten acres of land

Table 3.1: Percentage Distribution of Operational Holdings of India and Uttar Pradesh

Size of holdings (Acre)	*India*				*Uttar Pradesh*			
	Number (%)		*Area (%)*		*Number (%)*		*Area (%)*	
	90-91	95-96	90-91	95-96	90-91	95-96	90-91	95-96
> 2.5	59.0	59.4	14.9	15.1	73.8	75.6	31.4	34.1
2.5-5.0	19.0	18.8	17.3	17.4	15.6	14.5	24.4	23.8
5.0-10.0	13.2	13.1	23.2	23.2	7.7	7.3	23.4	23.1
10.0-25.0	7.2	7.1	27.2	27.0	2.7	2.4	16.9	15.8
Above 25.0	1.6	1.6	17.4	17.3	0.2	0.2	3.9	3.2
Average size (acre)	—	—	1.6	0.5	—	—	0.9	0.9

Source: Statistical Diary, State Planning Institute, Department of Planning, Govt. of Uttar Pradesh.

they amount to 2.6 per cent of the total number of holdings above ten acres. But the area of operational holdings that they possess amounts to 19 per cent of the total area of operational holdings. Quantitatively, it may appear less iniquitous for many of us but it needs a fresh assessment of the facts. Landholding size in the process of natural attrition has decreased, but the question of land controlled by the same privileged class still persists. Access to land resources enabled them to avail better opportunity and access in secondary and tertiary sectors. However, transfer of land has widened the land base among middle caste/class and other sections of the society also. Moreover, family participation irrespective of caste/class has also increased. As data suggest, majority of the farmers in state are marginal holders followed by small holdings. They together constitute about 90.1 per cent and possess 57.9 per cent of operational area. Semi-medium farms have almost equal proportion of holdings and area in their possession. Even if one ignores concealed tenancy, which is pervasive in Uttar Pradesh, there is apparent inequality in distribution of land, which explains the need for redistribution of land in Uttar Pradesh.

Concentration of landholdings measured in terms of Gini Co-efficient for quinquennial census data of agriculture suggest that Gini ratio for land concentration of operational holdings has been declining from 0.567 in 1980-81 to 0.505 in 1990-91 and 0.461 in 1995-96. Moreover, the gap between ownership and operational holdings may be explained through tenancy, and fluctuation in it suggests the prevalence of tenancy at will. However, individual research studies based on primary data and longitudinal studies show that Gini co-efficient with respect to land concentration in Moradabad district of West Uttar Pradesh has rather increased from 0.49 in 1957-58 to 0.52 in 1993. Although, value of co-efficients remained unchanged when landless households are excluded (Dreze, 1997). Similarly, another longitudinal study of Aligarh district of West U.P. suggests that percentage of households owning up to 25 *bigha* lands has increased from 36.4 in 1970 to 67.6 per cent in 1987. Of course, percentage of land owning households more than 50 *bigha* lands has declined. Overall Gini co-efficient in

1970 was 0.73 for the distribution of owned land on a household basis, and 0.63 on a per capita per household basis whereas corresponding figures for 1987 were 0.74 and 0.65 (Saith and Tankha, 1997; 100). Major concentration of land areas in Allahabad and Muzaffarnagar lies with Hindu upper castes and Muslims (Srivastava, 1997). Above analysis, thus, suggests that inequality in land distribution has not lost ground and much is yet to be done to restore land to the tiller in order to remove qualitative inequality in distribution of land.

Tenancy Reforms and Relations

Tenancy has a significant place in agrarian reforms in India rooted in the farm revenue system through formal introduction of intermediaries in agriculture in order to minimize uncertainty and risk in revenue collection in Mughal India. However, revenue farmers of the Mughal Empire gradually became owner of the land in their possession, with the decline in the authority of the Central Government. The British Company Government introduced Permanent Settlement in Banaras Province, which was later on ceded by the Oudh Government after the battle of Buxar. But land tenure system in Oudh was different from Agra. Oudh land was divided into two classes: (a) Khalsa (crown land) and (b) Huzoor (Tehsil land). The proprietary tenure was divided into four categories: (a) Taluqdari; (b) Zamindari; (c) Bhaeichara; and (d) Free Grants. Taluqdari tenurial system was most important among them. However, in Agra province limited rights were conferred to tenants through legislation in 1859 (Rent Act I of 1859) and later modified in 1901 (Rent Act II) further modified and repealed by the Agra Tenancy Act, 1926. The Agra Tenancy Act divided tenants into six categories: (1) Permanent tenure holders; (2) Fixed rate tenants; (3) Occupancy tenants; (4) Ex-proprietary tenants; (5) Statutory tenants; and (6) Non-occupancy tenants.

Congress Agrarian Reforms Committee (1934) headed by P.D. Tandon was another landmark in institutional reforms in agriculture of Uttar Pradesh. This was to assess the ground reality and recommend tenurial transformation to address the causes of peasantry to wield support of the masses in the Freedom Struggle. This Committee submitted its report in 1936. Institutional reforms relating to tenancy in U.P. began with submission of a report by the Zamindari Abolition Committee in August 1948. Zamindari Abolition Act (ZAA) based on the recommendation of the Committee was enacted in January 1951 and came in force from July 1952. This Act replaced a complicated tenurial system having forty types of tenures into four—Bhumidar, Sirdar, Asami and Adhivasi. Apparently ZAA was a major step to transform tenurial system. Partially it worked to reform institutional structure in U.P. and to some extent exploitation could also be eliminated (Shrimali, 1981, pp.227-228). However, larger beneficiary of this reform were rich farmers. Poor peasants subjected to numerous forms of exploitation remained vulnerable and could hardly mobilize funds to acquire status of Bhumidhari. Rather they were ejected and deprived from cultivation, the only source of their livelihood. Thus, ZAA could hardly transform agrarian institutions in favour of cultivators (Thorner, 1976, p. 27; Joshi, 1996; Mishra, 1996). Thus, in U.P. significant changes in tenancy relations have taken place. However, fact remains that tenancy is pervasive in one form or the other with a different magnitude and terms as a powerful mechanism to appropriate surplus from tenant farmers.

Magnitude and forms of tenancy discussed through National Sample Survey data suggest that magnitude of tenancy in terms of leased-in holdings and area has decreased between 1971-72 and 1981-82 but it registered increase between 1981-82 and 1991-92. NSS provides data on 'terms of tenancy' in terms of: (a) Fixed money; (b) Fixed produce; (c) Share tenancy; and (d) Other terms of tenancy. Inter-temporal changes in incidence of terms of tenancy suggests that changes in the incidence of terms under fixed money tenancy, number of holdings increased between 1971-72 and 1981-82 but decreased between 1981-82 and 1991-92. There was marginal increase in area during 1970s and 1980s. But there was significant increase in holdings under fixed produce tenancy and area as well. However, the incidence of sharecropping and other terms of tenancy has declined both in terms of holdings and area. Changes in distribution of leased-in holdings and area under fixed money tenancy indicate by and large an increasing trend. There has been significant change in terms of fixed produce tenancy over the years, particularly in 1980s. Holdings under sharecropping tenancy remained almost constant but there has been significant decline in area. Reverse tenancy has increased in 1991-92 over 1971-72 both in terms of leasing-in and leasing-out area. Thus, it appears that fixed money, fixed produce and reverse tenancies were on increase. Although sharecropping was declining yet its magnitude was much higher than that of other forms of tenancy.

Sharecropping remained dominant form of tenancy in Uttar Pradesh (Singh, 1984; 354-55) with considerable variations in terms and conditions in the lease market particularly with respect to process of production (such as cropping pattern, use of inputs, etc.), assured supply of labour, sometimes at lower wage than the market rate and sometimes free labour as well, seasonal and crop specific in view of the intensity of labour, caste network and linkages, etc. Besides 50:50 sharing of crops, rents vary in degree say 1/4, 3/8 and 2/3 of the output. It is worth mentioning that big farmers did not pay more than 50 per cent of the output as rent to the lessors. However, *vice versa* was not found. System of contract rent in cash also emerged to minimise the risk of uncertainty towards returns through rents. There was hardly any significant let up in the intensity and extent of tenancy. However, the change was perceived with respect of creating balance between land and labour in order to cope with insufficient progress in mechanisation and deficiency of working capital. A shift from leasing out as a means of appropriating rents to leasing out as a form of securing control over labour power and the appropriation of its produce was also witnessed (Srivastava, 1997; 214-16). Those households, who were not operating their land personally and were absent from the field as it did not remain their main occupation, behaved as absentee landowner in order to exercise control over the lands through manipulations and they kept on changing their tenants, executed bonds to treat them as their servant (not tenant) so that the tenant might not prove their tenancy right over the land. The tenants were generally at their (landowners) will and also remained at lower profile to avoid the complication and ejection from the land, which remained the only option for their survival strategy due to lack of other opportunities in non-agricultural sectors. Ruling class biases towards landowners were often compounding uncertainty of tenants in lease markets and sometimes intensified their hardships (Kripashankar, 1997).

A study of selected sample villages (Mishra and Diwakar, 2005: ch. iii) suggested that tenancy was very much prevalent in the sample villages of Uttar Pradesh. Magnitude of tenancy was closer to the level of tenancy in Uttar Pradesh as a whole reflected in NSS data. About 9.7 per cent households of the sample villages reported leasing-in tenancy. Sample district of Gorakhpur indicated higher presence of tenancy than other sample districts. Higher percentage of households reported leasing-in irrigated land than unirrigated land. Moreover, sum total of leasing-in households was lower than that of irrigated and unirrigated households. This suggested that lessee households were operating more than one quality of land. Percentage of households of lessor was lower than that of lessee. This implied that one household was leasing-out land to more than one households. Thus, network of lessor reflected its alternative dominant choice in the tenancy market. So far the tenure of tenancy was concerned, it was widely spread ranging from one crop to more than three years. One crop/season and annual tenancy showed nature of tenant at will under which lessee remained vulnerable to eviction subject to satisfaction of the terms of tenancy imposed by the lessor. Depending upon the agreement and satisfaction of the lessor, lessee had to prove his trustworthiness, subservience and higher rate of return. The lessee as such are allowed cultivating beyond one year also but his continuance was always subjected to loyalty and performance of lessee.

Existence of tenancy indicates process of historical development of a society and reveals modes of surplus appropriation and production relations. Lessor and lessee both are guided by their self-interest of maximizing their gain. However, the gain is defined differently. Lessees in the sample villages reported tenancy for their livelihood, employment, income and repayment of loan as they hardly found any other viable alternative. Majority of the households reported tenancy to support their livelihood followed by employment and income. Only a few households admitted tenancy to repay loan in Gorakhpur and Chandauli districts. Lessors were having different sets of objectives to lease-out land. Dominant objective was to collect rent followed by supplementing income through cultivation as they were absentee land owner engaged in business or services or both combined with absence of male family members (Bharadwaj and Das 1975; Swain, 1999) and non-availability of labour to operate their farm. Therefore, leasing-out was also intended to secure labour supply (Pearce, 1983). Some of the households were unable to operate their field due to sickness, handicapped member or they could not afford the cost of cultivation as they lacked resources. Thus, the objective of lessor is primarily to maximize their gain and make their interlinkages stronger.

Due to lack of viable alternative for lessee, the lessor was always in advantageous position to impose conditions and the lessee was left with no option but with compulsive contractual choice (Swain, 1999). In order to maximise gain, lesser operates various forms of tenancy with varying terms and conditions. Details of output and input sharing terms of tenancies (Mishra and Diwakar, 2005) suggest that sharecropping tenancy was a dominant form in terms of output and input sharing mechanism. However, fixed money rent after harvesting and payment of money rent in advance was also reported. Output sharing in terms of crop was generally 50 : 50 with an exception in Hamirpur where a few cases were found where output and input sharing were 66 per cent and 33 per cent respectively. In general cost sharing was also 50 : 50 but not in all types of costs. The cost sharing in terms of irrigation, chemical fertilizer, cost of seeds, and now a few cases of sharing cost of ploughing were also found (Diwakar, 2001). In case of irrigation cost, Gorakhpur and Rae Bareli did not provide any evidence.

Sharing cost of chemical fertilizer was common in all sample districts with varying percentage of households. Landowner of Chandauli and Muzaffarnagar did not share cost of seeds. Cost sharing for ploughing was found only in Gorakhpur. None of the households reported any adjustment about labour cost involved in cultivation.

Interlinking market and interlinked transactions were very much found in the sample villages of Uttar Pradesh. Rent in advance was emerging as one of the most secured modes of appropriation of surplus. This also led to alienation of poor peasantry from lease market, as they could hardly afford to pay rent in advance. Only resourceful could now enter into the tenancy market. This made poor peanants worse as they gradually lost avenues to supplement their income (Diwakar 2001). Value of rent varied in case of money rent, either pre-paid or post-paid. Depending upon the quality of land it varied from Rs. 1200 per acre to Rs. 720 per acre (Ibid, 2001). Inter-linkages were found in terms of credit and wage. Loyal lessee got credit at concessional rates of interest if they worked to the lessor's field. But they were paid lower wage, as they were considered closer to lessor's goodwill and hardly reacted keeping in view of leasing-in lessor's land as an obligation and opportunity to supplement their income. Thus, lessor maintained dominance and lessee remained dependent on lessor's will. Thus, despite the fact that government of U.P. declared complete elimination of intermediaries in this state long ago, concealed and sharecropping tenancy was very much pervasive in agriculture, which was a basic feature of pre-capitalist land relations in agriculture. It also appears from the above analysis that pre-capitalist tenancy relations are still prevalent and dominant form of capitalist lease market is yet to emerge.

New forms of tenancy relations—contract farming with corporate regulation, however, have also emerged. Contract farming in modern sense is a kind of capitalist penetration in agriculture for accumulation of capital and exploitation of farming sector through monopolistic corporate control imposed by the agribusiness companies (Singh, 2005).

Multinational Companies (MNCs) have entered in the contract market. Major players among them in India are: Cadbury in cocoa, Pepsi Co in potato, chillies and groundnut, Unilever in tomato, chicory, tea and milk, ITC in tobacco, wood, trees and oilseeds, besides Cargil, Monsento and Synzenta in seeds (Oxfam-centad, 2006). Domestic corporate sectors have also made their presence. For instance, Ballarpur industries, JK Papers and Wimco in eucalyptus and poplar trees, Green Agro Pack, VST Natural Products, Global Green Intergarden India, Kempsci Agro Exports and Sterling Agro in gherkins, United Breweries in barley, Nijjer Agro in tomato, Tarai Food in vegetables, M.Todd in mint, and Naamdhari Seeds in seeds. In Uttar Pradesh also MNCs: ITC—E-Chaupal, DCM-Haryali Kisan Bazar, Tata—E-Seva, have started corporate contract agriculture.

III. Growth Performance of Agriculture

We do not intend to negate the facts of the progress that agriculture of U.P. has achieved in due course of time since 1947 when the political power of the country was transferred from the British to Indian ruling class. There are indicators of agricultural development and growth in this state (Diwakar, 2005). Net Sown Area (NSA) has increased from 162.3 lakh hectares in 1950-51 to 165.97 lakh hectares in 2002-03. Percentage of net area irrigated to NSA for corresponding period has also increased from 29.8 to 77.4, irrigation intensity has been raised from about 108 per cent to 138 per cent. As a result, cropping intensity has also increased from 123 per cent to 146 per cent during reference year. However, micro study also suggests that cropping intensity in many parts of the State has remained constant (Saith and Tankha; 86). Needless to say that repeated occurrence of flood and lack of effective water management has been major deterrent for this stagnation.

Technological progress in terms of farm implements was witnessed. Introduction of iron plough and then tractorisation, gradually replaced the draught cattle in post-green revolution period (Ray, 1996: 621-27). It has resulted in structural change significantly. Introduction of energised pumping sets, thresher, crusher, harvesting combined devices, added with the application of HYV, etc., has changed the cropping pattern. But technological development was generally confined to a few sub-regions, which were endowed with infrastructure facilities like irrigation, credit, market, etc. (Sharma and Haque, 1996: 639-44). Use of chemical fertilizer, pesticides, and weedicides, have induced agricultural production and productivity particularly in rich peasantry whereas poor peasants were constrained due to lack of input and credit at the right time of the season of the crop. Intensity of technology witnessed increasing trend but replacement remained very slow (GoUP, 2003). Tractor per hundred hectare increased from almost non-existent in 1966 to 2.67 in 1997. However, wooden and iron ploughs together were 48.98 per hundred hectare in 1966 and by 1997 still these were 40.95. Bullock carts remained major transport. Number of bullock carts in 1966 was 12.39 per hundred hectare and in 1997 it was 8.95. Diesel pump sets per hundred hectare were 0.16 which increased to 13.25 and electric-driven pump sets increased from 0.06 to 2.42 only. Region-wise intensity of technology data suggest that 43 per cent of wooden ploughs were used in eastern UP followed by western UP using about 28 per cent. Among the users of iron plough distribution suggested that western UP took about 40 per cent as the largest share followed by eastern UP. About 54 per cent of tractors were used in western UP only. But so far cart as transport was used, western UP shared 56.66 per cent. In case of use of implements for irrigation, major share was of western UP. Lowest share in technology was of Bundelkhand region and central UP had second lowest figure. Fertilizer consumption has increased but still it was very low. During 1970-71 it was 2.37 per hectare to 19.94 kg per hectare. Most disturbing fact was that NPK ratio, which should ideally be 4 : 2 : 1, was 7 : 2 : 1 during 1970-71, became worse, (i.e., 25 : 8 : 1) in 2000-01. Region-wise distribution of (Nitrogen Phosphate-Potash) NPK remainedextra ordinarily alarming, particularly in Bundelkhand Region (431 : 280 : 1).

Estimates of sectoral net state domestic product of agriculture and allied activities available at different constant

Table 3.2: Annual Average Growth Rates of Agriculture NSDP of Uttar Pradesh at Factor Cost by Industry of Origin at 1993-94 Prices

Sector/ Period	*1960-61 to 1970-71*	*1971-72 to 1980-81*	*1981-82 to 1990-91*	*1991-92 to 2000-01*	*1960-61 to 2000-01*
Agriculture & Animal Husbandry	1.29± .0086	2.45± .0102	2.96± .00303	2.15± .0036	2.63± .0011
Forestry & Logging	5.75± .0054	(-)2.65± .0048	(-)11018± .0142	(-)2.33± .028	(-)3.85± .0044
Fishing	7.97± .0061	4.44± .00161	12.48± .01345	6.87± .0042	7.54± .0019

Source : Calculated from the data published by EPW Research Foundation.

prices have been spliced at 93-94 prices and their growth rates have been calculated. Result suggests that agriculture of U.P. has grown on an average of 2.63 per cent per annum between 1960-61 and 2000-01. During 1960s, agriculture grew by merely 1.29 per cent, 2.45 per cent in 1970s and touched its highest rate of 2.96 per cent in 1980s. During 1990s, growth rate has decelerated to 2.15 per cent. Fishery has maintained its impressive growth rates at 7.5 per cent per annum but forestry has registered negative rate of growth. Value of standard error attached with estimated growth rates suggests that possibility of variation in estimated rate of growth has been nominal (Table 3.2).

Performance of agriculture may be examined in terms of area expansion, volume of production and productivity. It may further be categorized in food crops and non-food crops. Data provided for different crops by the Directorate of Agriculture of Uttar Pradesh form basis to analyze the facts. Average annual rate of growth of the area under foodgrains production has been declining and turned to be negative in 1990s (Table 3.3) and in the case of production rate of growth has declined from 3.05 per cent per annum during 1970-71 to 1990-91 to 1.78 per cent in the 1990s. However, overall production during 1950-51 to 2000-01 has increased by 2.59 per cent per annum. Productivity has increased in post-green revolution period until 1991, which subsequently could not be sustained later and witnessed declining trend. However, if one takes account of triennium ending average at two points of time it suggests

Table 3.3: Average Annual Growth Rate of area Production and Productivity during 1950-51 to 2000-01

Period	Average Annual Growth Rates (per cent)		
Food Crops	Area	Production	Productivity
1950-51 to 1970-71	0.65	2.55	0.95
1970-71 to 1990-91	0.23	3.50	2.88
1990-91 to 2000-01	(-) 0.14	1.78	1.91
1950-51 to 2000-01	0.33	2.59	2.26
Non-Food Crops			
1950-51 to 1970-71	2.19	3.16	1.88
1970-71 to 1990-91	1.77	3.43	2.82
1990-91 to 2000-01	3.03	2.65	(-) 0.38
1950-51 to 2000-01	1.69	2.77	1.07
All Crops			
1950-51 to 1970-71	0.79	3.00	1.18
1970-71 to 1990-91	0.42	3.33	2.85
1990-91 to 2000-01	0.07	2.10	1.16
1950-51 to 2000-01	0.47	2.72	2.20

Note : Food Crops include cereals, pulses and non-food crops include sugarcane, oilseeds, potato and other crops.

Source : Calculation is based on data from *Uttar Pradesh ke Krishhi Ankre*, various issues.

differently. Data for triennium ending 2002 suggests that nearly 80 per cent of total cropped area in U.P. is under foodgrain production. If one compares this situation with triennium ending 1976 (72.6 per cent), there is an increase of about 8 per cent. Another state, which has similar trend, is Punjab. Punjab registered 8.8 per cent increase. At the all India level, there has been decline in general in area of food grains. However, 64.4 per cent of total cropped area in India is still under food grains production (Vyas, 2004). This indicates that value added agriculture is yet to make dent and market driven production in this sector is yet to dominate over subsistence agriculture.

Growth rates of non-food crops reveal decline of area until 1990-91 and subsequent increase in coverage of non-food crops. This explains substitution of the area under food crops. So far production of non-food crops was concerned there was increase in productivity until 1990-91 and subsequently it registered significant declining trend. As a result, productivity had a negative trend during 1990s. Details about access to technology, credit, input and production markets need to be explained and examined. Non-food crops particularly, potato and sugarcane growers have been facing critical situation. At the time of harvest, price of potato touches the lowest point quite below the level of minimal cost. In absence of retaining capacity, proper storage, credit and insurance farmers are left in the lurch. Limited accessibility of inadequate facilities and infrastructure further aggravate the situation of majority of farmers belonging to small and marginal groups. In such a precarious condition, farmers prefer to leave the crops in the field itself to avoid further aggravation of crisis. Thus, in absence of proper infrastructure development it appears that technological effects of green revolution could not be sustained in either foodgrains or non-food crops, which resulted into declining area, production and productivity of entire agriculture in 1990s in Uttar Pradesh. Moreover, supply elastic nature of agricultural prices due to lack of sufficient supporting infrastructure such as storage, credit, insurance, etc., amidst unmet pressing need resulting into distress sales even by the net buyers worked as disincentives in absence of retaining capacity of the farmers.

IV. Emerging Relations

There are a number of empirical studies, which accept the qualitative differences and variations in production relations in agriculture of Uttar Pradesh. West U.P. is characterised as more productive and developed than the rest of the state not only because of variations in social composition but also discriminatory tenurial systems and investment pattern rooted in the history of the colonial rule of British India. As a result capitalist base of changes in agriculture was faster in West U.P. where hard working Jats could reap the advantages of modern technological improvement introduced in agriculture. (Stokes, 1978; Patnaik and Hassan, 1995; 85). Whereas agriculture of East U.P. remained by and large in the trap of landlord based semi-feudal relations who stuck to unproductive rent appropriation, continues to prevail in the most of the east. (Patnaik, 1988; 23-24). Land reforms however could introduce a new dimension towards changes in agriculture with the rise of middle peasantry which has started challenging the dominance of upper caste based landlord production relation (Lerche, 1998 : A-30). This phenomenon has contributed significantly not only in production and productivity but also in terms of family labour participation in agriculture, particularly of east U.P. (Srivastava, 1994 : 168, 170; 1995 : 230). However, this has led to a horizontal growth and not significantly resulted into vertical liberation of the lowest rung of the society. Emergence of middle caste based neo-rich peasantry does not appear different than upper caste landlord.

A tendency of increasing wage rate and use of hired labour is also witnessed but output, wage and employment effects of technological change are difficult to observe in agriculture, in view of the uneven base of capitalist penetration in agriculture. In fact, inter-district variation presents a composite picture of production relation, more a case of semi-feudal relations than capitalist relation despite the emergence of capitalist relations in a few districts of Uttar Pradesh (Mishra, 1990, 198-99). As a result, landlord-cum-big peasants could earn not only without any significant investment through usury, trade and leasing out land but also calculate comparative advantages in respect of investment on land (Davey, 1975, 173).

Traditional institutions and identities of social organisation are yet to be transformed into bourgeoisie institutions. Caste and religion dominate the psyche of the rural masses. Of course, there is assertion from below not only to participate but also to exercise hegemonic role to control over these institutions. Symptom of capitalist changes is not enough to replace these institutions through bourgeoisie institutions. Technological advancement in one field may not be enough to sustain the capitalist feature in the economy as a whole. Massive loss of production not only because of recurring flood, due to lack of proper and effective water management but also because of the absence of proper infrastructure, are a few indications, which suggest that capitalism in agriculture is yet to replace pre-capitalist relations of production in U.P. There is an imperative need to re-assess the situation of forced commercialisation, which does not necessarily lead to capitalist transformation. This may pose questions for other parts of the country as well where farmers are getting frustrated, committing suicides in this form of productive organisation.

Undoubtedly symptoms of transitions are reflected in terms of increasing production and productivity, introduction of machine, displacement of labour through machines, marginal increase in wages, use of modern inputs, family participation, and now contract and corporate farming, etc. One should not overlook the phenomenon of increasing money-lending usury network leading to farmers' suicides in the country, including Uttar Pradesh. In my opinion indicators of emerging capitalist relations in limited pockets do not indicate any dominant sign of replacement of pre-capitalist relations of production in agriculture through capitalist mode. Of course this form of social formation has acquired some special features, which appear horizontally different but this is not enough to present a new kind of production relation as market biases are yet to be seen in favour of direct producers and particularly in terms of commodification of agricultural labourers. Moreover, "the powerful combinations of peasant proprietors-*cum*-moneylender-*cum* traders hand in gloves-with state apparatus has adopted subtle devices to divide and confuse the oppressed by exploiting caste and religious sentiments. It has also evolved legal as well as extra legal apparatus in the form of private armies to suppress any kind of mobilisation or resistance on the part of rural poor who may be either agricultural workers, sharecroppers, backdoor tenants or poor cultivators, to redress their just grievances" (Mehta, 1990 : 228). Therefore, in the light of the above discussion if one attempts to conclude this exercise a broad criterion is to be laid down in terms of concrete indicators even in those parts of the state where transition is witnessed, emergence of factor markets and distribution of surplus among the forces of production are yet to be seen in correspondence with social, economic and political institutions which ultimately decide the forms of productive organisations and not only by the production and productivity.

REFERENCES

Banaji, J. (1972): For a theory of Colonial Mode of Production, ed. in Patnaik, U., *Agrarian Relation and Accumulation*, Oxford University Press.

Breman, J. and Mundle, S. (Ed. 1991): *Rural Changes in Asia,* Oxford University Press, Delhi.

Breman, J., et al. (Ed. 1997): *The Village in Asia Revisited*, Oxford University Press, and New Delhi.

Byres, T.J., Political Economy, Agrarian Question and Comparative Method, *Economic and Political Weekly*, March 11, 1995.

Davey, B., (1975): *The Economic Development of India*, Spokesman Books.

Diwakar, D.M. and Sanatan Nayak (2007): *Development Challenges Afflicting Uttar Pradesh*, Manak Publications, New Delhi.

Diwakar, D.M. and G.P. Mishra, (2006): *Deprivation and Inclusive Development (Ed.)*, Manak Publications, New Delhi.

Diwakar, D.M., (2005): Growth Linkages of Agriculture of Uttar Pradesh: Constraints, Options, and Strategies, *Convention Journal, Lucknow Management Association*, Vol. 1, No. 1.

Diwakar, D.M. (2000): *Emerging Agrarian Relations in India*, Manak Publication, New Delhi.

Dreze, J. Occupational Change, Land Ownership and Social Inequality in Preman, J. *et al.* (Ed.) *The Village in Asia Revisited,* Oxford University Press, 1997.

Frank, A.G.: On Feudal Models and Methods of Escaping Capitalist Reality in Patnaik, U. (ed.) (1990): *Agrarian Relations and Accumulation*, Oxford University Press.

Geertz, Clifford (1972): Village, in David L. Sills (ed.) *International Excyclopaedia in Social Sciences*, The MacMillan Company & the Free Press, New York, Reprint.

Jual, B.N., Social Mobilization and Distributive Justice: Responding Some Questions in Diwakar, D.M., (Ed.): *Distributive Justice Through Social Mobilisation*, Manak Publications, 1998.

Kripashankar, (1997): *Bataidari ki Samsya* (Hindi), Paper presented in the workshop on Social Mobilisation and Effective Land Reforms in U.P. at Gandhian Institute of Studies, Varanasi, December 19-20,

Lerche, Jens, (1998): Agriculture Labourers, the State and Agrarian Transition in Uttar Pradesh, *Economic and Political Weekly*, March 28, 1998.

Marx, K. (1970): *Critique of Political Economy*, Progress Publishers, Moscow.

Marx, K. (1954): *Capital*, Progress Publishers, Moscow, Vol. I, reprint 1986.

Mehta, Uday, (1990): Indian Agriculture since Independence, G. Shah (ed.), *Capitalist Development*, Popular Prakashan, Bombay, 1990.

Mishra, G.P. and D.M. Diwakar (2005): *Land Reforms and Human Development*, Manak Publications, New Delhi.

Mishra, G.P. (1990): Output Growth, Wages and Employment in Agriculture, *The Indian Journal of Labour Economics*, Vol. 33, No. 3.

Nadkarni, M.V. (1991): The Mode of Production Debate: A Review Article, *Indian Economic Review*, Vol. 26, No. 1.

National Council of Applied Economic Research, (1996): Human Development Profile of India, Main Report, Vol. 1, November, 1996.

Patnaik, U., (1971): Development of Capitalism in Indian Agriculture, *Social Scientist*.

Patnaik, U. (1990): *Agrarian Relations and Accumulation*, Oxford University Press.

Patnaik, U. (1988): Some Aspects of Development in Agrarian Sector in Independent India, *Social Scientist*, No. 177, Vol. 16, No. 2.

Patnaik, U. and Joya Hassan (1995): Aspects of Farmer's Movement in Uttar Pradesh in the Context of Uneven Capitalist Development in Indian Agriculture in T.V. Sathyamurthy (ed.) *Industry and Agriculture in India since Independence: Social Change and Political Discourse in India, Structure of Power, Movements and Resistance*, Vol. 2, Oxford University Press, New Delhi.

Prasad, Pradhan H. (1989): *Lopsided Growth*, Oxford University Press.

Prasad, Pradhan H. and G.B. Rogers (1983): *Class-Caste and Landholdings in the Analysis of Rural Economy*, ILO, Working Paper No. 140.

Ray, A.K., *et al.* Matire pf cjamges om Draigjt amo,a; {pwer om Omdoa" A State-wise Study, *Agricultural Situation in India*, December 1996.

Redfield, Robert (1930): *Tepoztlan, a Mexican Village: A Study of Folk Life*, University of Chicago Press.

Redfield, Robert (1941): *The Folk Culture of Yucatan*, University of Chicago Press.

Redfield, Robert (1956): *Peasant Society and Culture: An Anthropological Approach to Civilization*, University of Chicago Press; Cambridge University Press.

Reserve Bank of India, Report of the Sen Committee on Agricultural Productivity in Eastern India, 1984, Vol. II, Ch. 25, See also Ch. 4, part-I.

Rudra, A. (1990): Indian Capitalism and Marxist Theory in G. Shah (ed.): *Capitalist Development*, Popular Prakashan, Bombay, 1990.

Rudra, A. (1969): Big Farmers of Punjab, *Economic and Political Weekly*, September 27 and December 27.

Saith, A., *et al.*, Longitudinal Analysis of Structural Change, in Breman, J. *et. al.*, (Ed. 1997): *The Village in Asia Revisited*, Oxford University Press, and New Delhi.

Sharma, H.R. (1994): Distribution of Landholdings in Rural India, *Economic and Political Weekly*, March 26.

Sharma, V.K., and T.K. Haque, Perspective of Technological Change in Indian Agriculture—A case of HYV Technology, *Agricultural Situation in India*, December 1996.

Singh, A.K. (1984): *Agricultural Development and Rural Poverty*, Ashish Publishing House, New Delhi.

Singh, B., and S. Mishra (1964): *A Study of Land Reforms in Uttar Pradesh*, Oxford Book Company, New Delhi.

Singh, Sukhpal (2005): *Political Economy of Corporate Farming in India*, Allied Publishers, New Delhi.

Srivastava, R.: *Change and Resilience in Producer Strategies in Uttar Pradesh Agriculture in Breman*, et. al. (Ed.) op. cit.

Srivastava, R. (1994): Planning and Regional Disparities in India in T.J. Byres(ed.) *The State and Development Planning in India*, Oxford University Press, New Delhi.

Srivastava, R. (1995): India's Uneven Development and its Implications for Political Process: An Analysis of Some Recent Trends, in T.V. Sathyamurthy (ed.). *Industry and Agriculture in India since Independence: Social Change and Political Discourse in India, Structure of Power, Movements and Resistance*, Vol. 2, Oxford University Press, New Delhi.

Steward, Julian H. (1955): *Theory of Culture Change: The Methodology of Multilinear Evolution*, Urbana: University of Illinois Press.

Steward, Julian H., et al. (1956): *The People of Puerto Rico: A Study of Social Anthropology*, Urbana: University of Illinois Press.

Stokes, E. (1978) *The Peasant and the Raj: Studies in Agrarian Society and Peasant Rebellion in Colonial India*, Cambridge University Press, Cambridge.

Wolf, Eric (1955): Types of Latin American Peasantry: A Preliminary Discussion, *American Anthropologist*, New Series 57: 452-471 in Sills, David L., (1972): *International Encyclopaedia in Social Sciences*, Reprint Edition.

4

Villages and Villagers of the Naugarh Region in Chandauli

R.C. MISHRA

Introduction

This paper reports a study carried out with villagers of the Kharwar community residing in Naugarh region of Chandauli district of Uttar Pradesh. Over the last two decades the villagers have been exposed to a variety of developmental porogrammes initiated by the government and non-governmental organizations. For a long time, the author has been involved in understanding the nature of physical and socio-cultural changes going on in that region, the way people enter into and adapt to various changes, and the way in which processes of social and cultural changes influence the psychological make-up of villagers.

Study of social and cultural change has been an interesting theme of research in the discipline of social sciences for a long time. Psychologists are not interested in the study of small-scale changes that take place slowly in the life of people. They are mainly interested in the study of changes that are large scale, and occur in the life of people suddenly without any previous warning (e.g., setting up of an industry or hydroelectric project in the region, or displacement of people due to construction of a dam, etc.). Such changes generate new demands of adjustment on the part of people, who may adopt different psychological strategies to deal with the problems of change.

Studies of social and cultural change have been carried out in two broad traditions of research. One is known as "modernization tradition" (Inkeles & Smith, 1974) in which changes are viewed as movement of individuals from a less desirable to a more desirable state. The journey of change is characterized by people's movement from a "traditional" state to a "modern" state. A basic assumption of this approach is that modernity is a valued goal which people in different parts of the world have been trying to achieve and that the journey between the two states takes place in a linear fashion. In a number of studies psychologists have attempted to study the process of modernization, the factors that facilitate this process, and the psychological consequences that emerge due to the pressure of modernization. Another tradition of research on social and cultural change is that of "ethnic group relations" in which changes in the life of a group of people are viewed as resulting from their "contact" with members of other cultural groups. Generally known as "acculturation" the process refers to culture change as a result of continuous first-hand contact of two independent cultural groups over an extended period of time (Redfield, Linton & Herskovits, 1963). Individual members of the groups in contact also experience change; this phenomenon is termed "psychological acculturation" (Graves, 1967). In this research tradition, changes are viewed as people's adaptations to the demands of the situation. They are considered to be multidirectional without placing any value on any one direction. The individuals seem to enjoy considerable freedom of choice to move in any one direction.

Contact lies at the heart of research in acculturation framework. Many times people seek these contacts voluntarily by moving out (e.g., in the life of education, trade, employment). On other occasions, the contacts are brought to people in an involuntary manner (e.g., by setting up an industry in their region, forcing education under a government policy). These situations pose different demands on people in the process of acculturation. Hence, the nature of changes in these situations are likely to be different.

A distinction has to be made between "acculturative changes" and "developmental changes". The latter refers to changes that take place due to the programmes organized by State and Central Governments to bring about changes in the life of selected groups of people (e.g., in the case of Scheduled Castes and Scheduled Tribes). In this case, the direction of change is well-defined, and a deliberate effort is made to achieve a certain level of change during a specified period of time. The glimpses of these intended changes can be found in Five-Year Plans of the Government of India. Berry (1980) prefers to call these changes as "acculturation-by-design", because in this case, the contact is brought in deliberately, and the nature of changes can be predicted well in advance, which usually does not happen in the case of general acculturation.

Psychological studies indicate that in the process of acculturation, the acculturating individuals hold different attitudes towards the way they would like to relate to individuals or groups who bring on to them the pressure of acculturation. These attitudes, referred to as "acculturation attitudes" (Berry, 1990, 2005), involve orientation of people towards two general issues facing all acculturating people: *cultural maintenance* (of one's own group) and *contact* (with other groups). These questions are of central importance in culturally plural societies in which more than one cultural group is represented in the population, and in which there is also some likelihood that these groups will continue to maintain them in future as well.

Individuals in such societies are usually confronted with two important questions in the process of culture change: (1) whether their traditional culture and identity is of value and to be retained, or whether these are not valuable and be given up, and (2) whether positive relations with the larger, dominant society should be sought, or the dominant group should be kept as distant as possible. A positive or negative response to these questions may indicate four varieties of acculturation orientations: integration, assimilation, separation and marginalization (see Figure 4.1).

In the "integration" mode, maintenance of one's cultural identity as well as movement to become an integral part of a larger societal framework is the option taken, whereas in "assimilation", relinquishing cultural identity and moving into

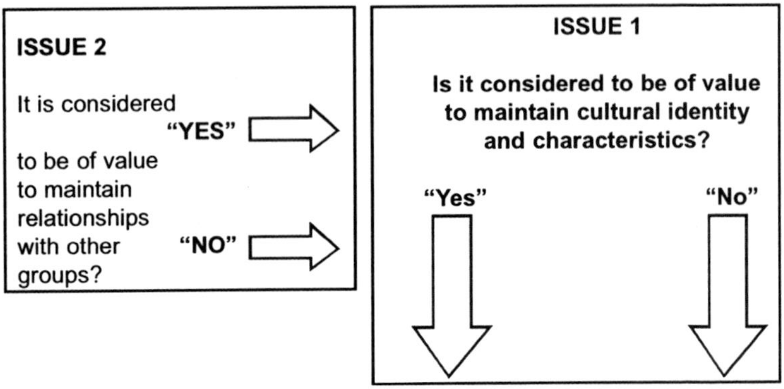

Fig. 4.1: Acculturation attitudes

the larger society is the individual's option. "Separation" refers to a self-imposed withdrawal from the larger society. However, when imposed by the larger society, it becomes one of the classical forms of "segregation". In "marginalization", the groups lose cultural or psychological contact with either their traditional culture or the larger society. When stabilized in a non-dominant group, it constitutes the classical condition of "marginality".

Research in India has also identified "co-existence" as another important acculturation strategy (Mishra, Sinha, & Berry, 1996). It has been regarded as a major strategy displayed by Indian people for dealing with inroads from other cultures (Sinha, 1988; Sinha & Tripathi, 1994). In this case, no attempt is made towards synthesis or assimilation of new elements; instead they are "enfolded" in the system and kept side by side with the pre-existing elements without involving any evaluation or standards of comparison (Mishra, *et al.*, 1996).

Research studies indicate considerable individual and group differences in acculturation attitudes. One individual may follow a course towards assimilation, whereas another may not. Similarly, one group may opt for separation by developing its own formal organization, whereas another may seek integration. However, the choice of acculturating individuals or groups for one option or another depends on several factors (Berry, 1986). The nature of the dominant society and the nature of acculturating groups are important factors in this respect. While larger societies may vary with respect to tolerance for diversity, the acculturating groups may vary with respect to freedom of contact and mobility (Berry, Kim, Power, Young & Bujaki, 1989; Berry, 1990; Berry & Sam, 1997). The case of voluntary contact suggests that immigrants and ethnic groups may be more likely to integrate or assimilate than refugees or native peoples. In the case of sedentary groups, there is the possibility of establishing protective institutions, which enhance the likelihood of maintaining one's identity, language and culture. Hence, integration or separation are the most likely modes of acculturation.

Berry (1990) suggests that these options should not be viewed as independent of the nature of the dominant society. In societies where cultural diversity is valued, tolerated and encouraged (considering it as a resource, rather than a problem), integration and separation are more likely to occur. In societies that have expectations (and a policy) to reduce cultural diversity, assimilation and marginalization are the more likely options. Studies carried out with Aboriginal groups and Native people in Australia and Canada (Berry, 1976; Sommerlad, 1968; Sommerlad & Berry, 1970) and with tribal people in undivided Bihar (Mishra, *et al.*, 1996) offer support to these contentions.

Studies of acculturation attitudes have been extensively carried out with immigrants to western industrial societies (Berry & Sam, 1977). The generalizability of these findings to other societies (non-western) and other groups (e.g., tribal groups cannot be claimed. These two populations (immigrants and tribal) differ widely in terms of their experience of acculturation. While immigrants voluntarily accept acculturation because of their own desire to move to the respective country, acculturation generally comes to tribal people in an involuntary manner. This may generally imply that such groups in due course of time will get assimilated into the group that brings the acculturative influences. However, it does not mean that they would necessarily favour assimilation at the attitudinal level. While the option for integration or assimilation remains open, the groups may also opt for separation, particularly if they are strong enough to sustain on their own resources. Thus, the attitudes of tribal people towards acculturation may vary in a variety of ways (Mishra, et al., 1996).

A strong image of tribal societies projected on to us is that tribals exist as a tightly kint society and value relationships more than anything else in their life. Forest activities require them to move in bands and work collectively. Collective dance is a typical feature of a tribal community. Any book on tribals would necessarily have a picture portraying drumming and dancing of men and women. Reports indicate that it used to be a regular activity in villages, and it had an intrinsic value of connecting people of the community with each other (Mishra, *et al.,* 1996). In recent years collective dance is reduced to the level of a ceremonial activity, which is intentionally organized on special occasions (Mishra, *et al.,* 1996). The loss of such cultural practices is likely to lead to the weakening of social connections and relationships among members of the tribal villages.

In the present paper an attempt has been made to examine the nature of changes taking place in Kharwar villages of Chandauli district, and how these changes have affected the psychological life of people in those villages during the span of a decade. Attempt has been made to examine the changes at both the objective and subjective levels. Objective changes refer to those changes that take place in various aspects of an individual's or group's life, and can be easily spotted out (e.g., changes in language, dressing style, housing). Subjective changes refer to those changes that take place in the psyche of people, and can be discerned only with the help of a sensitive measuring instrument (e.g., changes in attitudes, values or perceptions). These changes were assessed twice at an interval of ten years. In light of the previous findings it was hypothesized that :

(1) With the passage of time the villages and villagers would demonstrate a considerable level of change in terms of objective indices of acculturation.
(2) With the passage of time the villagers would show an increase in the strength of co-existence, integration and

assimilation attitudes, and a decrease in the strength of separation or marginalization attitudes to acculturation.

(3) The degree of connectedness in villagers would reduce with the passage of time both at the group and individual levels.

Sample and Design

The study was conducted with male Kharwar adults living in nine villages of Naugarh region in Chandauli district of Uttar Pradesh. The economic pursuits, cultural practices and history of acculturation of this group is well documented (Dubey, 1991). In general, the Kharwar live a traditional life. It may be noted that the Kharwar are now classified as "Scheduled Caste" by the State Government, but their tribal identity is so strong that they clearly reject this caste status.

The report presented here is based on data collected at two different points of time. With the support of a NGO working in the region, a study of acculturation of the Kharwar (*N*=200) had been carried out in the year 1992. The author had another opportunity to work with the same group of people in the year 2002. The data obtained in 1992 were used as a baseline to examine the changes in villages and villagers during a period of almost ten years. In the second study also 200 subjects were tested. The participants' age in both studies ranged from 26 to 40 years. In both studies participants were selected from the same nine villages. Such data sets allow a reliable understanding of what had been going on in the villages as well as among villagers during the course of their acculturation.

The *Kharwar* represent a group of people whose origin is traced in Palamau region of Bihar (now Jharkhand). It also refers to a group of people who earlier resided in the Sone valley. The Kharwars of U.P. claim their origin in Rohtas, and their descent from the family of the Sun, although scholarly opinions about them vary considerably.

Kharwar economy today is mainly based on farming, but livestock, forest activities and seasonal wage earning provide them with other sources of income. The land holdings of the

Kharwar are generally devoid of irrigation facilities. They generally yield only one crop in a year, and that too depends largely on adequate rainfall. The yield is barely enough to support the family for a few months. For a number of months they mainly depend on forest resources for livelihood. Thus, their economy can be called as "farming-cum-forest economy". They are also engaged in hunting and trapping of wild animals and birds. Fishing is also an important economic activity.

High salt consumption characterizes the Kharwar food habit. People often take food with a mixture of salt and hot pepper (called *silchuran*). Each Kharwar family passes through "food months" and "hunger months". In the harvest months, when the house is full of grains, people may have several meals in a day. During the periods of food scarcity, on the other hand, they may often go without meals and survive mainly on wild vegetation, flowers, fruits, roots and barks of the tree. Because of their exposure to the outside world, the Kharwar lifestyle is changing considerably. Joint family has started disintegrating, and there are also reports about social violence in the community. Exposure to mass media has influenced them to such an extent that many young Kharwar now feel that changing their lifestyle is essential for economic development and a good life.

Measures

The following measures were used in the present study:

Personal Biographical Schedule

It consisted of information about the participant such as his name, age, family background, means of livelihood, year of schooling, and degree of urban exposure.

Village Acculturation Scale

It was used to assess changes taking place at the village level. Based on a pilot study 11 physical features were identified in which change at the village level could be assessed. These included: Approach to the village (paved road, unpaved road, path), nature of houses (old styled, new styled, mixture of old and new), facility of drinking water (running water tap, hand pump, well, river/stream/tank), electricity (available, not available), agricultural implements (traditional, modern, mixed), water pitchers (clay, aluminium, other metals), settlement (huddled houses, isolated houses), domestic animals (old breeds, new breeds, mixed), shop (available, not available), school (available, not available) and entertainment technology (radio, televisioin, others). Each village could be rated on these features to examine the degree to which it has been affected by the waves of change. The score range on this scale was 8-25 (non-availability counted as zero).

Contact Acculturation Scale

Developed by Mishra, *et al.* (1996), this scale was used for measuring the degree of change in people's life as a result of their contact with the outside world. The scale is based on a number of indicators of contact acculturation suggested by Berry (1976) and Berry, *et al.* (1986). At the same time, some new indices of contact have also been added drawing upon the features of tribal setting in India. The scale consists of a number of indices of contact such as knowledge of tribal language, knowledge of Hindi (official language), knowledge of English and other language, ownership of people such as utensils, ornaments, furniture, etc., dressing style, means of livelihood, use of technology, travel experience and exposure to movies. The scale has been used for assessing the level of contact acculturation of tribal people in Bihar and Nepal and found quite useful. However, its suitability for the present study was examined on the basis of a pilot study with Kharwar people. Each person was rated on each of the indices using a 5-point scale.

Acculturation Attitudes Scale

This scale was developed to measure the attitudes of people towards acculturation. The idea was drawn from other similar works (e.g. Sommerlad & Berry, 1970; Mishra, *et al.*, 1996; Mishra & Chaubey, 2002). Based on a field survey, nine areas were identified in which acculturation orientation of people appeared to be important. These involved the matters of dress, friendship, food, customs and rituals, residence, co-operation with groups, naming of the child, lifestyle, and community relationships. Five Likert-type scales were developed for measuring integration, assimilation, separation, marginalization and co-existence attitudes with regard to each of the key issues, and these were tried out on a sample (N=60) of Kharwar group. The Likert-type strategy of attitude measurement did not work well. Hence, a ladder-rating procedure (Sinha, 1969) was adopted. Internal consistency of the scale items was found to be satisfactory (*r* ranged from .43 to .86). The scale consisted of 45 items. The participant had to select one out of five statements, and then endorse his degree of agreement on a 5-point scale. The score range on this each attitudinal measure was 0-45.

Social Connectedness

This measure consisted of eight items that involved rating community on a 5-point scale on issues like the selection of spouse, decision for marriage, choice of child's work, naming of a child, matters related to residence, raising of children, kinship orientation, and social support. The score range was 8-40. A higher score on the measure indicated greater connectedness in a community.

Individual Connectedness

It was assessed with a six-item rating scale (5-point), which probed into the extent of an individual's participation in collective dance, birth, marriage, and death ceremonies, the frequency of visit to relatives, and visit to ailing neighbours. The score range was 6-30, a higher score indicating greater individual connectedness.

Data collection was accomplished with the help of local research assistants, who belonged to the same community. They were thoroughly inducted into the process of testing. It was expected that the participants would have no hesitation in expressing their attitudes and discussing other matters with the members of their own community, and thereby the reliability of data would be enhanced. Testing was carried out in the local language.

Results

The scores of village acculturation scale indicated that in the year 1992 all the villages scores very low (score range 10-14). Those closer to the town of Naugarh had moved little away from their traditional status than those that were away from the town. In 2002, the range of acculturation score for villages was found to be 17-22, indicating that all the villages were characterized by some degree of change in terms of their physical parameters, including the possession of goods and livestock. Villages near the town were again characterized by greater change than those away from the town.

The mean scores of group obtained on contact acculturation measure at two points of time are given in Table 4.1. It may be observed that scores of the group show considerable increase over the period of a decade. All mean differences were found to be significant. While on other indicators there was a general increase in scores, a decrease was evident on the measure of "own language" use.

Comparison of mean scores on acculturation attitudes (Table 4.2) revealed a significant increase in scores on co-existence and integration attitudes; the increase in assimilation scores was not significant. A decrease in separation scores was noted over the years, but the difference was not significant. On the other hand, marginalization attitude showed a significantly sharp decline, and reached a fairly low level of its existence.

The mean scores of the group on social and individual connectedness measures are given in Table 4.3. A significant decline on both the measures is clearly in evidence.

Discussion

The findings in general support our predictions about changes among villages and villagers over a span of ten years. A significant increase in scores noted on most of the indices of

Table 4.1: Mean score of the group on contact acculturation measure

Indices	*Mean scores 1992*	*Mean scores 2002*	*Mean difference*	*t-ratios*
Own language	4.80 (2.63)	3.20 (3.25)	1.60	5.71**
Knowledge of Hindi	1.35 (0.96)	3.15 (2.10)	1.80	11.25**
Knowledge of English	1.10 (0.87)	2.05 (1.26)	0.95	13.57**
Utensils	1.65 (1.10)	4.00 (2.05)	2.35	14.69**
Ornaments	2.10 (1.65)	4.35 (2.15)	2.25	15.00**
Clothes	1.90 (0.95)	3.80 (1.78)	1.90	13.57**
Furnitures	1.20 (0.90)	3.20 (2.16)	2.00	12.50**
Livelihood	1.30 (0.76)	2.95 (1.05)	1.65	18.33**
Use of technology	1.20 (1.10)	3.10 (2.16)	1.90	11.18**
Religious practices	1.55 (1.15)	2.90 (1.65)	1.35	9.64**
Dressing style	2.10 (0.97)	3.60 (1.36)	1.50	12.50**
Travel experience	1.60 (1.25)	3.25 (2.10)	1.65	9.70**
Exposure to movies	1.10 (1.00)	2.60 (1.90)	1.50	10.00**

** $p < .01$

Table 2: Mean score of groups on acculturation attitude measures

Attitudes	*Mean scores 1992*	*Mean scores 2002*	*Mean difference*
Integration			
Mean	9.15	10.65	1.50
S.D.	5.60	5.35	(t=2.78)**
Assimilation			
Mean	7.05	7.75	0.70
S.D.	5.45	6.60	(t=1.17)
Separation			
Mean	7.25	6.10	1.15
S.D.	5.25	3.80	(t=1.82)
Marginalization			
Mean	3.95	0.65	3.30
S.D.	2.60	1.80	(t=15.00)**
Co-existence			
Mean	17.60	19.85	2.25
S.D.	6.65	6.70	(t=3.41)**

** $p < .01$

village and individual level contact-acculturation suggests that the programmes of change and development being executed in these villages are working fairly well in terms of introducing the Kharwar people to the lifestyle of other groups of people.

Table 3: Mean score of groups on social and individual connectedness measures

Measures	*Mean scores 1992*	*Mean scores 2002*	*Mean difference*
Social Connectedness			
Mean	36.15	24.45	11.70
S.D.	15.60	14.35	(t=11.54)**
Individual Connectedness			
Mean	27.30	17.75	9.55
S.D.	12.45	9.60	(t=8.60)**

** $p < .01$

It also indicates that people have accepted these changes as a viable option for their life. On the other hand, a significant decrease on the index of "own language" is noted, suggesting that in the process of change people are giving up their own heritage language. Loss of one's heritage language is a clearly documented phenomenon in the course of acculturation (Berry & Sam, 1997). Kharwar community is no exception to this rule. The most important reason seems to be the *functionality* of people's own language. Since the members of other groups, either living in Kharwar villages or in adjacent villages, speak a dialect of standard Hindi, the Kharwar are gradually picking up this language for communication with members of other groups as well those of their own group. The heritage language does not seem to be of much use in the changed context. A slight increase in the "knowledge of English" again indicates that the Kharwar are keen to move out of the local context to interact and work with members of other groups and participate in wider economic life.

The findings with respect to acculturation attitudes indicate co-existence and integration modes of acculturation to be strongly placed in them. These have become further stronger over the years of change. In view of the government policy and the general programmes aimed at integration of Tribals in the mainstream society (with due regard for their cultural identity), this was the most likely expectation. To this extent, the findings are consistent with those of others who have attempted to assess and discuss peoples' acculturation attitudes in multicultural societies (Berry *et al.*, 1989; Berry, Phinnery, Sam & Vedder, 2006a, 2006b; Mishra *et al.*, 1996; Mishra & Chaubey, 2002). High co-existence orientation of the groups indicates that in the course of acculturation, the preference of the Kharwar is to keep the elements of own and external culture side by side. There is sufficient evidence to demonstrate co-existence of different cultural elements in various walks of life of the Indian people in general (Mishra, 1994; Sinha & Tripathi, 1994).

The prediction that acculturation of people over a longer period of time would encourage greater assimilation did not find support in this study. There was a slight increase in assimilation scores of people, but the difference was not significant. However, this points to the fact that if assimilation is to take place in the course of acculturation, it is likely to come gradually over an extended period of contact with more pervasive influences on people.

The evidence for marginalization, which was fairly weak in 1992, was found to show further decline to reach a very low level of its existence in 2002. The socio-cultural context in which the Tribal people in general are enfolded in India may be one of the plausible reasons for this finding. Slightly greater marginalization observed in the 1992 study points to the fact that this orientation is likely to develop in the early phases of acculturation when people are not able to decide upon the course of action for themselves. When the contact crosses a threshold point, marginalization orientation is taken over by other modes of acculturation, which carry enough potential to reduce the feelings of marginalization.

Social connectedness has been regarded as a major strength to tribal communities for a long time. Acculturation seemed to have worked as a catabolic process for this orientation among the Kharwar. The findings reveal a significant decline in social connectedness as well as individual connectedness scores over the span of ten years. The villagers now in general perceive others to be less involved in matters pertaining to the community at large. They also do not display as much involvement in such matters personally as they used to do a decade before. This suggests that the members of Kharwar community are gradually becoming less concerned with their group and matters related to it. There seems to be a decline in kinship ties and strength of other relationships, which happened to be a major resource of the community in earlier times. This suggests that the Kharwar are at the risk of being ridden by stress, which often occurs during the course of cultural change, especially in situations of breakdown of social and cultural resources of the groups.

If we look at the findings in the context of other research carried out on acculturation attitudes among indigenous/tribal people, and among those who are acculturating to Western societies as immigrants, refugees or sojourners, we find evidence for a substantial degree of generalization of the present findings. There is clear evidence for the existence of integration, assimilation, separation and marginalization attitudes on the part of groups. The degree to which these attitudes are likely to be reflected among individuals or groups in multicultural societies is also fairly comparable with other studies.

Looking into the history of culture contact and change in India it was felt that co-existence, rather than integration or assimilation, would be a more characteristic strategy of the Kharwar for dealing with influences from other cultures. Thus, the co-existence attitude was created on a priori basis, and it was assessed along with other four attitudes. Conceptually, co-existence was defined as an attitude of compromise between two cultural standards, putting them on a horizontal plane, without involving any attempt at their comparison or evaluation. Behaviourally, it was considered to be close to integration, since it involved the maintenance of elements of both the cultures.

As predicted, the findings revealed co-existence to be the most dominant acculturation attitude of the Kharwar in general with integration occupying the next place in hierarchy. Both these attitudes tended to show an increase during the course of acculturation over the period of a decade. In view of the negative correlations reported between integration and assimilation in other studies, and also those found in a previous study with the Kharwar people (Mishra & Chaubey, 2002), co-existence could be regarded as a novel strategy that cuts across the boundaries of integration and assimilation. However, more research is needed for validating this construct, and for accommodating it in the acculturation framework being used in research on acculturation attitudes.

What do these findings tell us about the life of people in tribal Indian villages? There is no doubt that the villages have changed over the years, and they are likely to continue to change in the forthcoming years as well either because of developmental programmes initiated by the government or because of other influences resulting from people's contact with the outside world. The changes that have taken place in various walks of life of the Kharwar during a period of ten years are remarkable. While most of these changes seem to bear positive outcomes, loss in people's heritage language needs to be taken with seriousness. Language is a major component of culture. Thus, by losing heritage language one remains at the risk of losing culture. The Kharwar need to understand the value of their heritage language and make effort to ensure its maintenance. They also need to recognize the strength of social relationships and collective living in order to guard them against the negative outcome of acculturation.

REFERENCES

Berry, J.W. (1976). *Human Ecology and Cognitive Style*, New York: Sage/ Halsted.

Berry, J.W. (1980). Social and Cultural Change. In H.C. Triandis & R. Brislin (Eds.), *Handbook of Cross-Cultural Psychology, Vol, 5.* Boston: Allyn & Bacon.

Berry, J.W. (1980). Multiculturalism and Psychology in Plural Societies. In L.H. Ekstrand (Ed.), *Ethnic Minorities and Immigrants in Cross-cultural Perspective.* Lisse: Swets & Zeitlinger.

Berry, J.W. (1990). Psychology of Acculturation: Understanding Individuals Moving between Cultures. In R. Brislin (Ed.), Applied Cross-cultural Psychology. Newbury Park: Sage.

Berry, J.W. (2005). Acculturation: Living successfully in two cultures. *International Journal of Intercultural Relations*, 29, 697-712.

Berry, J.W., Kim, U., Power, S., Young, M., Bujaki, M. (1989). Acculturation attitudes in plural societies. *Applied Psychology: An International Review*, 38, 185-206.

Berry, J.W. Phinney, J.S., Sam, D.L. & Vedder, P. (Eds.) (2006a). *Immigrant youth in cultural transition: Acculturation, identity and adaptation across national contexts*. Mahwah: Lawrence Erlbaum Associates.

Berry, J.W. Phinney, J.S., Sam, D.L. & Vedder, P. (Eds.) (2006b). Immigrant youth: Acculturation, identity and adaptation. *Applied Psychology: An Intemational Review*, 55, 303-332.

Berry, J.W. & Sam, D. (1997). Acculturation and adaptation. In J.W. Berry, M.H. Segall & C. Kagitcibasi (Eds.), *Handbook of Cross-cultural Psychology*, Vol. 3 (291-326). Boston: Allyn & Bacon.

Dubey, V.K. (1991). *The Agony of Life*. Varanasi: National Council of Development Communication.

Graves, T.D. (1967). Psychological acculturation in a tri-ethnic community. *Southwestern Journal of Anthropology*, 23, 337-350.

Inkeles, A. & Smith, D. (1974). *Becoming Modern*. Cambridge, Mass: Harvard University Press.

Mishra, R.C. (1994). Individualist and collectivist orientations across generations. In U. Kim, H.C. Triandis, C. Kagitcibasi, S. Choi & G. Yoon (Eds.), *Individualism and Collectivism: Theory, Method, and Applications* (pp. 225-238). Thousand Oaks: Sage.

Mishra, R.C. & Chaubey, A.C. (2002). Acculturation attitudes of Kharwar and Agaria tribal groups of Sonebhadra, *Psychology and Developing Societies*, 14, 201-220.

Mishra, R.C., Sinha, D., Berry, J. W. (1996). *Ecology, Acculturation and Psychological Acculturation: A Study of Adivasis in Bihar*. New Delhi: Sage.

Redfield, R., Linton, R. & Herskovits, M.J. (1936). Memorandum on the study of acculturation. *American Anthropologist*, 38-152.

Sinha, D. (1969). *Indian Villages in Transition*. Bombay: Asia Publication Company.

Sinha, D. (1988). Basic Indian values and behaviour dispositions in the context of national development: An appraisal. In D. Sinha & H.S.R. Kao (Eds.), *Social Values and Development: Asian Perspectives*. New Delhi Sage.

Sinha, D. & Tripathi, R.C. (1994). Individualism in a collectivist culture: A case of co-existence of opposites. In U. Kim, H.C. Triandis, C. Kagitcibasi, S. Choi & G. Yoon (Eds.), *Individualism and Collectivism: Theory, Method, and Applications* (pp. 123-136). Thousand Oaks: Sage.

Sommerlad, E. (1968). *The importance of ethnic identification for assimilation and integration: Study of Australian aborigines Attitudes*. Unpublished B.A. Honours dissertation, University of Sydney.

Sommerlad, E. & Berry, J.W. (1970). The role of ethnic identification in distinguishing between attitudes towards assimilation and integration. *Human Relations*, 23, 23-39.

5

Mapping Cultures: Modernity, Homogenisation and Change in Village Shahabpur

B.N. TEWARI

Rang-rang kai boli, Rang-rang kai bani
Rang-rang kai gahana guria, Ab ba eke thani
(song from Shahabpur)

The path of modernisation on which the nation embarked after independence has brought about many changes in socio-economic and cultural lives even in remote villages of the country. These changes are reflected in the popular culture and lifestyle of the people like their dresses, ornaments, housing patterns, sports, fairs and festivals etc. The changing patterns in these cultural artefacts can be traced by comparing their memories of the past with their contemporary lifestyle. A strong homogenisation and death of varieties in the cultural life of the people due to the growing influence of dominant and oppressive forms of modernisation on the lives of villagers, can be easily observed in villages. Many things that were unique to particular communities have been lost. Additionally, there has also occurred a loss in the variety of cultural artefacts of these communities. New cultural forms are being acquired, but the wide varieties of cultures that were earlier present in the village are slowly diminishing. Most studies till date have tried to record the new changes that have appeared in the arena of public culture, but there is very little data on cultural artifacts that have been waylaid in the process of modernisation.

This paper aims to present cultural data on the eroding multiplicity and emerging homogeneity in the lives of the people of a village, and also record the history of the changes that have appeared in the culture of the village over time. These changes have been documented through the oral narratives of the people themselves. The study was carried out in village Shahabpur in Phaphamau district near Allahabad. This is a tiny village in Central Uttar Pradesh, which is at a distance of twenty kilometres from Allahabad. It is located on the Allahabad-Lucknow Highway five kilometres to the north of Hathigarh Chauraha, lying in the *doab* area of the Ganga River. The village is nearly 2500 metres in length and has almost the same breadth.

Shahabpur village is inhabited by people of various castes, most of them belonging to the lower strata in the Indian caste hierarchy. Castes like Patels, *Pasis, Mauryas, Kumhars, Chamars, Turks* (Muslims) and *Dhobis* who are numerically stronger, are mostly settled in their own caste based *pattis* (small hamlets and subhamlets, also called *Poorvas* and *Tolas*). Other castes like Yadav, *Darzi, Lohar, Nai, Bhuja, Dafali, Churihaar,* who are less in number, live mostly in the Shahabpur Bazaar or are scattered in other *pattis.* There are thirteen *pattis* in the village. Most of the names of the *pattis* are based on the names of the castes that predominantly inhabit them. The average distance between each of the *Poorvas* and *Pattis* ranges between two to three kilometres, linked by narrow *kutcha* roads or furrows (*chauri aris)* within agricultural fields. All the *pattis* are surrounded by lush green fields growing crops like rice, wheat, mustard, pulses and vegetables that are consumed by the people themselves.

In order to compare the state of affairs at different points of time, some persons from each of the caste settlements belonging to three different age groups i.e., the older generation (seventy and above), middle generation (between the ages of forty and fifty) and younger generation (between the ages of twenty and thirty), were chosen for conversations. Some of the narrators had detailed narratives about the past of the village and the process of development, while others had fragmented and scattered narratives. These were then woven together to produce a comprehensive story about the changing culture and life patterns of the village.

Dresses, *Topis* and Hair styles

Villagers of Shahabpur remember that earlier the dress worn by the poor men was a half *dhoti* with bare bodies. They did not wear shoes on their feet. Children usually wore *langot*. Middle-income group men belonging to the upper castes wore *dhoti-kameez* with *mirzai* (*long shirt*) and *saluka* (*pyjamas*). Beards and moustaches with *pugrees* on their heads were common then. There were a wide variety of hairstyles for men at that time, said Ramnath Patel.[1] Describing the various hairstyles he said that, "Some men sported long hair till their shoulders. This hairstyle was called *patta* in which the hair was parted in the middle. Some men had short hair and the back of the heads was shaved off. This hairstyle was called *khat*. Another hairstyle found at that time was one in which a square patch was shaved off on top of the head. It was believed that the heat of the head would be released through this patch. Some men shaved off the hair in front of their heads, halfway to the back. A few others kept their hair long in the front while at the back they cut their hair short. Today, however, these various hairstyles are no longer found. All the men have the same hairstyle and the wide variety has disappeared."

There were also a wide variety of caps worn by men belonging to the middle income upper caste category, said Ramnath Patel. Some men wore *ruidar kantop* (cottonwool caps that covered their head and ears). Some other men wore *dupalli topi* (a cap with two layers). Some upper caste men wore *chaugosia* caps. In addition, another kind of cap was found at that time called *gol topi*. This was made of a material called *sujni* on which floral designs were made. After that a fashion appeared in which two finger long tassels were attached to these caps. Even old men wore these fashionable caps then.

Another fashionable cap found at that time was one that was round in shape and had intricate designs on it. These kinds of caps were worn during marriages and other festive occasions. After a few years some men started wearing *Kishtia* or *kishtidar* caps that were made of velvet and were shaped like a boat. When these caps were made of thin cotton, they came to be known as *Gandhi topis*. Patel added that these varieties of caps are also not found today. Very few men wear caps on their heads, preferring to leave their heads bare.

Children belonging to this category wore *knicker* (half pants) and *banyan* (vest). Small girls wore *chaddi* (bloomer) and frock before their marriage, while after marriage which took place around the age of seven years, they wore *dhoties* or sarees. Women, both poor and rich, wore sarees. People used to colour their *dhoties* and sarees either at home or by the *Rangreja* (dyers) to give them a longer life. Women belonging to well-off families often wore colourful *lehengas* (long skirt with gathers) whose pleats were nearly 3 to 4 gauze in length. They also had a four finger wide frill at the bottom. But they were not allowed to enter the kitchen wearing the *lehengas* since stitched clothes were considered to be impure. In such situations they used to cover themselves with a *dhoti* worn like a saree. The brides of rich families wore *angiya* and *maharam* (inner garments) underneath their clothes while women of poor families wore *jhulla*, which was a small sleeveless buttoned shirt (*kurti*). They had small openings in front and had *ghundi tukma*, or small hangings in the front. Gradually the *jhullas* went out of fashion and after that women started wearing shirts without buttons.

Hindu women belonging to rich families did not wear slippers or shoes on their feet. Women belonging to lower and middle castes used to wear ordinary *chattis* (hand made slippers) made in the village itself. These used to be also called *latari, khatari* or *badhauri*. Gradually women of higher castes started wearing half-slippers. When women of the city started wearing designed shoes, the women of the village also started wearing them.

In the present times, dresses have undergone a considerable change. Even poor people wear clothes whereas earlier they usually kept their bodies bare. Some people buy clothes while others receive clothes as a part of their work condition. Senior men wear *dhoti-kurta* (long piece of cloth around the lower portion of the body, worn with a long shirt) or *lungi-banyan* (long piece of cloth wrapped loosely around the lower portion, worn with a vest) while men of the younger generation wear shirt and pant. Children wear half pant-*banyan* or shirt, or knicker and shirt. Middle class men of the older generation wear *dhoti-kurta* or *pyjama-kurta,* and *sadari* (a kind of jacket), over the *kurta.* A few men also wear shirt and pant. Middle generation men wear mainly shirt-pant or *pyjama-kurta.* At home they usually wear *lungi-banyan.* Young boys wear shirt-pant. Jeans is also a popular dress among them. They also sometimes wear *lungi-banyan* at home. Children of the middle income group today wear shirt-pant or half pant.

Women today wear mostly colourful synthetic sarees that they buy from the market. Older women still wear cotton sarees while widows wear light coloured cotton sarees. Poor women seldom wear blouses with their sarees. The style of tying the saree has not changed much, with women still using the *dehati* (village) style. Young married girls are still not allowed to wear *salwar kameez* (loose *pyjamas* and long shirts), although a few young girls wear them when they visit their natal houses. Unmarried girls wear frocks when they are small and *salwar kameez* when they are older since the age of marriage has been raised. Ramnath Patel's wife, Chameli Devi[2], who is nearly eighty years old, narrated that when she was young, Hindu women did not wear sarees but wore cotton *dhoties* in the style of sarees. Muslim women wore *churidar pyjama* and *kameez* with their heads covered with *orhnis.* They took to wearing sarees before Hindu women, who started wearing them much later.

Ornaments in Three Generations

Ramwati[3] an old woman of Shahabpur narrated that earlier both males and females wore ornaments made of gold and silver though they were more popular with women. Silver ornaments used to be very heavy and covered the entire body starting from the toes to the top of the head. She described that on the feet, women wore silver *gorhara* (anklets) that covered the top of the feet, attached to the toes with the help of *authana*. Other ornaments worn on the feet were *paladi*, *genua* and *purhaia* that were different kinds of anklets. Around the waist women wore a thick band of silver called *kardhani* that weighed between three *pau* to one *ser* (between three-fourth and one kilo). On the neck they wore *hasuli* which was made of either gold or silver and also weighed between three *pau* to one *ser*. Another ornament worn around the neck was called *habel*.

On the arms women wore many kinds of ornaments like *bahutha, paubaju, bairakkhi* and *pahuchi*, all of which were made of silver. The ornaments worn on the wrists were *agela, chhanna, tora* and *pachhelia*. Glass bangles were not worn at all then. On the palms and hands, women wore an ornament called *chavanni* that was attached to the thumb by *arangurtana* and to the middle finger by *arsi*.

On the nose the women who had their noses pierced, wore a *pulli*, a kind of nose ring. The ornaments worn in the ears were *dhar*, *jhumka* and another ornament called *bandi*, that was used to hold the *katiya*, a silver band like ornament covering the head. Many women also pierced the top of their ears to wear tiny rings made of either gold or silver. The number of rings worn was an odd number with three rings in one ear and two in the other. On the head women also wore a *teeka* in the parting of their hair.

Giving an account of the ornaments possessed by women of the middle generation, Nirmala Devi[4], a forty year old woman living in Godam patti, said that both the quality and quantity of ornaments have changed. Only silver ornaments are worn today in the village. On the feet women wear ornaments called *lachchha, chhagal* (pajeb), and *payal* on their ankles and *bicchuas* on their toes. On the waist women still wear *kardhani* or a thinner version called *peti*. On the throat they wear an ornament that consists of many chains made of gold or silver held together at one point, called *jajir*. Other ornaments worn on the neck are *gatia* and *haar*.

Ornaments worn in the ear consist of *jhumkas* made of gold or silver and silver rings on the top of the ears. On the arms women wear *kangan, chhanni* and *pachheli. Agela* is worn by a few women of the older generation. Most women commonly wear glass bangles that were considered to be taboo earlier. On the hands women wear *haath phul* at the time of their marriage. On the head they wear a *maath beni,* though a few women also possess *katiya* and *bandi.*

Nirmala Devi's daughter-in-law, a young woman in her twenties possesses only silver *lachchha, kardhan, beni, jhumka, jajir* and a *haar.*

Table 5.1 : Ornaments possessed by women of three generations

Part of body	*Nirmala Devi's mother*	*Nirmala Devi*	*Nirmala Devi's daughter-in-law*
Feet	Gorhara, authana, paladi, Genua, purhaia, thhos(jhanjh), Karha, Paijeb,chhara, lacchha, Chhaagal, chhalla, bichhua	lachchha,chhagal, payal, bichhua,	lachchha
Waist	Kardhani	Kardhani, peti	kardhani
Neck	Hasuli, Tabeej, Dholna Hamel, jugnu, Kathula	jajir, gatai, haar	jajir, haar
Hand/wrist	Agela, Chhanni, Tora,	kangan, haathphul,	bangles
Palm/ fingers	Pachhelia, Mutehra, Angurtana, arsi, mudari, Angoothi, chavanni, Kara, Kangan	chhanni, pachhelia	
Arms	Bahutha, paubaju, Baurakkhi, Pahuchi, Tandiya, Jausan		
Nose	Bulak	Phulli	Phulli
Ear	Dhar, jhumka, bandi Karnaphool	jhumka, chandi rings	Tops, bali
Head	Katiya-bandi, teeka	maath beni, katiya-bandi	Maath beni

The number of ornaments worn by people in the rural societies has gradually decreased with the decline in the spirit of celebration and festivity among the people. Earlier ornaments were worn to decorate and beautify the body on the numerous festivals and cultural occasions celebrated there. With growing acculturation and homogenisation on the path of development the number of festivals and rituals have undergone a steady decline. People no longer find the correct occasion to exhibit and demonstrate their clothes and ornaments before the rest of the community. In the words of Nirmala Devi, earlier ornaments were regarded as a symbol of affluence that was used to exhibit the prosperity of a household. At that time almost all economic transactions were in kind with little monetary exchange involved. The families were also self-supporting, growing almost everything they needed. People had surplus income to invest in gold and other ornaments. With growing commercialisation, the need for liquid cash has greatly increased. This has led to a situation where many households are forced to sell off their family ornaments to buy land and other assets. Skyrocketing increase in the prices of gold and silver have also debilitated the capacity of people to buy new ornaments except when they are forced to invest for their daughter's wedding.

The kinds of ornaments worn by women today have undergone considerable change. The ornaments worn by Muslim women are now also worn by Hindu women, e.g., *bali* on the ears and *tauk* on the neck. Upper caste women did not wear bangles earlier since they were commonly worn by lower caste women like *Pasi, Ahir* and *Chamar*. Today almost all the women in the Shahabpur village wear glass bangles, which they buy from the Muslim Maniharan women (bangle sellers), who visit their *Pattis* regularly to sell bangles. The older women in most of *Pattis* of the village were found to wear *agela* and not bangles. Silver or *Phool* (a kind of metal) *Agelas* were earlier the specific ornaments of *Ahir* women, but later women of lower castes also started wearing them. *Karhas* made of brass or *Phool* were also worn by lower caste women which later diffused among women of other castes also. Earlier *bulak*, which was worn on the nose by Muslim women, were not worn by Hindu women. Due to a process of cultural interaction between various communities, a composite culture of ornaments developed in the recent past because of which Hindu women also started wearing *bulak*. Although this is not commonly worn by women anymore, a few women still wear them in their noses. Earlier ornaments used to be made of metals like gold, silver, brass and *phool*. Gradually, ornaments made of brass and *phool* disappeared leaving behind only gold and silver.

Male Ornaments : Lower Caste and Higher Caste

According to Ramnath Patel[5], earlier males also used to wear rings with stones (*naginedaar anguthi*), but under the influence of the British, they started wearing simple rings with the first letter of their names engraved on them. Earlier rings used to be worn on the right hand, but seeing the British, they started being worn on the ring finger of the left hand. People of the *Ahir, Kurmi* and *Kachi* castes used to wear gold locket (*dholna*) in gold chains around their necks and tiny rings in their ears. In addition, the *Kahar* community also wore silver bangles called *dharkauwa* on their wrists. *Baniyas* and *Kalwars* used to wear twisted gold rings on their fingers that were called *pherwa*. They also wore silver *kardhani* on their waists. Jagroop Saroj[6], a 50 year old man of the Bazar informed that he used to wear *lorki* in his young age which he had sold to fulfil the economic requirement of his everyday life. He pathetically says, "*sab kha pi dale, lorki pahanne ka man karta hai par ab kahan mile*" (Everything has been eaten up. I feel like wearing a *lorki* but where will I get it now). Among the people belonging to upper castes, there was also a tradition of wearing rings on their thumbs.

At the present juncture, all the male ornaments have disappeared except for small earrings, rings and gold chains worn by rich people. It is noteworthy that earlier even poor people of lower castes could afford to wear gold and silver jewellery whereas today even people belonging to affluent middle and upper castes can no longer afford them.

Table 5.2 : Male Ornaments—then and now

Then	*Now*
naginedaar anguthi, rings on right hand, *dholna, dharkauwa, pherwa, kardhani,* rings on thumbs, *loriki* (made by gold)	earrings, rings, gold chains

Housing : Then and Now

The older residents of the Shahabpur village remember that earlier most of the houses built during earlier period were *kutcha* houses. The walls were one *gaj* (guaze) thick. The roofs were made of bamboo on which were placed tiles. The gap between the bamboo and the tiles were filled with *thaat,* a kind of structure made of dry branches of *arhar,* mustard, *sarkanda* and *jhau* (kinds of plants with long reeds), that were tied together tightly so that rain water could not soak through. These roofs were durable enough to last for fifty or sixty years since they were constructed. The *thaat* in the houses of rich people of that time were made of thin strips of wood that were held together with nails and covered with thick tiles called *Allahabadi tiles.*

At that time the roofs of the houses of poor people were made of straw (*phoos*) and there were no doors in their houses. Jagroop Saroj[7], a resident of Pasiyapur, said that the doors were only a thin panel made of dry reeds of wild grass like *sarkanda* and *jhau,* that were tied together to keep away cats and dogs. In front of the houses there used to be an open space called *osar* or *chaupar* (chaupal). Often cows and buffaloes used to be tied there. Affluent people housed their cattle in special sheds called *goruwar* and *bagar.* Big sheds were called *bakhri.*

He added that the houses of that period were made of mud and *kutcha* bricks. Some of the houses were made of stones, which were ordered from Shivrajpur of Shankargarh and Manikpur. These stones were also known as *imarati patthar* which were soon replaced by *pucca* bricks and cement. The roofs were also converted to iron ones. One of the important features of big houses were the courtyards (*angan*) in front of the houses. For sanitation big holes were dug in the corner of houses called *sandas.*

At present, the newly constructed houses of Shahabpur village are made of bricks and cement. Many old mud houses are being replaced by bricks and cement. Tiles of mud houses are also being renovated by the owners which they buy from *Kumhars.* The earlier price of tiles ranged between Rs. 10 and Rs.15 for 1000 tiles, whereas now the price is Rs. 300 to Rs. 350 for 1000 tiles. Sometimes, the owners themselves make their own tiles.

Many of the houses in the Murain Tola, Jurupur and Bazaar are *pucca* houses with their own bathrooms and kitchens inside them. In Godam Patti, which is inhabited mainly by *Chamars,* most of the houses are *kutcha,* although a few *Chamar* houses are also *pucca.* In Pasiyapur and Lakhanpur, the maximum number of houses are *kutcha,* while one or two are *pucca.* Kohran patti and Inara patti have equal number of *pucca* and *kutcha* houses. There are a few *sarkari* houses in the Godam patti, which are occupied by Harijan families. In Pasiyapur, which is an Ambedkar village, a few *sarkari* houses are lying in a semi-constructed condition.

Musical Instruments: A History of Disappearance

People narrate that earlier a large variety of musical instruments like *dhol, kasha, turahi-dafla, shahnai, roshan chauki, harmonium, majira, khanjari, bansuri, hauda, kasawar, mridanga, daf, rawana, been, nagara, masak been, huduk,* etc. used to be played in the village. It is interesting to know that earlier different communities had their own instruments, e.g., *turuhi* was played by the *Mehtars,* the *Kahars* played the *huduk, Chamars* and *Dhobis* played the *kasawar* and *mridanga.* The *Daf* and *Rawana* communities played the *dafli.* Each kind of folk song had its own particular instrument for accompaniment, e.g., *alha geet* was accompanied by *dholak* and *majira.*

Today very few of these instruments are played in the village. Ramkisun Patel[8] narrated that harmonium, *dhol, jheeka, kartal, jhanjh, khajari* and *daf* are the only instruments that are played at present. Banjo has now been introduced in the village, which is played by a band party that performs in the village. This band party is hired to play at marriages, *pujas* and functions held in the village.

Table 5.3 : Musical Instruments then and now

Then	*Now*
dhol, kasha, turahi-dafla, shahnai, roshan chauki, harmonium, majira, khanjari, bansuri, hauda, kasawar, mridanga, daf, rawana, been, nagara, masak been, huduk	Harmonium, dhol, jheeka, kartal

Documenting Sports

The kind of games played in the village has undergone a great change since earlier times. Earlier *akharas* where wrestling was taught, were common features of the village. There were many *akharas* present in the village near each of the *pattis.* Regular competitions used to be organised by the *akharas* where the wrestlers used to display their skills. Jagroop Saroj [9], a resident of the Bazaar, said that the wrestling ring was prepared by digging 15 by 15 feet of land with a shovel many times till it became soft. All the pebbles and stones lying inside the ring were removed. This process was known as *akhara bandhna*. The land for this ring was selected slightly outside the settlements where people, especially ladies, did not visit very often. The ring was bound on all four sides with hard clay. This was called *merh bandhi.* On one end of the *merh bandhi* a heap of clay was piled high, which was called *Pahalwan Baba.* This *Pahalwan Baba* was a kind of deity who used to be garlanded and worshipped by lighting incense sticks before it. Before stepping into the ring to fight, each wrestler used to pour a handful of clay from the wrestling ring on top of *Pahalwan Baba,* rub the clay that was remaining in their hands, on their bodies, and pray to *Pahalwan Baba* for success. By continuous pouring of clay, *Pahalwan Baba* became quite high.

The *akhara* ring was a popular venue for men where they used to also play traditional games and do exercises like *dand baithak*. In the process they also rubbed their bodies with mud which was considered to make their bodies strong. Each *akhara* was regularly visited by a few men of the *Nat* communities, a traditional acrobatic community, who taught the students of the *Akharas* special skills of wrestling. The *Nats* came to the village in autumn and stayed till spring. *Nats* were considered to be the *gurus* of *Pahalwans* and their visits were greatly welcomed by the villagers. Each family of the students learning wrestling, used to donate 10 or 20 kilogrammes of rice or wheat (*do dhara/char dhara*) at the time of their leaving, as a form of payment.

Each year a competition was held between all the *Akharas* in the village and in the neighbouring villages. This was known as *dangal*. *Dangals* were commonly held in Shahabpur, Shivgarh, Dehriawan and Kaurihar where wrestlers exhibited their wrestling skills. The *dangals* in Shahabpur were earlier organised enthusiastically by the villagers but they have gradually disappeared due to the changing taste patterns of the people. *Nats* also no longer visit the village. The indigenous games like *gilli-danda, goli, kabaddi, tash, kabootar urana* (pigeon flying), *erhi koodna* (long jump), *surra, cheel jhapatta* , *tahat* etc., were commonly played by both children and adults of the village are also no longer played in the village except during some functions when children demonstrate their wrestling skills.

The children of the Shahabpur village now commonly play games like cricket, volleyball and badminton. A few children play *gilli-danda* and marbles. Cricket is the most popular game in the village and there are three cricket teams existing there. Cards are commonly played by adults.

Table 5.4 : Sports—then and now

Then	*Now*
Akhara, gilli-danda, goli, kabaddi, tash, and marbles *kabootar urana* (pigeon flying), *erhi koodna* (long jump), *surra, cheel jhapatta*	cricket, volleyball and badminton

Sources : Field Interviews

Dhobiha and *Chamraua* and *Ramlila* : Remembrance of Cultural Performances

Ramlila used to be put up in the village by the *Raja Sahab* and his *Mukhtar.* The people of Inara Patti, who were then only three families, were the most active participants and organisers of the *Ramlila.* It used to be held at the Primary School in the Bazaar and all the villagers used to contribute to it. *Ramlila* companies also used to come from outside the village to perform *Ramlila.* The *Dhanush Yajna* incident of the *Ramayana* was the most memorable episode that is still remembered by the villagers. Pitambar Patel[10], who also acted in the *Ramlila* in both female and male roles as Sabari, Sampati, Manthara etc., said that nearly ten years ago there was a conflict between the people of the Inara patti who were in the forefront of the management of the *Ramlila,* and people from the other pattis, which led to the stopping of the *Ramlila.*

Apart from the *Ramlila,* each caste had its own performing arts in which they were skilled. The *Mehtars* used to play a musical instrument called *turhi.* The *Kahars* played the *huruk,* also called *ardh pakhawaj.* They adorned themselves in colourful clothes and *ghungrus* (anklets). The *Ahirs* had a special dance called *Ahirwa,* in which the men wore a *lehenga* with many gathers and danced exuberantly while playing a drum called *nagara* or *bagheli.* They also performed many acrobatics while dancing. The songs that were sung were called *biraha.* Another dance particular to the *Dhobi* community was the *Dhobiauwa* in which instruments like *kasawa* and *mridanga* were played.

They sang the *Dhobia's biraha* which were love songs associated with the *dhobi ghat* or the banks of the river where the *dhobis* (washermen) washed their clothes.

The *Chamars* had the most well-organised dance troupe called *Chamaraundha.* The main instrument used during this performance was a flat bowl made of brass or *phool.* It was hung from one hand while it was beaten with sticks by the other hand. This instrument was called *kasawar.* In addition they also played the *mridanga.* The men who danced had shaven moustaches and long hair on their heads, which they sometimes covered with a cap. On their feet they wore anklets and wore long colourful *lehengas.* They also sang songs while dancing, said Bhullar[11], one of the members of the erstwhile *Chamar* dance troupe.

Narrating about the performances Bhullar said, "This *nautanki* was performed on the occasion of marriages and other festive occasions. There were two characters in them called *Karinga* and *Bolkaha.* One of the characters spoke the dialogue correctly while the other inverted it. *Mridangas, Kesarwas* and a flute made from a deer's horn were played during the *nautankis.*" Narrating why these performances were no longer held in the village, he said, "Earlier when these dances were held in our *patti,* the upper caste men also used to join in attracted by the cheerful sounds. They used to get so hyped up while seeing the performances that they used to misbehave with our women. Sometimes these led to unmanageable brawls between the *Chamars* and the upper caste men. So since the last twenty or twenty five years we have decided not to have these performances any more." Bhullar added that some *Chamars* in the neighbouring villages still hold these performances.

The *Pasis* also had their own caste based performance called *Panwara. Panwara* was a musical cultural performance in which only males participated. This is a very energetic and vibrant song routine for which it is necessary for the men to consume country made liquor to shed their inhibitions. They are usually in the form of a duet in which two persons engage in questions and answers about the glory of a *Pasi* king. No musical instruments are used as accompaniments. Shobhnath Pasi[12], a forty year old *Pasi* living in Pasiyapur narrated that "Most of the stories sung in the Panwaras narrated the valour and chivalry of our ancient *Pasi* kings so that the people of our caste feel inspired to attain the same glory. Panwara was a symbol of our cultural identity that was unique to our own caste. The *Panwara* performers were highly acclaimed in our society and they were invited to perform at various functions, especially marriages and other social gatherings. *Panwaras* were also performed whenever there was any gathering of the caste like Panchayats, community feasts, or on happy occasions after harvesting. Even in summer when mangoes were ripe, people used to gather in the mango orchard, eat mangoes, drink wine and sing *Panwara.* Women did not sing and neither did they join the men as listeners. They usually hid themselves behind the men to listen. But today the singing of *Panwara* is no longer considered to be fashionable. Only a few *Panwara* singers are left in our village and they also have not passed down this artform to their sons. We are afraid that very soon this specialised cultural form will disappear altogether from our society."

Shobhnath Pasi narrated that the *Pasis* had another cultural activity in their repertoire, which was called *Pasiyauwa* dance. These dances were performed at the time of marriages and other religious functions for praying to *devi-devta* (gods and goddesses). The goddesses to whom these prayers were offered were Kali, Sharada and Sheetalamata. Describing the dance he said, "First one man used to walk for sometime on his hands. This was called *phari maarna.* At one point he stood up on his feet while walking on his hands. This was called *ulti phari maarna. Phari maarna* was also known by some as *bichhu chal* (scorpion walk). A musical instrument called *huruk*, which was a percussion instrument shaped like a small drum was played continuously by another man called *hurukaha*, as background music, saying *'himmat kar koowat kar'* (have courage, keep jumping). The man doing the *phari maarna* used to keep time with the beat of the *huruk.*"

Another item performed during the *Pasiyauwa* dance as narrated by Shobhnath Pasi[13] was the *Karinga.* In this item, the performer who was called *Karinga* used to play the flute and also sing in between. The *karinga* used to wear a special kind of tight half pants upto his knees that had *ghungroos* (bells) stitched at the bottom. He used to sing songs about all the gods and goddesses. A third item forming a part of the *Pasiyauwa* was the *Gujaria* dance. In this item two men donned the garb of women like *dhoties* or sarees and danced on the beats of the *hurukwa.* All the items of the *Pasiyauwa* were performed at the same time after consuming country made liquor by the performers. Shobhnath Pasi lamented that the *Pasiyauwa* was also not performed by the *Pasis* of Shahabpur any more. If they felt like arranging a *Pasiyauwa* routine they usually hired performers from neighbouring villages like Faridpur, Gadhina, Motilalpura or Bhuwanpur.

Although these cultural performances are specific to each of the lower castes, some performing arts like the *Gujariya* dance was performed by almost all the lower castes. Some castes like the *Dhobis* performed this dance from *patti* to *patti* to collect money from the castes living there, usually after the crops were harvested. All the people of these castes used to gather around the dancers at the entrance of the *patti* and donate small amounts of money to them. Some were so happy that they even donated their clothes to the dancers. These cultural forms are now slowly disappearing from the village. An important reason for this could be the changing socio-cultural scenario and the rising consciousness among the lower castes. Earlier each caste had an assigned location in the village social structure and the caste based performances were an integral component of their own desire for festivity and enjoyment, which was respected by the other castes. But with the falling respect by other castes for their art and culture and the rising sense of humiliation and self-dignity within the lower castes due to the atrocities and oppressions of the upper castes, they no longer perform these specific dances. Thus, the cultural scenario of the village has become less colourful with their disappearance.

Festivals : Changing Modes of Celebration

Guriya (Nag Panchami), *Phagua* (Holi), *Barhka Amavas* (Deepawali), *Janamashtami, Shivratri, Barhka Itwar* etc., are some of the festivals celebrated by the people of Shahabpur. These festivals have been celebrated since a long time but the mode of celebration has gradually undergone a change because of the changing living patterns of the people. People say that earlier there used to be a great deal of festivity on these occasions when most of them were celebrated collectively. Ramnath Patel[14], who belongs to the older generation, observed that when they were young the whole village celebrated each of these festivals together. This spirit of community participation is now slowly declining with most people celebrating the festivals in their own houses with their own family members. The only occasions that are celebrated collectively today are Republic Day and Independence Day, which are celebrated with a great deal of patriotic fervour in all the schools of the village.

The present *Raja* of Shahabpur, Akhil Pratap Singh, in a bid to foster community participation among the people, started organising *Holi Milan Samaroh* in the village since the last two years. This *Samaroh*, which is more like a *Darbar* celebration, is held in the school started by the *Raja*, called Ajit Pratap Higher Secondary School. Male members from both Shahabpur village and the surrounding villages and also the male members of the family of Raja Akhil Pratap Singh, participate in the ceremony. Music groups and folk song groups living in the various *pattis* of the villages, perform popular items on the stage. The King of Pratapgarh also attends the function, where he is treated as a royalty by the villagers. This *Samaroh* has now become a political gathering where the *Raja* tries to mobilise people to build up a mass base in order to fight the elections. Many local political leaders also attend this *Samaroh* to meet and interact with the people.

The Muslim community living in the Turkan patti are closely linked with the Muslims living in the neighbouring villages of Sarai Phatte and Kanjia. They celebrate all their festivals like *Moharram, Barawafat, Id (Ramzan), Gyarahvi, Shabbe Barat*, together. Many Hindus also participate in their festivals though the number is less. Muslims also participate in Hindu festivals like *Holi, Guriya* etc.

Conclusion

The study of making and changing of the culture usually focuses on the 'culture now', ignoring the 'culture then' and highlighting the new entries due to the influence of urbanisation and modernisation of the life of people living in villages. Without studying the culture as it was then one cannot study the process of change in the culture over time. The most important source of studying 'culture then' of peoples' lives is the remembered narrative about their own cultural past as narrated by them. The process of modernisation has caused a reduction in the variety of cultural artifacts of the people, which is an irreparable loss in their lives. Most studies on changing cultures, however, usually only mention in passing that increasing modernisation has caused a decrease in the cultural resources of people, without specifying the exact losses that have taken place. Documentation of the data of disappearance of various forms of cultural life is an important issue in the study of the process of homogenisation that people underwent during the process of modernisation oriented development over the time.

The evolution of the culture of the village over the years shows a great deal of cultural exchanges, interactions and adaptations of the cultures of the various communities coexisting together. The intermingling of the lifestyles of British, Muslim, upper caste and lower caste Hindu into one composite culture is plainly visible in the village. For example, imitating the British, the males of the village started wearing rings on the ring finger of their left hand whereas earlier they used to wear rings in their right hand. Among the women too, glass bangles are now popularly worn irrespective of the caste, whereas they were considered to be taboo by upper caste women since they were worn by lower caste women like *Ahir, Pasi* etc. only. It is commonly believed that culture usually moves in the upward direction with the lower castes adopting the culture and lifestyles of the upper castes but a study of the Shahabpur village shows that quite often the upper castes have also borrowed and assimilated the culture of the lower castes.

Cultural homogeneity and disappearance in the cultural resources in the village can be observed in other spheres also like dresses, kinds of houses, sports, festivals, musical instruments, performing arts etc. The tables in the text show the decline in the varieties in these spheres. Thus, in conclusion we can say that increasing modernity is compelling us to live with only a few cultural resources which are also in grave danger of disappearing soon from the domain of public culture. The new culture that is emerging as a result of new socio-economic changes would be another dimension in the study of the process of homogenisation in rural areas.

REFERENCES

1. Ramnath Patel: Time: 11 AM Date: 24.1.03 Place: Tali, Shahabpur Cassette No. 1A, 20 AB.
2. Chameli Devi Patel : Time: 12.00 noon, Date: 6.2.03 , Place: Tali, Shahabpur, Field Diary (MM).
3. Ramwati : Time: 1.30 P.M Date: 6.2.03, Place: Godam Patti, Shahabpur, Field Diary (MM).
4. Nirmala Devi : Time: 1.30 P.M, Date: 6.2.03, Place: Godam Patti, Shahabpur, Field Diary (MM).
5. Ramnath Patel, *ibid.*
6. Jagroop Saroj : Time : 11.30 AM, Date: 8.3.03, Place: Bazaar, Shahabpur, Cassette No. 2.
7. Jagroop Pasi : Time: 12.00 noon, date: 8.3.03, Place; Pasiyapur, Cassette No. 3 .
8. Ramkisun Patel : Time: 10.35 AM, date: 12. 3. 03. Place : Inara Patti, Cassette No. 1A.
9. Jagroop Saroj, *ibid.*
10. Pitambar Patel , Time: 11.00 A.M, Date: 20.2.03, Place: Inara Patti, Cassette No. 6A.
11. Bhullar, Time: 11.00 AM, Date: 8.2.03, Place: Godam Patti, Cassette No. 1 (small).
12. Shobhnath Pasi, Time : 2.30 PM, Date : 6.2.03, Place: Pasiyapur, Cassette No. 2B.
13. Shobhnath Pasi, *ibid.*
14. Ramnath Patel, *ibid.*

6

Baigapada : A Biography of an Indian Village

RAJ KUMAR

> *My study has convinced me of the enormous value of studying Indian sociological problems in single villages. I do not say that all sociological problems can be studied in the village. But those that can be studied in single villages or in small clusters of neighbouring villages will yield rich insights into Indian social life.*

M.N. Srinivas, Village Studies and their Significance, 1962:135

> *The Indian village as the symbol of a tyrannical system that obligingly conforms to nineteenth-century left-Hegelian depictions of feudalism, the Indian village as the obstinate symbol of mindless homicidal patriarchy, the Indian village as the depot of 'pure' environmental-cultural sensitivity and people's critique of conventional development, and, above all, the Indian village as the counter-city and escape from the city—these are all markers of the changing political-cultural status of the village.*

Ashis Nandy, An Ambiguous Journey to the City, 2007: 75-76

The primary objective of the article is the study of the changes in an Indian village. For the purpose of the study, I have chosen my village named 'Baigapada', which is a part of the erstwhile Kalahandi district of Orissa. I chose to study Baigapada because I know my village intimately for the last four decades and hopefully will be able to document the changes the village has witnessed over the years.

Several sociologists and social anthropologists have emphasized the need of studying an Indian village to understand the dynamics of Indian social life. My focus in this essay is not just to explore and understand sociological problems of my village. The reason for doing so is simple. Sociological problems have their origin in certain social structural factors and the interplay of these factors in time. Structural factors and their interplay have their roots in particular historical condition and are both undergirded by and reflect certain cultural, economic and political factors. Moreover, there is involved time span in which the interplay of structural factors develop, take certain shape, and yield certain consequences for individual lives and social relations. As such, a simple sociological approach to the ever developing pattern of individual and communal life does not and cannot fully illuminate the experiences the interplay of the factors that have made and are still making deeper impact on daily lives of the people. In view of this, I will cast my net wide and include historical, political, economical, cultural and religious factors that have impinged on the life of the village and shape its onward movement in time.

Since the time-period of this study spans over four decades, it is difficult to encapsulate the complex process of change and the evolving life patterns in the village. However, even a brief account of the village caught in the process of change will go a long way not only to enhance our understanding but also help us to properly evaluate it. The time-span of forty years relate to a village that was stationary or exemplified what economists call "steady state" for long. It was then suddenly exposed to external forces, for as that a long way in rousing it up from its long slumber. Inescapably then it must have been jolted by the impact of these forces which it had to react or respond to. For example, one can immediately think of such external forces impinging on the village as the various welfare programmes undertaken by the Government of India after independence and their impact on the placid life pattern that characterized Indian villages as 'little Republics". Further, the liberalized economy introduced in India some fifteen years back has already brought several changes in the lives of the people all over the country. These two examples are enough to show that the lever of change in the Indian villages in general in the modern time is primarily economic. It is through the modification, alternation and even overturning the pre-existent patterns of social life and relation in different spatially organized entities that it is expected to bring into being the kind of society that has been the preferred goals since Enlightenment. As such, in order to apprehend the character and the significance of the economically induced social change, it is desirable to focus on those economic factors that impinge heavily on village life today.

Though no concrete study is yet available on the impact of the liberalized economy on Indian villages, I will try to have a closer look at this phenomenon in order to highlight some of the salient feature of changes going on in my village. This, I propose to do not with the help of aggregate data or abstract ideas. Instead, I will document the day-to-day life-experiences of the people of my village and critically interpret them so that they become intellectually relevant. In other words, what I intend to do in the following pages is, in a way, to try to bring out a biographical account of my village, which has remarkably undergone changes over the last four decades. This account, with all probability, may also prove to be the biographical account of my Indian village, which has undergone similar changes over the last forty or fifty years. However, it is also true that no two Indian villages are identical because of the differential location and inherited past of each village. But one can still generalize the prominent features of a particular village in the case of other villages because, except for the time and situation, the humane experiences reflect a similar quality across geographical boundaries. This is the reason why most of the social scientists generalize their findings even though their studies are located in a particular set-up.

History

As mentioned earlier, Baigapada is a part of the erstwhile Kalahandi district of Orissa, which now falls under Nuapada district (since it was divided in 1992), and inherits all the stereotypical images of what Kalahandi, in general, has been known for: poverty, backwardness, corruption and mass migration. Baigapada is an average village consisting of 75 families. The caste characteristics of the village is like this: five families out of the total belong to Brahmans, four *Telis* (oilmen), seven *Malis* (gardeners), two *Adivasis*, sixteen *Dombs* (Dalits) and the rest belong to *Gaudas* (Yadavas). Like any other Indian village, the settlement-pattern of Baigapada is characterized on the basis of caste. Each caste group has separate dwellings, which is collectively known as a *pada*. Thus, the village has several *padas* such as, *Brahman pada, Mali pada, Teli pada, Gaud pada* and *Gana pada*. Each caste group, while interacting with others, strictly follows caste rules. Thus, caste system with its various practices is very much prevalent in the village.

So far as the history of the village is concerned, it will be little more than 150 years old. People in and around the village believe that Baigapada was founded by an *Adivasi* named Baiga. As such, there is no evidence to ascertain who this Baiga was; where did he come from and what happened to his family members, etc. But even today, there proudly stands a hillock at the outskirts of the village named *Baiga Dongri* as a memorial to the founder. Actually, according to the ethnographic records 'Baiga' is the name of a tribal community who lived in many parts of Kalahandi district in the past. It might so happen that this community once lived in and around Baigapada village. Though no proper archaeological survey has been done by any agency to ascertain this fact. People of Baigapada, at times, especially while ploughing their fields or digging soil from the earth have come across several artifacts used by a generation several years ago. Today, the villagers remember that a certain gentleman belonging to the Yadava caste came to the village as the founder-member, who eventually became the *Gauntia* (headman) of the village. He, later, invited several families from outside to settle down in the village. Accordingly, he brought a family each of *Mali, Teli, Adivasi* and *Domb,* who were put into different services of the village. For example, the duty of the *Malis* was to supply the villagers *murhi* (puffed rice) and *chihra* (flattened rice). The *Teli* was responsible for supplying oil. The *adivasi* gentleman was made the village priest. He was in-charge of worshipping village deities. The *Domb* was the messenger for every errand. He was also responsible for doing all kinds of menial works such as sweeeping village roads, clearing dead animals, etc. Later, a Brahman family was brought in to help the Gauntia collect revenues. The number of families that exist today in the village are the successors of those six families, who came to settle down in the village from the very beginning.

Officially, Baigapada is a revenue village. Before India's independence, the revenue of the village was collected by the Gauntia, who was directly appointed by the King of Khariar, under the *Zamindari* system. The King of Khariar was responsible to collect and deposit revenue to the King of Kalahandi, who was a direct appointee of the British government for the purpose. It may be mentioned here that British government took over Kalahandi only in 1818. Prior to the British occupation, Kalahandi was under the Mughals and the Marahattas from the seventeenth century to the beginning of the eighteenth century. As a part of the deal, the King of Kalahandi agreed to pay a nominal annual tribute of Rs. 4000 to the British. Accordingly, Kalahandi was recognized as a feudatory state with full control over the internal administration but the British appointed a political agent at Bhawanipatna, the capital of Kalahandi, to introduce their ideas of law and order and revenue administration.

The consequences of the deal made between the King of Kalahandi and the British government were several. One of the immediate results was that each and every villager had to compulsorily pay the revenue amount fixed up by the revenue collectors appointed by the King. Sometimes, repressive measures were taken by the revenue official to collect the maximum revenue from the villagers. If the villagers could not pay the amount in time they lost the ownership rights of their lands. In that case, the ownership of the land got transferred to the person who instantly paid the revenue as demanded by the official. This was contrary to the land rights that prevailed before the coming of the Britishers to Kalahandi. It may be recollected here that the Permanent Settlement Act and the Ryotwari Act introduced by the Britishers during the eighteenth century direcly affected the autonomy of Indian villages. According to these Acts, land became a commodity so that it could be bought and sold anytime in the market, if the owner desired so. Further, heavy taxes were imposed on the farmers and those who could not pay, had to lose their land to the British government. The village land or the community land also became the land of the government. Thus, the traditional ownership of the land was lost and a new land policy came into effect.

In the case of Kalahandi the result was worse. The land rights newly introduced by the Britishers severely affected the farmers of the district. Local historians like Fanindam Deo who have done research on Kalahandi have found out that till the eighteenth century Kalahandi was ruled mostly by the Kandhas, an *Adivasi* community. There were as many as thirty-two Kandha clans ruling all over Kalahandi during the eighteenth century. Each clan ruled over a territory that was called a *desh* and was comprised of between 12 to 84 villages. The chieftain of each *desh* was called *Umrao*. The *Umrao* had all the power to control over the land of the entire *desh*. In order to run the administration smoothly he appointed a *Mukhia*, the headman choosing one of the elderly persons amongst the villagers called *Majhi*. Thus, the villagers who were mostly *Adivasis* owed allegiance to *Majhi*, the village head and the *Majhi* owed it to the *Umrao*.

This traditional set-up immediately changed when the King had a pact with the Britishers. The King no more consulted the *Umraos* when he took any decision on land. Instead, he initiated several measures that went against the interest of the Kandhas. For example, in order to collect more revenues he invited skilled cultivators from outside the district. Now, the village, instead of *desh* became the unit of revenue administration. Fanindam Deo and Padmalochan Barma in their joint article titled, "Roots of Poverty: Historical Contexts in Kalahandi, Orissa" underline the following changes:

> Village was auctioned for three-year term. Nazrana or levy was demanded at the time of auction from the thekedar/gaontia or leaseholders. The old system of one "Umrao" one "desh" one single patriarch or a circle of a village was abandoned. The effects were wide-ranging. Umrao, Majhi and Kandh in general, unaccustomed to regular revenue payment, now became liable to pay it. These traditional heads failed to collect revenue from their own clansmen. They could not compete in the auction, and moneyed men mostly outsiders (Kultha, Su(n)dhis etc.), gradually took the village in auction and became gaontia/thekedars. Not only Kandh headmen were removed, but they also lost their power, position and prestige. The Kandhas revolted in 1850s but were suppressed. Very little attempt was made to educate the Kandhas. (p.3)

Due to the reorganization of land rights in Kalahandi, people of Baigapada were also affected. The immediate result was that the *Yadava Gauntia* was now replaced by a Brahman, who was directly appointed by the King of Khariar. The change of the guard was, perhaps, more to do with the demand of the situation than the caste factor. Actually, the Yadava headman of the village was an illiterate person, who could not cope with the new regime. The *Gauntia* had to be a calculative person so as to devise the revenue policies from time to time and collect the revenues following few harsh measures, if necessary. In contrast, the Brahman *Gauntia* was not only a literate person; he was also well versed in the revenue policies introduced by the Britishers. His further advantage was that his forefathers were already working under the King of Khariar. Once appointed, the *Gauntia* used his power and position to his advantage and amassed lots of wealth—both in cash and kind. He also imposed his decisions in several spheres of village life, be it social, political or cultural. Thus, his monopoly continued in the village for more than five decades. After his passing away, two more generations of his family members succeeded his powerful position and ruled the village quite autocratically.

Today, the *Zamindari* system is a thing of the past. The *Gauntias*, the *Zamindars* and the Kings may still be around, but their official powers have long been cut down immediately after India's independence from the British Raj. Even though these people have already lost their official positions they still continue to wield power under the new dispensations and they have also donned new roles with the changing passage of time. Many of them are into active politics, thus, retaining their traditional power over people. Some of them have become social activists by setting up various voluntary organizations or Non-Governmental Organizations (NGOs) and collecting money in the name of the people. The scene at Baigapada is more or less the same. The *Gauntia* and his family members continue to be at the helms of affairs of the village, even today. For example, the post of the Ward Member of the village has always been occupied by a member of his family. Politically speaking, the family not only gained control of the village, they also extended their power outside the village. The fact that the elder son of the *Gauntia* once became the *Sarpanch* of the local panchayat proves this point. Interestingly, the present *Naib-Sarpanch* of the local panchayat happens to be the grandson of the *Gauntia*, who has also been elected as the Ward Member of the village for the last two consecutive terms. Thus, the political power of a family has been transferred from one generation to the next.

Apart from politics, the power of the *Gauntia* was also felt in other spheres of the village life. For long time nothing was done in the village without his consent. Even the local bureaucrats—be they from the department of forest, Block, panchayat or police—who came to execute different programmes in the village, entirely depended on his personal judgment. This process of dependence not only marred the development initiatives started by the Indian government after independence, but this also paved the way for corruption in the public arena. Personal recommendations were made by the village headman so that his loyalists got the maximum benefits from the various welfare schemes—be it Indira Awas Yojana, Antyodaya scheme or even a small loan to the farmers from various banks. The result was that the needy and deserving villagers could not avail the government assistance, which was their due. This phenomenon continues even today.

The *Gauntia* also presided over several committees of the village. He continued to become the Chairman of the village Primary School for as many years as he wanted. He was a natural choice for the head *panch* of the village council, if any dispute had to be settled down within the village. During various social functions, people at large paid respect to him, as if bound by tradition. For example, during *Nuakhai,* the new rice eating festival, all the villagers thronged to his house to pay their respect. On his part, the *Gauntia* would give them a token gift—a *bidi* (country-made cigarette) to the elderly male and a *pitha* (rice-cake) to the each female. This is undoubtedly an example *par excellence* of a patronizing role.

The economic condition of the *Gauntia* was far more visible than his socio-political power. Apart from owning several hundreds of acres of fertile land by virtue of *Zamindari,* the *Gauntia* also controlled the entire village land. It was he, who generously gave few acres of free land to *Jhankar*, the village priest, an *Adivasi,* who was made in-charge of worshipping the village deities and to the village chowkidar, a *Dalit,* whose duty was to guard the village at night, carry messages from place to place and do various menial works of the village as assigned to him from time to time. The *Gauntia* also had an influence over the local administration. Whenever there was any public works like making of roads or digging up the village ponds sanctioned either by the Panchayat or by the Block, he or his family members were assigned the contract work. Thus, the *Gauntia,* apart from being a very powerful man, was also very rich and wealthy.

The family members of the *Gauntia* continued to enjoy their power and privileges till the 1960s. Thereafter, there were serious contestations at several power-points of the village. The first power-contest was for the post of the Ward Member of the village. Defying the dictates of the *Gauntia*, the villagers, for the first time elected a *Yadav* person who continued to become the Ward Member for the next two terms. Another Yadav became the Chairman of the Primary School. Four to five young men from different families came forward to take charge of the village's public works such as building roads or digging up the ponds. Thus, for the first time, people from different castes and communities came forward to get involved in the affairs of the village. It may be mentioned here that several forces were working at the same time to bring positive changes in the village. However, the role of education definitely becomes quite significant.

Politics

There was no school in Baigapada till the 1950s. Way back then, the idea of setting up a Lower Primary School was mooted out. Surprisingly, the proposal came from the *Gauntia* of the village, who had already lost his formal power by then. This is indicative of the fact that not all the Gauntias were exploiters; many of them were also reformers, who took developmental initiatives in their areas. Once the school was established, people irrespective of their caste affiliations came to help it run. Thus, with the participation of the villagers at large, the Lower Primary School was upgraded to become an Upper Primary School. Later, in 1989, a Middle English School was also established and the State Government sanctioned full grant to the school in 1991. All these small details about the school are important because without education, the villagers would have continued to be illiterates. Earlier, being illiterates, they accepted their existential conditions passively. Now the education was within their reach, they could not only feel the wind of change blowing but also help it to gather strength and momentum by assimilating the impulse in their own being and re-orienting their orientation and behaviour in accordance with their self-understanding.

The beneficiaries of the school education were mostly the children of the marginal farmers, wage labourers and girl children, who, due to several socio-economic problems, never attended any school earlier. Before the school was established, there were several schools, but they were located in far-flung villages. Only a few rich farmers could afford to send their male children to such far places. These students were required to stay in a mess and they needed money to meet the expenses that living away from the family setting involved. Naturally, the poor farmers had no money to spend for educating their children. Now once the school was located in their village, the poor farmers were able to send their children—mostly the male children—to study. They hoped that after the completion of school education, the boys would, at least, become government school teachers and bring economic security to their respective families. Today the village is proud of having at least a dozen school teachers who are also agents of social change. There is another half-a-dozen government employees who are also the products of the same school.

Girl children going to school was definitely another big achievement. Earlier, they could not dream of going out of the village to study. Like elsewhere in India, the patriarchal social order was very strong in Baigapada. Except for the working class women, who came out to work in agricultural fields, the rest of the women were confined within the four walls of their houses. The women, especially from the upper castes, were in the most pitiable conditions, because they were in *purda*. They had hardly any interaction with the outside world. And the lower middle class women imitated everything that the women from the upper castes did in the name of keeping up the so-called "tradition". All these stereotypical roles of women started changing, once the girl children started going to school. Several girls who completed their school education later entered into public domain, mostly becoming *Anganwadi* workers. Becoming *Anganwadi* workers may not be a big achievement but, it clearly shows that if equal opportunities are given to women, they can always do better. Education among girl children is definitely a desirable step in the direction of bringing gender equality in a society.

Apart from women, another section who made use of education for the benefit of its members was comprised of

Dalits. It may be stated here that the caste system was very much prevalent in Baigapada. And as a corollary to this, there were instances of very crude forms of untouchability being practiced by the upper caste people. There were clear segregations on all fronts. For example, *Dalits* were living in the outskirts of the village. They were not allowed to draw water from the common wells used by the upper castes. *Dalits* had separate bathing *ghats,* cremation grounds etc. They were also not allowed to participate in any religious functions of the village. Since most of them were landless they did not have many options but to do menial works in the village for their survival. They were daily wage labourers, drum beaters, domestic servants, etc. Almost for everything they used to depend on the mercy of their upper caste masters. Their dignity and self-respect were at stake. Once formal education was opened up for them, they sent their children to the village school with a hope that education would bring among them a social mobility and finally a social change. The *Dalit* children worked very hard and most of them completed their school education. Some of them, later, joined High schools, colleges and even some premier universities of the country like Jawaharlal Nehru University, Delhi. After completion of their education few of them have succeeded in getting government jobs. Thus, education not only gave them opportunities to better their economic situations, it also brought in its wake social awareness.

Once *Dalits* were conscious of their rights, they were quite assertive about achieving them. When the *Dalits* made their claims for basic human rights, initially, there were retaliations from the upper castes. There were even social boycotts. But eventually, *Dalits* obtained what was their due. For example, *Dalits* are now allowed to take water from the same tube wells which was denied to them earlier. They are also participating in various social and religious functions organized in the village from time to time. This does not mean that atrocities against *Dalits* have come to an end, the upper caste people still find their ways and means to subjugate them. But *Dalits* are no more mute spectators to the injustices perpetrated against them by the upper castes. They have been protesting against all forms of inequalities so to have dignity and self-respect which they had lost in the past.

The overall effects of all these changes mentioned above signified some positive results insofar as the question of the deprived and the depressed social sections are concerned. The villagers, now, were no more passive onlookers. Instead, they were actively participating in the decision-making processes as they affected village life and relations. Thus, a democratic environment emerged gradually out of the earlier frozen traditional society based on separation and suppression in the village. The immediate result was that in the 1980s, the youths of the village came together to set up a club. Named as *Beenapani Yuvaka Sangha,* the main objective of the club was to organize socially sensitive cultural events through dance, drama etc. The *Sangha,* at one point of time, started a library movement, which eventually had to be closed down because of differences among the members. However, the initiatives taken by the villagers had long-lasting effects, the results of which are now being enjoyed by today's youths.

Economy

In the past, people entirely depended on agriculture. Therefore, the village economy revolved around the land. Forest was everywhere and people cleared parts of the forests to create agricultural land. The various grains they cultivated were: paddy, *mandia, kodo, gurji, suan,* and several kinds of pulses and cereals such as, *chepta chana, nak chana, matar chana, leher* and *mushri.* Crops such as wheat, *jowar, bajra,* etc. were hardly cultivated. Apart from agriculture people are also entirely dependent on forest for their day-to-day needs. They collected several edible roots, fruits, leaves and nuts for their consumption. It may be mentioned here that there are as many as fourteen to fifteen kinds of green leaves which people collect from the fields even to this day for cooking. Some of the names go like: *chakoda, chench, dahipatual, kena, sirial, kulher, musakani, sunsunia, kosla*, etc. They also collected several forest products either for consumption or for selling them in local markets. Some of these included: *mahul, chahanr, dhoop, kardi, kunjher,* etc. In addition, they also collected various kinds of medicinal herbs and plants from the forest. Thus, in the past people never had any problem getting food and medicine. It was only after the population grew up that resources became scarce and people thought of expanding their agricultural and homestead land. But the forest reservation laws were already in execution. So people had hardly any options but to depend entirely on whatever resources they had for their livelihood.

The land of the village was unevenly distributed. Except for the *Gauntia* family who had more than hundred acres of land a few farmers had more than ten acres of land and the rest were marginal farmers, who had between two to five acres of land. There were also a good number of landless households, whose sole earnings came from working in the agricultural fields as daily labourers. Basically, the village had subsistence economy till the forties and fifties of the twentieth century. However, from the sixties onwards, people were faced with uneven rainfalls and uncertain monsoons; this brought regular droughts and sometimes, famine. Since there was no irrigation facility available, people could not depend fully on agriculture in the aftermath of the failure of the monsoon. Thus, people were forced to switch on to many non-agricultural activities, which provided them alternative sources of income and livelihood. It was during this time that many landless agricultural workers and marginal farmers from the village migrated in bulk to the nearby towns or even outside the state to work as menial workers, factory labourers, hotel attendants, rickshaw pullers, servants, domestic maids and so on and so forth. With the continuous failure of both rains and crops in the recent years people now are accustomed to migrate to far distant places than earlier. It is, therefore, hardly a surprise if, today, we happen to meet people from Baigapada as rickshaw pullers in Raipur, the factory workers in Bhopal, the brick makers in Andhra Pradesh or even as daily wage workers in some remote parts of Delhi or Mumbai. Poverty is one of the main reasons for mass migration.

It may be mentioned here that poverty that we see in a village like Baigapada in particular, and erstwhile Kalahandi district in general, is more of a man-made phenomenon than a natural calamity. In the past, Kalahandi was very rich with plenty of natural resources. At one point of time, 60 per cent of its total area was covered by rich forest. Kalahandi was also known for its best rice, particularly its *Dubraj* variety, an equivalent of *Basmati*. For several years, the district had records of yielding more rice per hectare of land compared to the state as well as national average. For example, even in 1989-90, the per capita production per year was 331.86 kg compared to 253.03 for Orissa and 203.13 for India as a whole. In fact, the meaning of the term "Kalahandi" states the obvious: "*kala*" means black and "*handi*" means pot. This implies that the soil of Kalahandi was very fertile. In fact, it continues to be so even today. Except that there is no regular rainfall now. To find its reason, one has to go back to the past and unravel the history of Kalahandi's poverty.

The fifties and sixties of the twentieth century was the time when India went through a series of changes under the dynamic leadership of Jawaharlal Nehru. The welfare economics which Nehru propounded and propagated during his premiership was supposed to have brought 'development' in all spheres of life of the people. But that did not happen, especially for the people of Kalahandi. Instead, in the name of development "the worst" came to Kalahandi region. It was as if a coincidence that when India was, after a decade of her Independence, celebrating the glory of Freedom, the people of Kalahandi suddenly witnessed hundreds and thousands of trucks plying days and nights together on its rough and uneven roads. People still describe the scene with awe about how these trucks took away all the valuable woods — including teak— from their deep, green jungles. This was purely a loot. The looters were builders, contractors, bureaucrats and politicians, who together, hand-in-glove, worked out the plan. Kalahandi, they thought, was a "goldmine" and they extracted as much as they could to amass wealth for themselves. They left Kalahandi only after it became grey, barren and useless.

This is not to say that there was hardly any exploitation of forest before the independence. In fact, the depletion of forest started during the British rule in the district when the King of Kalahandi invited non-*adivasis* contractors to exploit the forest resources primarily to increase the revenue collection. This was the first instance of commercial exploitation of Kalahandi's forests. Fanindam Deo and Padmalochan Barma document the inevitable fall-out of such a callous action:

> (T)he feudatory chief in order to enhance his income encouraged the non-*adivasis gaontia* to cultivate wasteland. He also opened forest to commercial exploitation, which led to the denudation of *sal*, and teak forest of Kalahandi. Forest contractors used the cheap *adivasis* labour in their missioin. Gradually, minor forest produce, an important source of livelihood of the *adivasis*, was taken over by the traders. This reduced the means of livelihood of *adivasis*, on the other hand indiscriminate felling of trees and over-exploitation of forest resources led to the breakdown of ecological balance. This was one of the reasons for the frequent drought and famine in the last decade of the 19th century. Earlier the *adivasis* withdrew to the interiors, into the deep forest. In the 20th century, this avenue was closed for the *adivasis*. Due to forest reservation laws, construction of dams, and declaration of wildlife sanctuary etc. land became scarce, on the other hand population of Kalahandi grew. This contributed to the unequal distribution of land. Scanty irrigation provision to agricultural land made the problem more complicated and created vexed problems. (p.5)

Thus, the infamous phenomenon called "Kalahandi"—known for its poverty, backwardness and child selling—is very much the making of the so-called "civil society". In the name of "development", the entire region had to be deprived of its rich and varied natural resources. The creation of wealth for others meant the complete depletion of the natural wealth of Kalahandi. It is rather a contradiction that while independent India gave the people of Kalahandi the idea of "Freedom", it took away their rights to livelihood thus making them "slaves" in their own country. Government after government, both in the centre and the state have, of course undertaken several measures to correct the wrongs done to the people of the regions. Changes also have come on their ways. But these are only cosmetic changes. The much-talked Central Government assistance towards the implementation of Kalahandi-Bolangir and Koraput (KBK) project has hardly yielded any desired result in spite of several thousands of crores rupees being pumped into the region for the last several years. As more money has been injected in the region, more and more cases of corruption and nepotism are coming to limelight. There are also evidences of more and more people in the region becoming thieves, dacoits and cheats.

Before talking about the political economy of the village at present, it may be relevant here to mention about how people managed their economic life in the past. As stated earlier, the village was characterized by subsistence economy. Barter system was the common practice among the villagers. The villagers got almost all their household needs from their fields. Only for a few items such as salt, oil, clothes, kerosene and medicine, they had to depend on the outsiders. Luckily, these items also came to their door-steps through the vendors, who went from village to village to sell their goods. Moreover, there were weekly markets in nearby villages, where people went to buy and sell their goods. The circulation of money was very much limited. It was only during the seventies and eighties of the twentieth century that people started using money in a big way.

Where did this money come from? People remember that during the seventies and eighties of the last century, several welfare schemes were undertaken by the Indian Government, particularly in the rural areas, when money was distributed on a very large scale for the first time. Earlier, government had introduced "food-for-work" programme and as the part of the payment, the workers were given wheat, *gur* and rice. It may be a coincidence that with the circulation of money, there came corruption in public life. So much so that when Rajiv Gandhi, after becoming the Prime Minister of the country, visited Kalahandi district, he publicly acknowledged the bureaucrats-politicians nexus eating away as much as 90 per cent of the public money and spending only 10 per cent for the people. Today people, in fact, believe that the proportion of corruption has gone up. There is corruption everywhere: in government offices, whether it is police, forest or revenue department, Block, panchayat, banks, even in schools. For instance, in schools teachers eat away the money meant for the mid-day meals; in banks loans are sanctioned only when the officials are given certain percentage of loans; in government offices no file moves unless the concerned officials are given bribes. With corruption everywhere one does not know how to bring a positive change in the region.

In spite of a grim future the village has undergone remarkable changes in different spheres of life in the last few years. These changes are due to the new economic policy, which was introduced in India in the nineties of the last century. With the new economic policy, money is seen circulating everywhere including in the remote and rural villages like Baigapada. This has resutled in people to enhance their ability to buy more and more of market products. As witnessed elsewhere, consumerism has, in a way, become the rule of the day even for these rural village folk. For instance, till a few years back, the village did not have a single motor vehicle. Today, it has at least half-a-dozen four wheelers, 15 motorcycles, 9 television sets and 20 mobile phones. The statistics given here may not be sufficient to prove the point that the liberal economy has entered even the remotest corner of the nation. But it does reveal that people are accepting changes. It is another matter that these changes are market-driven and hence, people have, sometime, no choice but to accept it. In the process, however, the people's culture becomes a casualty. I turn in the following section to exploring the ways in which it is happening.

Culture

Culture can be anything; it can be food, dress, language, religion, festivals, etc. It is also defined as a way of life, i.e. the way people live, think, behave and conduct themselves in different spheres of their life: whether public or private. Thus, it is through people's culture that we come to know about their world-views and civilizational ethos. Raymond Williams in his essay titled, "Culture is Ordinary" endorses this view when he writes:

> Culture is ordinary: that is the first act. Every human society has its own shape, its own purposes, its own meanings. Every human society expresses these, in institutions, and in arts and learning. The making of a society is the finding of common meanings and directions, and its growth is an active debate and amendment under the pressure of experience, contact, and discovery, writing themselves into the land. (p.11)

Of course, most of the cultural habits of the people are determined by several factors, such as their geographical locations, economic conditions, their mindsets etc. Considering the importance of culture in the life of the people, it is better to describe a few characteristics of the village culture and its changing character in the remaining pages.

It has already been mentioned earlier that agriculture plays a dominant role in shaping people's lives in Baigapada. That is why most of the cultural activities are centred around agriculture. But with the change of time there have been several changes in the village life as well. Thus, the oral community which had earlier been isolated from the rest of the world is now a community living side by side with both tradition and modernity. In other words, there is change as well as continuity in the village culture.

To begin with, let us discuss first the housing patterns of the villagers. Till very recently only four to five rich families had big houses made of bricks. The rest of the people had mud houses. The poor people lived in huts. Today almost all houses of the village are made of bricks. This is, no doubt, a sign of prosperity. But the prosperity has also brought along with it a calamity which is far more dangerous than one can imagine. With the making of the new houses hundreds and thousands of trees have been cut without bothering about the consequences. This has severely affected the ecology of the area bringing regular droughts.

Earlier the village was totally cut-off from the rest of the world. There were no roads and hence no vehicles. People used to walk several miles barefoot which took lots of their time and energy. A few rich people used to travel far away places by bullock carts. Now with *Gramya Sadak Yojana* and other projects the village is connected by both *kachcha* and *pucca* roads. There are at least half a dozen buses plying everyday connecting the village and the district headquarters. People now can travel far more distance by other means of communication as well, such as, cars, scooters and motor vehicles. Thus, the villagers can avail various avenues in nearby towns and cities.

With the coming of urbanization and modernization to the village the traditional methods of agricultural works are getting replaced by new techniques and methods. Earlier farmers used cow dung to make their land fertile. Now more and more farmers are using chemical fertilizers. They are also using chemical pesticides instead of natural pest control methods, such as using ashes, *neem* leaves, etc. With the use of chemical fertilizers and pesticides more and more village land is slowly turning barren and useless.

Another change is clearly visible in the choice of seeds. Several varieties of indigenous paddies have already vanished due to the introduction of hybrid paddies in the market. For example, *dasramatia, chinger, lochei, kalikhuji, jhipri, hiran, baksel, suantoti, puagi, maharaji, haldi guala, dumerphuli, kabrichini, nenka, mirchamanji, beganmanji, sankri, huna* and *dubraj*—to name a few have already disappeared from the region. Also, earlier the farmers manually harvested their crops which naturally took a long time. Now-a-days people use machinery, tools and techniques to harvest their crops. Even small farmers are seen using tractors for various agricultural works.

Since paddy is the main crop of the region, the staple food of the people is rice. *Dal* and curry made of vegetables are taken along with rice by the well-to-do families. *Dal* is generally prepared from various pulses and lentils such as, *leher, mung, chana,* and *mushri.* Sometimes, rich people are seen eating *dal* prepared from *semi* and *jhudanga,* which belong to beans family. Poor people, however, manage with only one item: either *dal* of lesser varieties of pulses such as, *cheptra kulath* or even *jhilo,* a wild and coarse pulse. Since the majority of the people are poor, to secure two square meals per day is considered to be a luxurious thing in the region. Since there are droughts regularly in the area, there is always food scarcity, and hence, it becomes difficult for the poor to manage a good living throughout the year. Even if there is a normal monsoon, they always suffer during the lean season. That is because neither do they have any stock of paddy nor do they get any work to support their families. During such difficult days, they usually have *pakhala* i.e. watered rice with or without salt, chilly and onion simply to keep their body and soul together.

Hence it may be worth noting that Kalahandi is a dry region. Its water table level has gone down very deep (sometime, you do not get water even after digging up as much as 260 feet or more). Such a situation makes it difficult for people to grow vegetables, which demand regular water. It is only during the rainy and winter seasons that people eat varieties of vegetables, grown by themselves and also by others. Some of the common vegetables produced by the villagers in their fields are: *bhendi, janhi, lau, kumda, bardal, kakharu, sapua, semi, jhudanga, korkoet, kundru, karla, bheja, began, koche, saru* etc. In other times, they somehow manage to eat rice along with *dal* or potato which was introduced in the area fifteen or twenty years back only. In the past, because there was forest everywhere, people managed to collect several varieties of green leaves (namely, *chakoda, chench, dahipatul, kena, sirial, kulher, musakani, sunsunia, kosal, mungna, bhaji, kunjher,* etc.), fruits (such as, *kendu, chandhar, boer, aam, jam, lanka bhulia, kusum* etc.), roots (for example, *kardi* made of bamboo shoots and *pita kanda*), flowers (for example, *neem*) etc. as part of their food items. However, with deforestation they have been deprived of that opportunity. Since green leaves and vegetables are only seasonal, people try to preserve them through traditional methods. For example, *kumda, baral, began* and *bheja* and made *sola* by using some spices, salt and rice powder. *Hanua* is made out of *kardi*. *Badis* and *aachars* (pickles) of different varieties are also made to be used from time to time.

Along with vegetarian dishes people also, by and large, enjoy non-vegetarian dishes. In the past, people used to go for hunting to obtain meat as their staple food but now with the enactment of forest laws hunting is forbidden. Therefore, a majority of the villagers rear poultry, birds, goats, sheep, etc. in their homes to have their meat. It may be mentioned here that during various festive occasions such as *nuakhai basi, pupuni, chhadkhai* and *dussehera*, people make it a point to have at least some non-vegetarian food as a part of their celebration.

Apart from meat and chicken people are fond of fish. When there is a good monsoon people catch varieties of fishes of small sizes such as, *kotri, balia, tengna, jian, magur, singi, rohu, bhakur*, etc. from various water sources and prepare curries. Poor people even collect crabs and snails from the fields to prepare dishes. But now with uncertain rainfalls people are deprived of getting these free gifts from nature. Of course, at times fishes are available in local markets, thanks to the Fishery Department of the State Government which is trying to bring blue revolution even to the remote parts of Kalahandi district. But, people's purchasing capacity is very low and therefore, they can hardly afford to buy them.

One cannot deny the fact that there is the impact of urbanization and modernization in the village. This process has already brought several changes in the life-styles of the people. For example, in the past, people used less edible oil and spices for cooking. Oil extracted from *til*, groundnut or *mahua* seed called *tol* was used as edible oil. Now, people are found using edible oils belonging to some well-known brands such as Dhara, Fortune etc. Earlier people used turmeric, chilly, garlic, *jeera* and *dhania* as spices. Now they are using varieties of spices including *garam masala* and meat *masala*. People earlier used unprocessed sea salt. Now they are using iodised salt processed through machines. There are two big shops in the village catering to the demands of the villagers.

It may also be pointed out here that a small percentage of the people have developed the habit of taking tea (generally black tea in big quantity) at least once in a day. Coffee has not yet entered into the life of the villagers. However, one thing, which can be seen, is the increasing tendency among the villagers to replace tea and sometimes *suji* for the *basi pakhala* (leftover watered rice from the dinner) they used to take as breakfast before leaving for their work. As far as the drinking habits of the people are concerned, a good number of people take wine regularly. It may be stated here that in the past, it was part of the rituals to offer wine to gods and goddesses during the worship. People also used to take wine during various festivals and social occasions including marriage ceremonies. This practice has already been stopped over the years. Now, drinking has become a fashion with more and more young men getting addicted to it. As a result, more anti-social elements can be found in the village. Earlier, people used to drink country liquor prepared out of *mahua* flower. Now-a-days, apart from the country liquor, several shops are also selling cheap foreign liquor.

Like the food and drink habits, the dress patterns of the villagers are also changing. Men generally wear *dhoti* with *kurta* on special occasions. On other days, they use *lungis* and carry towels with or without *banyans* on their bodies. Women in general, use *sarees*, blouses and petticoats. But poor women are seen wearing single *sarees* without any blouse. Earlier, people were buying hand-woven coarse cotton clothes directly from the local weavers who were either *Dombs* or *Bhulias*. Now-a-days, they prefer buying factory-made printed colourful clothes available in the local markets and also gifted and donated by migrant relatives and friends coming back from various towns and cities. It may be mentioned here that with more and more garment factories taking over the markets handlooms are about to disappear from the region. As an evidence one can see the youths of the area putting clothes from some of the international brands like Peter England.

There are also changes in costumes and toiletry. Women earlier used to wear several ornaments in different parts of their bodies made of gold and silver. Many of these ornaments are no more in use now. For example, some of the fascinating bracelets such as *katria, bandria* (worn on hands), *paunji* (worn on legs), *mathamani* (worn on head) and *kamarmani* (worn on waist) have already disappeared. *Chaunri* and *ribbon* earlier used by women to tie up their hair are also disappearning. Instead, new modern toiletries are being used. Some of the cosmetics commonly being used by village women are: powder, cream, nail polish, *bindi*, colourful rubber bands, etc. The use of foot wears by both men and women is also slowly gaining popularity.

As regards language, the spoken language of the people is *"Koshali"*. In fact, *Koshali* is used by the people of Western Orissa as a whole, which is comprised of predivided Kalahandi, Bolangir and Sambalpur districts. However, the written language of the people is Oriya. It may be relevant here to note that in recent years there has been a systematic attempt by the people of western Orissa to unitedly protest against the imposition of language and culture on them by the coastal Orissan people. Named as *"Koshal"* movement, it demands to divide Orissa into *"Koshal"* and *"Utkal"* to have separate linguistic and cultural identities. The movement, in the meantime, has invented its own scripts to write *Koshali* language and is trying to rediscover its glorious past. However, Oriya still continues to be text book language in the region. Apart from the spoken and written languages mentioned above, every community has very distinct dialectic-form to communicate among themselves. For example, communities such as *Teli, Mali, Bhunjia* and *Domb* have their own dialects which might be difficult for other communities to understand. Sadly, these dialects are slowly disappearing as they are considered to be inferior as compared to the spoken language used by the hegemonic upper caste people. Unfortunately, no attempt has been made so far either by any person or institution to preserve this dying cultural tradition.

So far as the religious tradition of the village is concerned, it has the presence of both what social anthropologists call "the little tradition" and "the great tradition". Being a tribal dominated area, almost all the gods and goddesses of the village are of tribal origin. The villagers still believe in "totemism", according to which a particular god or goddess is personified through a form, the structure of which is made of either stone or wood. Some of these prominent gods and goddesses are : *Budharaja, Dokribudhi, Pardashen, Jhitku, Gangadi, Chhotibudhi, Kulaten, Jakenjiren,* etc. The villagers attribute to each god or goddess a supernatural power and worship him or her for securing their own well-being. People worship them round the year by sacrificing hens and goats. If they do not find any bird or animal to sacrifice, they offer them coconuts or even areca nuts with flowers and *bel* leaves and worship them. Since the village life is centred around agriculture, no agricultural produce is consumed by the villagers before offering it to the village deities. In the past, elaborate arrangements used to be made by the village priest to offer any new grain to the village deities. Now that fervour is no more there. Except during *nuakhai* and *dussehera,* in no other time people at large come to worship the village deities together. It may be stated here that *nuakhai* is the main festival of the region. During the festival, *prasad* made from the new rice is offered to the village deities as well as to the ancestors. Since this is the main festival, people celebrate it for three long days (called *upas nuakhai,* and *basi*) with elaborate arrangements.

Dussehera is another festival when people worship the village deities with lots of zeal and enthusiasm. The festival sometimes lasts for a month when the deities wish to visit people from door to door and from one village to another giving *darshan* to everyone, irrespective of caste, class or gender. This, in local term, is called "*boel*". During these visits people come close to their deities and ask for several favours. *Dehuris,* who are supposed to be possessed by the spirits of different deities give them boons and wish them good luck. Critically speaking, these festivals are some of the examples of how the members of an oral community imagine things and arrange their immediate world and beyond.

Though various ritualistic practices have changed over the years, the faith of the people has remained more or less the same. For instance, when they fall ill, instead of directly going to a doctor, they go to the village priest or the traditional medicine man, who, in order to cure the illness, sacrifices a chicken or a goat to appease the evil spirit. People still believe that it is the wrath of the gods and goddesses that brings them suffering. This may be due to blind beliefs and lack of scientific education.

Apart from believing in totemism, the villagers also worship some of the so-called mainstream Hindu gods and goddeses such as *Shiva, Rama, Krishna, Durga, Ganesh, Laxmi, Parvati, Saraswati,* etc. Perhaps, it is due to the dominant influence of the Brahman families that the rest of the villagers worship these gods and goddesses mentioned above. This process can be seen as a part of Hinduization. Many tribal regions of the country have undergone similar processes over the years. There is also other evidence of how people are now exposed to new religious orders. It has been observed that after the campaigning of the Ram temple movement by the Hindu fundamentalists, more and more religious functions are being organized in the village so that people, irrespective of faiths, could be attracted into the Hindutva fold. For such purposes, *Yuga Shakti Gayatri,* a religious organization is openly indoctrinating followers from all castes including *Dalits.* It may be remembered that earlier only the upper caste people, those who had the right to wear the sacred thread were its followers. In many villages of Kalahandi district, including Baigapada, some *Dalits* also now wear the sacred thread; they also become priests and perform various religious duties, thus challenging the hegemony of the Brahman priests.

The villagers celebrate several festivals round the year. Some of the popular festivals are: *nuakhai, dussehera* and *chherchhera.* Earlier we have already described at length about *nuakhai* and *dussehera*. *Chherchhera* is also another festival related to agriculture. Once the harvestings are over, people try to relax after several days of hard work. To celebrate this festival people select a day and enjoy by eating varieties of food including non-vegetarian dishes. Generally, the harvestings are completed by the end of *Pausa*, one of the Hindu calendar months and the first day of *Magha* is selected for this celebration. Young children used to visit singing and dancing from house to house to collect foodgrains. This feature of the festival is no more visible. Apart from these festivals, there are several social occasions, which people celebrate with customary rituals. But with the change of time these rituals are also undergoing changes. For example, in the past people strictly followed certain taboos especially during birth and death. There are laxities in their observance now. Marriage as a social function in the past used to be celebrated for several days. Now the function is reduced to either one or two days. Unfortunately, certain rituals like *kunabera* are no more celebrated.

Earlier people celebrated every festive occasion as a mark of friendship and goodwill. They wholeheartedly devoted their time and energy to enjoy the spirit of the festivals. But now-a-days, the very character of the festivals is somehow lost. There is always the display of ostentation which brings commerce in every function and people's participation is becoming less and less meaningful. For instance, now-a-days, during the festivals video shows are organized by collecting money from the people. Thus, people's participation is confined to mere time passing entertainment rather than collective social celebrations. Often, the villagers are seen fighting over certain trivial issues. Factionalism is increasing in the village. Thus, instead of a harmonious peace-loving village, we often find the conflict-ridden communal village.

Conclusion

The objective of this essay was to study the changes in an Indian village. Baigapada, a village in the erstwhile Kalahandi district of Orissa was chosen for the purpose of understanding the situation. After documenting the various changes in the village spanning over forty long years, it is now fairly clear that some changes were inevitable, whereas some other changes were definitely unwarranted. For example, the upsetting of the power-centre was definitely a revolutionary step taken by the villagers to create a democratic environment so as to assert their rights. But, later, in the same environment, they became selfish, individualistic and so much corrupt that there came disunity and disharmony in the village. This analysis is not to suggest that the villagers need to go back to their good old days, to their "golden past". In fact, there was never a golden past. Yes, there was less competition in the past and still less was ill feeling towards each other. There was exploitation of the poor by the rich, but there was also protection of life from time to time. Thus, every change has its own logic and consequences.

Finally, no one can predict what will happen to a village like Baigapada in the next couple of years. Now that the government-backed liberalization, privatization and globalization processes are going very strong, more and more changes are in the offing. Whether the coming changes will lead to better or worse, only time will tell.

Glossary

Mandia, kodo, gurji and *suan*	:	These are names of some coarse grains produced in the fields within two months. Poor people substitute them for rice
Pada	:	hamlet
Dongri	:	hillock
Chana	:	pulse
Kulath	:	horsegram
Bhendi	:	ladies finger
Janhi	:	ridge gourd
Lau	:	gourd
Kumda	:	pumpkin
Kasharu	:	water gourd

Karla	:	bitter gourd
Bheja	:	tomato
Began	:	brinjal
Boer	:	berry
Aam	:	mango
Jam	:	guava
Lanka bhulia	:	cashew nut
Pita kanda	:	bitter tuber
Jeera	:	cumin
Dhoti	:	a long piece of cloth worn by Hindu men. It is sometimes tied round the waist, with the lower part passed between the legs and put into the cloth at the back, so that the knees are usually covered.
Kurta	:	shirt
Banyan	:	inner cloth worn by men
Lungi	:	a piece of clothing worn in South and South-East Asia consisting of a piece of cloth, usually worn wrapped around the hips and reaching the ankles.
Kunabera	:	a ritual part of life cycle. Usually, girls before attaining puberty tie their knots with the branches of mango tree as a symbol of marriage.
Leher	:	arhar dal
Gur	:	jaggery
Upas	:	fasting
Dehuri	:	men or women supposed to be possessed by supernatural spirits act as gods or goddesses.

BIBLIOGRAPHY

Bailey, F.G. *Caste and the Economic Frontier*. Manchester University Press, Manchester, 1957.

Bailey, F.G. *Tribe, Caste and Nation*. Manchester University Press, Manchester, 1960.

Bailey, F.G. *Politics and Social Change: Orissa in 1959*. University of California Press, Berkeley, 1963.

Beteille, Andre, *Caste, Class and Power: Changing Patterns of Stratification in a Tanjore Village.* Oxford University Press, Bombay, 1966.

Chakravarti, Anand. *Contradiction and Change: Emerging Patterns of Authority in a Rajasthan Village.* Oxford University Press, Delhi 1975.

Chowdhury, Anwarullah. *A Bangladesh Village: A Study of Social Stratification.* Centre of Social Studies, Dacca, 1978.

Currie, Bob. *The Politics of Hunger in India: A Study of Democracy, Governance and Kalahandi's Poverty.* Macmillan Press Ltd., London, 2000.

Das, Arvind N. *Change: The Biography of a Village.* Penguin, New Delhi, 1996.

Deo, F. *"Tribal-Non-Tribal Interaction with Special Reference to Nawapara Sub-Division, Kalahandi District in Western Orissa".* M. Phil. Dissertation submitted to Centre for Historical Studies, Jawaharlal Nehru University, New Delhi, 1984.

Deo, F. and Padmalochan Barma. *"Roots of Poverty: Historical Context in Kalahandi, Orissa"*, an unpublished article written in 1997.

Dube, S.C. *India's Changing Villages: Human Factors in Community Development.* Routledge and Kegan Paul Ltd., London, 1958.

Dumont, Louis and David F. Pocock. *"Village Studies". Contributions to Indian Sociology,* No. 1, 1957.

Madan, Vandana (ed.). *The Village in India.* Oxford University Press, Delhi, 2002.

Misra, Sarat Chandra. *Kalahandi and the Rain God.* Ankur Publication, Noida, 2000.

Nandy, Ashis. *An Ambiguous Journey to the City: The Village and other ruins of the Self in the Indian Imagination.* Oxford University Press, New Delhi, 2007.

Omvedt, Gail. *"Worst in a Hundred Years: The Kalahandi Drought".* Manushi, Issue 97, November-December 1996.

Pati, Biswamoy. *"Environment and Social History: Kalahandi, 1800-1950".* Environment and History. No. 5. 1999.

Pradhan, Jagdish. *"The Distorted Kalahandi and a Strategy for its Development".* Social Action. Vol. 43, July-September 1993.

Samal, Kishor C. *"Drought and its toll in Kalahandi."* Mainstream, New Delhi. Vol. xxxii, No. 14, February 19, 1994.

Srinivas, M.N. (ed). *India's Villages.* Asia Publishing House, Bombay, 1955.

Srinivas, M.N. *Caste in Modern India and other Essays.* Media Promoters and Publishers, Bombay, 1962.

Srinivas, M.N. *The Remembered Village.* Oxford University Press, Delhi, 1976.

Williams, Raymond. *"Culture is Ordinary"* in the Raymond Williams Reader. Edited by John Higgins. Blackwell, Oxford, 2001.

7

Living Conditions of People in Village Bhaganpur : Some Observations

BHASKAR MAJUMDER

'The apparently unknown geographic space becomes known by human settlements. The geographic space by human settlement comes to be identified as a country, a district, a block, a town, a village etc. This geographic-administrative division depends on a number of indicators, like the number of population settled in a particular region, physical infrastructure etc. When we consider a particular village, we consider also the socio-economic-cultural dimensions. Some regions show settled population, while some difficult regions (like hills, deserts, and forests) show population often unsettled (not permanently settled). Village as a unit gets converted into an economy, by entry and adoption of technology of higher order, expansion of market, movement and mobility of individuals. There exists a close association between economic hierarchy and social hierarchy in villages in India' (Dasgupta, 1977, p. 9).

This paper deals with the living conditions of people settled in a particular village in Uttar Pradesh. The village is located in the block of Karchhana in the district of Allahabad in Uttar Pradesh. The village is Bhaganpur. We select the village such that it has a high number of tribal households.

The rest of the paper will have five sections. In Section I we present a review of village in India. In Section II we present the objectives, methodology and sample of the study. In Section III we deal with the facts about the living conditions of people in village Bhaganpur. In Section IV we offer some general lessons on the living conditions of people in village Bhaganpur. Finally, in Section V we offer concluding comments.

I. Village in India : A Review

The Kautilyan analysis on (village) society, that reflects the society of a time period between 4th century BC and 150 AD, is one of the world's oldest treaties on the economic administration of the state. In his description of the economy, 'power comes from the countryside, which is the source of all activities. An ideal *janapada* (human settlement) was one which was easily defended and which had a lot of productive land with cultivable fields, mines, timber forests, elephant forests and pastures' (Rangarajan, 1992, p. 77). 'Agriculture was the most important economic activity. Cultivable land was considered better than mines, because mines fill only the treasury while agricultural production fills both the treasury and the storehouses' (Rangarajan, 1992, p. 77). In Kautilya's view, land is the most important natural resource. Land in his time was primarily in the public sector, with the state holding all virgin land, forests and water resources. Arable land, however, was both in the public and the private sectors. Regarding village life, Kautilya suggests that a lot of responsibility fell on the *gramika,* the village headman and the *gramvriddha,* the village elders. The village headman was responsible for maintenance of the village boundary pillars, controlling grazing and ejecting undesirables...Usually everyone in the village has to contribute his share of the cost of common projects, festivals and entertainments (Rangarajan, 1992, pp. 57-58).

There is now a vast literature available on village studies. Srinivas (1976) has elaborated the experience of a village in the state of Karnataka in South India. He has shown that the life in a village in terms of animals, plants also show the life of human beings in the village, the former providing the physical basis for the latter. Within the physical-cultural existence of people in a village, strict caste hierarchy observes 'togetherness' and 'separateness'. Each man belongs to a caste, which forms part of a system of ranked castes. 'Purity' and 'Pollution' of individuals are determined by 'structured' castes. There is also land-based hierarchy. There is an element of overlap between the twin hierarchies of caste and land. 'Ideas of hierarchy derived from the *varna* model of five-layered India-wide castes are not only simple and clear-cut but misleading in understanding the caste system as it operates at the village level' (Srinivas, 1976, pp. 169-170). Of the five all-India castes, the fifth one (the untouchables) are regarded as outside the system. Manual work is regarded as menial labour, esteemed as 'low' job in the village. 'Unlike caste, the hierarchy based on ownership of land was a secular one, and, in theory, everyone was free to acquire land though the higher castes had more resources as well as opportunities for it' (Srinivas, 1976, p. 211). There exists patron-client relationship in the village. This relationship stemmed directly out of possession of differential rights in land. The patrons are expected to protect the clients, while the clients are compelled to obey the patrons (Srinivas, 1976, pp. 177, 180, 181, 183, 187, 195, 211, 216, 264). The inequality in the village is not always manifest, and not always institutionalized. This covers areas, which are not directly in the caste and land net.

In his village studies in Karnataka (Tumkur district) in South India, Ramachandran (1980) has examined the process of integration of rural and urban areas based on the exchange of surplus production. One of his premises is that 'the characteristics of and happenings in the non-rural segment are to a large extent responsible for the development of underdevelopment in the rural segment' (Ramachandran, 1980, p. 21).

The use of the term 'village' in various Indian languages denotes 'place of origin' that reinforces the silence of native locality, for which the village is paradigmatic (Lambert, 2002, p. 146). With respect to a study of a village in west India, Lambert takes the assumption that 'within Indian culture, kinship is necessarily secondary to (or encompassed by) caste and...the emphasis on *jajmani*-type relations in accounting for, then discrediting, the phenomenon of multicaste village 'solidarity'' (Lambert, 2002, p. 156). Inter-caste relations in villages are described primarily by reference to economic relationships and in particular the *'jajmani* system', an economic/ritual model that emphasizes occupational role separation and status differential, whether within a model of 'hierarchy' (Lambert, 2002, p. 156). As Lambert reads Srinivas, 'Srinivas's conception of village solidarity was predicted on the assumption that it resulted from the inter-caste cooperation consequent on patron-client relations' (Lambert, 2002, p. 156). Lambert believes that the supposed 'solidarity, of the village was in fact contingent on the coercive power of the dominant caste'. Lambert suggests that the identity of an individual and social identity is very much linked in India with the place of origin (Lambert, 2002, p. 157). In his view, for the majority of the people in India, the villages where people are born and brought up or have lived for a long time is home in the full sense of the word. Also, for most of the women, 'home' means two villages rather than one (if not throughout their lives then for a large part) (Lambert, 2002, p. 158).

Menchel observes the socio-economic structure of a village in South India, a Tamil village. He hardly found any change in the relationships between those at the top and those at the bottom. In his study, whatever change has occurred is between castes close to one another in the hierarchy (Menchel, 2002, p. 176). Menchel questions the possibilities of economic development keeping caste hierarchy intact (Menchel, 2002, p. 180).

Madan visualizes caste as a social organization (Madan, 2002, p. 298). He explains community divisions among people settled in rural Kashmir (the state in extreme North India), in terms of their identities. He concentrates on examining the mutual and sharp exclusion between Kashmiri Pandits and the Muslims. He shows that the Pandits do not get engaged in certain activities, which they consider as either polluting or manual. The Pandits consider the Muslims as ritually impure (Madan, 2002, pp. 311-312). As observed by Madan, Kashmiri Muslims enter into relations with Pandits, which they view as traditional economic transactions. It is a relationship of mutual dependence, but is asymmetrical (Madan, 2002, p. 320). As commented by Madan, 'at the ideological level there is complete mutual exclusion. .. both ideologies command identical behaviour towards non-believers — total exclusion — and are in that sense mutually reciprocal and reinforcing. ... The relationship of the ideological and empirical situations may thus be seen as one of complementary opposition' (Madan, 2002, pp. 322-323). Srinivas (1996) shows that 'in contrast to the village, caste has social reality. The village is only the dwelling place of diverse and unequal castes' (Srinivas, 1996, p. 2). In view of Srinivas, 'individual villages in India are far from self-sufficient economically... Caste ties stretched across villages ..' (Srinivas, 1996, p. 20). Srinivas says that 'the members of the dominant caste are in a privileged position *vis-à-vis* the other local castes, and its leaders wield considerable power. These leaders have the greatest stake in the village, have command over resources and, generally, it is they who organize local activity... They dominate the traditional village council or panchayat' (Srinivas, 1996, p. 25). Srinivas suggests that in the past villages functioned as a unit irrespective of caste and other affiliations of individuals, perhaps because of a sense of belonging to a local community having certain common interests overriding caste, kin and factional alignments (Srinivas, 1996, p. 27). This inclusion in village society, however, may be questioned by the revealed exclusion of Harijan castes from access to wells and temples used by the others in the same village (Srinivas, 1996, p. 28).

In any case, caste and community were the institutions in village society that regulated the village people. These institutions by moral code (oral and often through meetings of village elders) framed by the dominant castes were also executed by the dominant castes (Srinivas, 1996, p. 74). The very existence of caste as hierarchy as well as an institution shows caste-based pyramidal local power structure that at the same time shows absence of equality among people/units forming the whole of village society. Thus, accommodating caste and community, with hierarchic caste in power ladder in village India, shows community also as working within a hierarchic frame, and hence unequal. Sometimes village community is seen as 'stable' and known to be of immense antiquity (Srinivas, 1996, p. 6). This stability is really concealed stagnation, a life projection that shows resistance to change, restraining the mindset within lowest possible hole, living under traditions-belief-custom immobility, a world of the self-subjected by and subjugated to destiny. Even the mode of production gets submerged into this caste-community hierarchy, so that the system goes unquestioned and unresisted by the instrument of heredity and superstition. What could be revealed as social division of labour gets revealed as caste-cum-gender division of labour. While science (and technology) has developed externally, scientific outlook is yet to develop internally, so that belief gets domination over science. The ideological questions remain a far cry when the very basis of development of consciousness is far off. In a state of questions unearthed, the dimensions on individual identity, collectivism and related questions remain unexplored. In a blurred state of private-public relations, the progressive forces (by institutions, property, law etc.) do not carry much meaning for most of the people in village India.

In view of Fuller, 'villages are normally recognized as significant social units, which are defined and constituted by relationships among villagers themselves, their local deities, and the land on which they live' (Fuller, 2002, p. 271). In Fuller's view, (despite all variations), 'villages (in India) are still generally recognized as local communities, rather than places in which people merely happen to live and work. For the majority of Indians, including many urban migrants, the village where they were born and brought up or have lived for a long time is home in the full sense of the word. Village rituals are one manifestation of the social significance of the local community, and in much of India the unity or solidarity of the community is most strikingly expressed in the celebration of village festivals' (Fuller, 2002, p. 272). Fuller questions the organic solidarity of village India also by the visible exclusion of the Harijans (the untouchables) as members of the village (Fuller, 2002, pp. 280-281). Fuller examines these questions with respect to villages in both south and north India.

On the basis of a study of 153 villages in North India (Uttar Pradesh) Dube suggests that 'An individual and his family belong also to a village, which is often multi-caste in its composition. The village itself is a part of the network of neighbouring villages, the region, and the nation. ...Caste is perhaps the most important single organizing principle in these communities, and it governs to a very considerable degree the organization of kinship and territorial units...The caste divisions are regarded as divinely ordained and are hierarchically graded (Dube, 2002, p. 353). He also shows the patron-client relation in rural UP explained in ethnographic terms as the '*jajmani* system'. Also, that 'caste largely determines occupational choice...Within a village the caste system manifests itself as a vertical structure in which individual castes are hierarchically graded and kept permanently apart (Dube, 2002, p. 354). Dube also points at 'local conditions of the villages as binding conditions for even the more progressive people settled inside the village' (Dube, 2002, p. 355).

With respect to the study of Karchhana tehsil, Jaer (1995) says that 'caste is the inter-subjective fact which governs the *jajmani* system. ..caste also provides a model of the social world as well as a model for social action within it. As an information and value system encompassed by a very pervasive ideology and other strong mechanisms of social control, caste determines to a great extent the social destiny of villagers. Caste affiliation, determined through birth, identifies the person. However rich, educated and otherwise high-ranking a low-caste person might be within the national setting, caste is beyond comparison the intersubjective fact which defines a person's social identity and identifies his rank in the local hierarchy. Within the local setting, caste still clings to a person as a stigma. The only way for an individual to escape the iron law of caste is to leave his native place, change name and move to one of the big cities' (Jaer, 1995, p. 54). As observed by Jaer in Karchhana tehsil, ' the *jajmani* system, an aspect of caste which organizes production, distribution and consumption without the intervention of the impersonal forces of the market, is a typical example of a division of labour based on heredity and personal relations....*Jajmani* regulates economic exchange as a direct function of social structure — as a form of mechanical solidarity. Social relations organized by caste exhibit furthermore the characterizations of separation in interdependence' (Jaer, 1995, p. 64). On the contrary, as observed by Jaer, 'social relations organized by class are impersonal, not hereditary and based on contract. Economic exchange organized by class is furthermore mediated by money via the impersonal price mechanisms of the market. Class regulates economic exchange indirectly as a form of organic solidarity' (Jaer, 1995, p. 64).

Dasgupta analyses the functioning of villages by economic parameters. He suggests that 'the propensity to migrate is high in villages characterized by land-scarcity, inequality of land distribution, moderate but not great proximity to urban centres, and a relatively high educational level. However, it is not necessarily the poorest who migrate; given the high costs of transport to, and subsistence in towns, and then relatively low differences (and perception of differences) in earning possibilities between villages and towns among the poorest sections in the village, the propensity to migrate to towns is higher among groups other than the very poorest in a village' (Dasgupta, 1977, p. 15).

Srinivas (2003) explains how the (caste-based) hierarchic mode of local production is breaking down to the emerging forces of market-based division of labour. Thus, he explains how caste-division of labour centred on local (localized) production of basic needs (goods for subsistence or self-sufficiency in consumption) gives birth to impersonal (market) division of labour. The emergence of market division of labour is not only because of cash needs of individuals but also because of developing techniques of production, improved communication etc. In fact, the changed and changing mode of production led to displacement of caste (status) division of labour (and social relations) to product-*cum*-market division of labour and economic relations. Technology played a great role in this conversion from caste relations in production to economic relations in production (Srinivas, 2003, pp. 455-457).

The Individual, the Family, the Group, and the Society in Village India

Generally, an individual is an element of a family. A family constitutes the lowest unit of any economic-sociological study. The formation of groups by individuals may seem to be independent of the families. However, the targets and mode of operation of the groups will reveal at some stage that the families are there at the back. In fact, the society is the composition of individuals who come from the families. These individuals get involved in activities for economic survival and express themselves in practices that crop up from the types of economic practices that they perform.

It sometimes remains concealed why and how the identity of an individual remains an integral part of a village. In fact, in a relatively underdeveloped region (by conventional economic indicators) it is the village that shows the country ('desh') for an individual, more so for an asset-poor individual. The village shows the root of the individual. The 'root to the land is a fundamental distinction between a rural and an urban economy' (Ramachandran, 1980, p. 47). The root lies in collection of food, food habits, habits of childhood, adolescence, and youth. The root also lies in links with the members of families. The root also lies in links with neighbours, local rituals and festivals. The movement and eviction of the individual cannot remove from the mindset of the individual's past — the memories that she practiced in her early days. These practices were collective — sharing life experience with the relatives, friends, and neighbours.

The village that we talk about is really boundary-less. However, the village social accommodation is defined subject to the given caste-hierarchy or accommodating divisions along community line. Birth determines the social existence of individuals. The economic existence of individuals is a conversion of individuals in society by inclusion in areas that we call economic. The first one also includes categories like caste, community, tribe, gender, some of which are man-made. The latter includes occupation, conversion of nature by labour etc. While the society cannot exclude any individual, the economy can do it. The mechanism of exclusion, however, may remain implicit in the functioning of the society. Thus, the type of inclusion that we call 'social' may actually be pseudo-accommodative. This pseudo-accommodation may work within the village society by strict compartmentalization of castes. What is visible as local (village) unity is really unity within the caste. Unless there occurs a shock from outside in terms of new information (communication and mobility of people), the hierarchic relation remains undisturbed.

Physical and Cultural Existence of People in Village India

The living of any individual is not only physical but also cultural. Even when an individual works for living, it is conscious labour that aims at transformation of nature in which she lives symbiotically. Thus, the physical existence and living of an individual is not anti-nature. Culture of an individual gets the first expression in terms of how she accommodates the reality outside her. It also reflects how she interacts with the world outside her. The interaction includes many manifestations like dependence, interdependence, isolation, withstanding the aggression by others etc. This physical-behavioural world may be understood in a narrow space as well as in a broad space. The narrow space seems to be her root, her birthplace, may be the village. The broad space may be the visible and invisible realities on the ground of which she is a part.

The concept that comes while one concentrates on cultural dimensions of village life, one talks about vertical (upward diagonal) movement of individuals by mobility. The question comes what type of mobility it is. Is it mobility within the structure of casteism, or a mobility that attempts at breaking the caste structure? In this context, *'Sanskritization'* that came into analysis in India since early 1950s implies a process by which a low caste or tribe or other group takes over the customs, ritual, beliefs, ideology and style of life of a high and, in particular, a twice-born (*dwija*) caste. *'Sanskritization* of a group by caste or otherwise has usually the effect of improving its position in the local caste hierarchy' (Srinivas, 1996, p. 88).

While a rigid and systematized caste hierarchy obstructs the vertical mobility of low castes even after acquiring qualities like similar language, property (land etc.), it remains not clear the position of women along this caste hierarchy. Thus, *'Sanskritization'* works within the given frame of caste hierarchy with occasional scope for a section of the low caste to move up the ladder. In a given power structure, locally and local set in a regional/national context, the dominant caste-*cum*-economic group enjoys power and imposes wishes on others, so that the vertical mobility of the section in the lower caste remains a far cry. The upward movement of people of the low caste, if it can be called *'Sanskritization'*, thus depends on acquiring power. But if power is hereditary, by birth in a particular caste, and supported by ownership and control over land and major means of production in rural areas, then the very process of *'Sanskritization'* even by introduction of universal political process of voting remains questioned. Also, *'Sanskritization'* makes the context of upward movement of women obscure. Even the role and status of women as individuals with identities in the caste hierarchy is not very clear. Thus, by accepting village as a unit of study, we by no means accept caste hierarchy as an unquestionable organization nor do we accept 'standard' *'Sanskritisation'* as an unquestionable concept (Menchel, 2002, p. 180; Dreze, 2002, p. 219).

Perspective of the Study

We narrate four stories that present the perspective of the paper.

Story One: I was once told by one of my friends in Kolkata that the people of Bangladesh cross the 'border' frequently, come to India (Kolkata), do odd jobs and go back with the money that they collect to Bangladesh. I asked, 'Who are they?' My friend replied, 'they are the makers and menders of umbrella'. I asked, 'What is wrong in it?' The response was, 'These people are not only violating the 'visa' rules, but also eating away the job opportunities of the people settled in

Kolkata' (India). I assured my friend that the people were not crossing (illegally) the boundary of their country, they were only moving from one 'village' to another village/town. My point is that the village is the root of these people, the home for these people. Also, these people are not consciously competing with their fellow people in India, they are only struggling to survive by applying the expertise that they got probably by inheritance.

Story Two: I used to ask my grandparents, 'Where had been your 'desh'' (Bengali term for country)? The immediate response was, 'Barishal' (a region/village in Bangladesh). The fact is they had to leave Bangladesh following the declaration of independence and partition in 1947, and that even after coming over to West Bengal they could not forget their 'land' and perhaps people and associated culture. Given a chance, they would again like to go back to their land but for us, the next generation, we came to concentrate on state more than the land and the people.

Story Three: I used to accompany my friend to bring labourers (not acknowledged as dignified people) from a region called Nwada in Bihar to work in the brick plants in the sub-urban areas in West Bengal that my friend owned. I had listened to many of the well-wishers in Kolkata that people from Bihar were brought to work in the plants when there were available workers in Kolkata itself. The point that I would confess here is that it was cheaper labour working under extreme conditions of poverty. As far as the people who were being brought in were drawn through a 'Munsiji', who too was from a village in Bihar. Thus, the labourers could be from any village that is located anywhere in the world. What matters to the people, thus, brought into the brick plants is a temporary displacement from one village to 'in their supposition' another village, the latter offering them temporary monetary protection.

The point is that people who stay in a village do not like to get displaced permanently, unless compelled. This is because the village is the root for the people that take birth there, the root that covers all the components of nature there. The 'push' and 'pull' factors that make people move from the village is really an oversimplification of people at least in some categories. It is not always a mobility from village (rural) to town (urban) explained by presence (pull) of some facilities in towns that are not available (push) in villages. The reason for the movement of people may also be from village (in a relatively job-scarce region) to another village (in a relatively job-abundant region). The movement may also be socially apparently regressive and economically progressive. Let me tell a recent story.

Story four: A few months back when I was going to my village (converted now into a sub-urban area with the same mindset of most of the people of my childhood) along with my family, I hired a taxi from the Howrah railway station. As we started talking about different issues, the taxi driver joined us. We could little understand that he was a pure Hindi-speaking person from the district Balia in east Uttar Pradesh. Ultimately we came to know that he is an individual with surname 'Upadhyay', that is a high caste Brahmin. While strict caste hierarchy obstructed him to do any 'socially considered' menial job, he being a Brahmin by birth, in the town of Kolkata he could easily do the same with pride. Thus, he converted himself from a mere social being to an active economic being, without, however, loosing his social identity. However, that social identity in Kolkata was not based on caste.

Among the lessons that may be derived from all the stories told, the significant ones are that man-made divisions by social parameters like caste etc. are visible in the village and less visible or concealed in the town. Conversion of social village individuals into economic/town individuals also conceals social/caste categories as locally operating forces. The social relations, thus, depend not only on visible social parameters by birth but also by economic parameters. The conversion from a 'pure' social to an economic identity is not an easy one. It depends on learning, training, development of skill, mobility, job opportunity etc. Traditional (village) India—traditional production (by products for subsistence) and barter-based exchange—and immobility (economic and non-economic) are inter-linked.

II. Objectives, Methodology and Sample

We will examine the living condition of settled people in village Bhaganpur

(i) by fulfilment of basic needs,
(ii) by ownership over residential and agricultural land,
(iii) by availability of physical and social infrastructure.

In case of fulfilment of basic needs we will look into access of people to elementary education, food, clothing, housing etc. For access to food, we will look into the type of card holding in the public distribution system. We will also see the availability and use of fuel for cooking food. In case of clothing, we will see the number and quality of clothes that the local people purchase and use. In housing, we will see the type of residential houses that the local people have, by durability and facilities.

Regarding objective (ii), we will see the ownership and use pattern of productive assets related to cultivable land. These assets will cover water for different purposes, tractor, thresher, pump set, crushing machine, commercial vehicles etc. In case of availability of water, we will see sources of water.

Methodology and Sample

We consider the state of Uttar Pradesh and consider the district of Allahabad purposively. UP is a relatively underdeveloped state in India. The district of Allahabad is relatively more developed in the eastern part of UP. Within the selected district, we consider a particular block, Karchhana. We select a particular village, Bhaganpur, purposively.

Bhaganpur is a small village by size of population and number of households. Following 1991 Census, the number of households in Bhaganpur village was 57 and a population size of 445. Of this total population, the ST population was 73, that is, 16.4 per cent of the total village population. In Karchhana block, the percentage of ST population was 0.10. Thus, relative to the block, the village has high concentration ratio of tribal population. We will, thus, study the life environment of people settled in the village, with a focus on the tribal people.

The village being very small by number of households (57 following 1991 Census), we intend to select all the households in the village. One reason for this is that it will enable us to cover all the tribal households, which is small in absolute number (though the ratio is high). This will enable us to have a comprehensive and comparative look at the life environment of people settled in the village.

III. Living Condition of People in Village Bhaganpur : Some Facts

The village Bhaganpur has 88 households that cover a total population of 684. Thus, the size of each household on average is 7.7 (number of individuals). Of the village total population, male population is 54.68 per cent and female population 45.32 per cent (Table 7.1).

Table 7.1 : Gender Composition of Population in the Village

Total Households	*Total Male Population*	*Total Female Population*	*Total Population*
88 (100.0 %)	374 (54.68 %)	310 (45.32 %)	684 (100.0 %)

Source : Field Survey, 2003.

The caste-*cum*-tribe composition in the village shows percentage of ST population at 15.8 (which is 14.8 per cent for households). The castes and tribes in the village are *Adivasi* (tribes), *Mallah* (Backward caste), *Brahmin* and *Bhumihar* (General), *Thakur* (General). The households in general castes (*Bhumihar, Brahmin, Thakur*) constitute 51.14 per cent of all households. The *Mallah* (fishermen dependent on water-centric economic activities) constitute as high as 34.09 per cent of all households (Table 7.2).

Table 7.2 : Tribes and Castes in the Village
(Percentage share in all households and population)

Castes/Tribes	*Households (%)*	*Population (%)*
Adivasi (Scheduled Tribes)	13 (14.8)	108 (15.8)
Mallah (Backward Classes)	30 (34.09)	230 (33.6)
Brahmin and Bhumihar (General)	41 (46.6)	315 (46.1)
Thakur (General)	4 (4.5)	31 (04.5)
Total	88 (100.0)	684 (100.0)

Source : Field Survey, 2003.

In the village the Mallahs are in backward castes while *Adivasi* are tribes (as they claim) and *Brahmins, Bhumihars, Thakurs* constitute general caste. The distribution of households by size-class (number of individuals in households) is similar for all the caste-*cum*-tribe groups in the village.

Of all the population in the village, one-fourth is illiterate and another one-fourth has education up to primary level. There is high illiteracy among female population in the village, it is nearly two-fifth of the total female population.

More than half of the female population in STs is illiterate while one-third of population in STs is illiterate. Nearly one-third of the population in BCs is illiterate, where female illiteracy is 44.0 per cent. In population in general caste, female illiteracy is a little more than one-fourth, so that total illiteracy in general caste comes down to less than one-fifth of total population in general caste. There are no graduates from STs and no female graduates from any of the households covering STs, BCs and general castes. There is only one woman from STs, two from BCs who have high school standard certificate. Female illiteracy is major phenomenon among all the population, though more prominent among STs and BCs.

Agriculture is the main occupation for all the households in the village that covers 80.0 per cent of all households. There is nobody employed in the organized service sector from *Adivasi* (tribe) and *Mallah* (BC). In the service sector an insignificant percentage of households from general castes are employed. The occupations of tribes (*Adivasi*) and non-tribes (General castes) are similar, both being land-*cum*-cultivation dependent. There is nobody working as agricultural labour in the village from BC (*Mallah*) and general caste; only one household from ST is employed as agricultural labour. From only four households engaged as non-agriculture labour, 75.0 per cent come from STs (*Adivasi*) and 25.0 per cent from BCs (*Mallah*) (Table 7.3).

Table 7.3 : Households by Castes and Main Occupations
(Percentage Distribution)

Occupations	*Households by Castes (%)*			
	Scheduled Tribes	*Backward Classes*	*General*	*All Households*
Agriculture	9 (11.3)	29 (36.3)	42 (52.5)	80 (100.0)
Agricultural labour	1 (100.0)	0	0	1 (100.0)
Non-agricultural Labour	3 (75.0)	1 (25.0)	0	4 (100.0)
Service	0	0	3 (100.0)	3 (100.0)
All Households	13 (14.8)	30 (34.1)	45 (51.1)	88 (100.0)

Source : Field Survey, 2003.

67.0 per cent of the households belong to the income bracket, Rs. 1,000-2,500 p.m. 17.0 per cent of the households earn income p.m. below Rs. 1,000. Thus, 84.0 per cent of the households in the village earn income below Rs. 30,000 per household per year or approximately below Rs. 3,896 per capita per year, or below Rs. 324.6 per capita per month or below Rs. 10 per capita per day. 14.77 per cent of the households earn income between Rs. 2,501 and Rs. 5,000 per household per month, while only one household (in general caste) earns income per month between Rs. 5,001 and Rs. 10,000. No ST household in the village earns income per month above Rs. 2,500 (Table 7.4).

Most of the households depend on agriculture. Hence, we enquired into the type of residential plot of land and agricultural land holding that these households have in village Bhaganpur.

Table 7.4 : Households by Castes and Income
(Percentage of Households)

Income Group (Rs. Per Month)	*Households by Castes (%)*			
	Scheduled Tribes	*Backward Classes*	*General*	*All Households*
Below 1000	01 (6.7)	07 (46.7)	07 (46.7)	15 (100.0)
1001-2500	12 (20.3)	19 (32.2)	28 (47.5)	59 (100.0)
2501-5000	0	04 (30.8)	09 (69.2)	13 (100.0)
5001-10000	0	0	01 (100.0)	01 (100.0)
All Households	13 (14.8)	30 (34.1)	45 (51.1)	88 (100.0)

Source : Field Survey, 2003.

Residential Land Ownership

There is no landless in the village by residential landholding. There is also no household owning more than 20 *biswa* of land per household for residential purposes. 69.3 per cent of all households in the ST (*Adivasi*) and BC (*Mallah*) own land less than 2 *biswa* per household for residential purposes. Only the households in general caste have residential land per household more than 5 *biswa*. The category that is 'land poor' most is the ST (*Adivasi*). In general, most of the households by residential land ownership are bracketed between 1 *biswa* and 2 *biswa*, it is 72.0 per cent, that shows the modal class of residential landholding (Table 7.5).

Table 7.5 : Residential Landholding of Households by Castes

Landholding in Biswa	*Households by Castes (%)*			
	Scheduled Tribes	*Backward Classes*	*General*	*All Households*
Landless	0	0	0	0
Less than 1 Biswa	08 (61.5)	10 (33.3)	01 (2.2)	19 (21.6)
1-2 Biswa	03 (23.1)	17 (56.7)	22 (48.9)	42 (47.7)
2-5 Biswa	02 (15.4)	03 (10.0)	17 (37.8)	22 (25.0)
5-20 Biswa	0	0	05 (11.1)	05 (5.7)
More than 20 Biswa	0	0	0	0
All Households	13 (100.0)	30 (100.0)	45 (100.0)	88 (100.0)

Source : Field Survey, 2003.

There is no causal association between households in income brackets and residential landholding. The households in the modal class by income bracket between Rs. 1,001 and Rs. 2,500 own mainly residential land between 1 *biswa* and 2 *biswa.* The households with income less than Rs. 1,000 per month mostly own residential plot of land between 2 *biswa* and 5 *biswa.* In general, 72.7 per cent of the households own residential plot of land between 1 *biswa* and 5 *biswa.* Residential landholding below 1 *biswa* is covered mostly by households in income bracket between Rs. 1,001 and Rs. 2,500. (Table 7.6).

Table 7.6 : Residential Landholding of Households by Income

Residential Landholding (In Biswa)	*Households by Income (%)*				
	Below 1,000	*1,001-2,500*	*2,501-5,000*	*5,001-10,000*	*All Households*
Landless	0	0	0	0	0
Less than 1 Biswa	04 (26.7)	13 (22.0)	02 (15.4)	0	19 (21.6)
1-2 Biswa	14 (93.3)	22 (37.3)	06 (46.2)	0	42 (47.7)
2-5 Biswa	06 (40.0)	11 (18.6)	04 (30.8)	01 (100.0)	22 (25.0)
5-20 Biswa	01 (06.7)	03 (05.1)	01 (07.7)	0	05 (05.7)
More than 20 Biswa	0	0	0	0	0
All Households	15 (100.0)	59 (100.0)	13 (100.0)	01 (100.0)	88 (100.0)

Source : Field Survey, 2003.

Agricultural Landholding

There is no landless household by ownership of agricultural landholding from general castes in village Bhaganpur. The 'landless' are very few from BCs (*Mallahs*) and ST (*Adivasi*). More than 50.0 % of all the households have agricultural landholding between 1 acre and 5 acres. There is no household from ST and BC who own agricultural land above 10 acres. There are very few households (5.7 %) who own agricultural land more than 10 acres and that is cultivated by the households in general castes. 69.3 per cent of all ST households own agricultural land between 0.5 acre and 2 acres. Two-thirds of

BC households own agricultural land between 1 acre and 5 acres. Around two-thirds of the households in general castes own agricultural land between 2 acres and 5 acres. Thus, small size of agricultural land (less than 2 acres) is generally owned by households in STs (*Adivasi*), while medium size (1 acre to 5 acres) is owned by BCs (*Mallah*) and large size (between 2 acres and 10 acres) is owned by households in general castes (Table 7.7).

Table 7.7 : Agricultural Landholding of Households by Castes

Agricultural Landholding in Acre	*Households by Castes (%)*			
	Scheduled Tribes	*Backward Classes*	*General*	*All Households*
Landless	01 (07.7)	01 (03.3)	0	02 (02.3)
Below 0.5	02 (15.4)	06 (20.0)	01 (02.2)	09 (10.2)
0.5 to 1.0	06 (46.2)	02 (06.7)	03 (06.7)	11 (12.5)
1.0 to 2.0	03 (23.1)	17 (56.7)	07 (15.6)	27 (30.7)
2.0 to 5.0	01 (07.7)	03 (10.0)	15 (33.3)	19 (21.6)
5.0 to 10.0	0	01 (03.3)	14 (31.1)	15 (17.0)
10.0 Acre above	0	0	05 (11.1)	05 (05.7)
All Households	13 (100.0)	30 (100.0)	45 (100.0)	88 (100.0)

Source : Field Survey, 2003.

There is no causal association between households in income brackets and agricultural landholding. For example, agricultural landholding over 10 acres per households is owned only by the households in income bracket Rs.1,001-Rs.2,500. However, households in the low-income bracket own mostly agricultural land between 1 acre and 5 acres (52.5 % of households in this income bracket). This income bracket covers most of the households. More than half of the households with income per month less than Rs.1,000 own agricultural land between 1 acre and 2 acres. These households do not own agricultural land above 5 acres. For households in medium income bracket (Rs.2,501-Rs.5,000 per month) ownership over agricultural land is evenly distributed between 1 acre and 10 acres (77.0 per cent of the households in this income bracket) come under this range of agricultural land ownership. The single household in the village within the high income bracket own agricultural land between 5 acres to 10 acres (Table 7.8).

Table 7.8 : Agricultural Landholding of Households by Income

Landholding in Acre	*Households by Income (%)*				
	Below 1,000	*1,001- 2,500*	*2,501- 5,000*	*5,001- 10,000*	*All House-holds*
Landless	01 (06.7)	01 (01.7)	0	0	02 (02.3)
Below 0.5	03 (20.0)	04 (06.8)	02 (15.4)	0	09 (10.2)
0.5 to 1.0	02 (13.3)	08 (13.6)	01 (07.7)	0	11 (12.5)
1.0 to 2.0	08 (53.3)	16 (27.1)	03 (23.1)	0	27 (30.7)
2.0 to 5.0	01 (06.7)	15 (25.4)	03 (23.1)	0	19 (21.6)
5.0 to 10.0	0	10 (16.9)	04 (30.8)	01 (100.0)	15 (17.0)
Above 10.0	0	05 (08.5)	0	0	05 (05.7)
All Households	15 (100.0)	59 (100.0)	13 (100.0)	01 (100.0)	88 (100.0)

Source : Field Survey, 2003.

Productive Assets of Households

We have included here all types of assets, animate and inanimate, that the households maintain and use to earn income in cash and in kind. These include domestic animals like cow, bulls, buffaloes, goat, pigs that yield milk, meat, skin, work as draught animals. These also include ploughs, pump-sets, thresher, tractor, sewing machine, non-residential building, etc.

The households, in general, have some combination of domestic animals like cows, bulls, and buffaloes. The rare productive assets are non-residential building, pump-set, tractor, sewing machine, Jeep/Tempo. None of the households from STs (*Adivasis*) and BCs (*Mallahs*) owns non-residential building, pump-set, thresher, tractor, sewing machine, Jeep/Tempo. While 80.0 per cent of the households are cultivators, more than 80.0 per cent do not have even a plough per household. All the tractors in the village (a total of four) are owned by high caste households. The machines and equipments (capital goods) as productive assets are owned by high caste households, while the domestic animals as capital goods (multiple/durable use) and trees/garden/plantations are owned by all the caste/tribe groups in the village (Table 7.9).

Table 7.9 : Income Generating (Productive) Assets of Households

Assets by Types	*Households by Castes (%)*							
	Scheduled Tribes		*Backward Classes*		*General*		*All Households*	
	Owning Assets	*Asset less*	*Owning Assets*	*Asset less*	*Owning Assets*	*Asset less*	*Owning Assets*	*Asset less*
Cow	02 (15.4)	11 (84.6)	09 (30.0)	21 (70.0)	28 (62.2)	17 (37.8)	39 (44.3)	49 (55.7)
Bulls	03 (23.1)	10 (76.9)	14 (46.7)	16 (53.3)	07 (15.6)	38 (84.4)	24 (27.3)	64 (72.7)
Buffalo	04 (30.8)	09 (69.2)	24 (80.0)	06 (20.0)	31 (68.9)	14 (31.1)	59 (67.0)	29 (32.9)
Goat	01 (07.7)	12 (92.3)	10 (33.3)	20 (66.7)	02 (04.4)	43 (95.6)	13 (14.8)	75 (85.2)
Non Res. Building	0	13 (100.0)	0	30 (100.0)	01 (02.2)	44 (97.8)	01 (01.1)	87 (98.9)
Plough	03 (23.1)	10 (76.9)	07 (23.3)	23 (76.7)	06 (13.3)	39 (86.7)	16 (18.2)	72 (81.8)
Pump Set	0	13 (100.0)	0	30 (100.0)	03 (06.7)	42 (93.3)	03 (03.4)	85 (96.6)
Thresher	0	13 (100.0)	0	30 (100.0)	04 (08.9)	41 (91.1)	04 (04.5)	84 (95.5)
Tractor	0	13 (100.0)	0	30 (100.0)	04 (08.9)	41 (91.1)	04 (04.5)	84 (95.5)
Sewing Machine	0	13 (100.0)	0	30 (100.0)	05 (11.1)	40 (88.9)	05 (05.7)	83 (94.3)
Jeep/Tempo	0	13 (100.0)	0	30 (100.0)	01 (02.2)	44 (97.8)	01 (01.1)	87 (98.9)
Trees/Garden	09 (69.2)	04 (30.8)	24 (80.0)	06 (20.0)	42 (93.3)	03 (06.7)	75 (85.2)	13 (14.8)
All HHs	13 (100.0)	13 (100.0)	30 (100.0)	30 (100.0)	45 (100.0)	45 (100.0)	88 (100.0)	88 (100.0)

Source : Field Survey, 2003.

One direct corollary of this pattern of ownership over productive assets is that no household within STs and BCs earns anything from material capital goods like ploughs, pump-sets, thresher, tractor, sewing machine, Jeep/Tempo, and non-residential building. This is because either they do not own these and/or these do not yield any direct income (like ownership/use of plough). The households in STs and BCs earn most from ownership/use of buffaloes, per buffalo this annual income is Rs. 5,000 (net income over and above costs for maintenance of a buffalo at current prices). Owning/ maintaining cows shows differential income for households in STs, BCs, and general (high) caste. Bulls are used in drawing ploughs, carts, and for breeding. Thus, unless the net income from bulls falls drastically and unless tractors substitute bulls partially in some uses, bulls continue to be maintained as a productive asset in village Bhaganpur by the households. Maintaining goats is relatively easy and hence these are maintained as productive assets.

Residential Houses by Types and Facilities

In village Bhaganpur more than half of the residential houses were *katcha*, while nearly one-fourth was *pakka*. The rest were semi-*pakka* (one-sixth) and *jopri* (one-tenth).

The households in STs reside either in *Katcha* houses or in *jhopris*, the former type for a little more than half of all ST households. The households in general/high caste do not live in *jhopris*. The *pakka* houses are generally one-storey building made of bricks, stone, iron, sand, and cement. The *katcha* houses are generally made of clay/mud, tiles, leaves etc. The *jhopris* are mostly dilapidated. Half of the households in BCs (*Mallahs*) have semi-*pakka* and *pakka* houses (Table 7.10).

Table 7.10 : Types of Residential Houses of Households by Castes

Houses by Types	*Residential Houses of Households by Castes (%)*			
	Scheduled Tribes	*Backward Classes*	*General*	*All Households*
Katcha	07 (53.8)	13 (43.3)	25 (55.6)	45 (51.1)
Pakka	0	06 (20.0)	15 (33.3)	21 (23.9)
Semi-*Pakka*	0	09 (30.0)	05 (11.1)	14 (15.9)
Jhopri	06 (46.2)	02 (06.7)	0	08 (09.1)
All Households	13 (100.0)	30 (100.0)	45 (100.0)	88 (100.0)

Source : Field Survey, 2003.

Nearly three-fourth of the households that own *katcha* residential houses belong to low income brackets. More than half of all households who own *pakka* houses, half belong to the low income bracket, i.e., Rs. 1,001-Rs. 2,500. The reason why most of the households in both *katcha* and *pakka* houses come from this low income bracket (Rs. 1,000-Rs. 2,500) is that this income bracket covers most (two-thirds) of the households in the village. No households in income bracket above Rs. 2,500 reside in *jhopris* and no household in income bracket above Rs. 5,000 p.m. reside in *katcha* or semi-*pakka* houses. In fact, there is only one household in the village in this income bracket that reside in *pakka* house. Of the middle income bracket households (Rs. 2,501-Rs. 5,000), more than half reside in *pakka* houses. 84.0 per cent of households in the village have income per month less than Rs. 2,500 and most of them are settled in *katcha* houses (Table 7.11).

Table 7.11 : Types of Residential Houses of Households by Income

Types of Houses	*Residential Houses of Households by Income (%)*				
	Below 1,000	*1,001-2,500*	*2,501-5,000*	*5,001-10,000*	*All House-holds*
Katcha	10 (66.6)	32 (54.2)	03 (23.1)	0	45 (51.1)
Pakka	02 (13.3)	11 (18.6)	07 (53.8)	01 (100.0)	21 (23.9)
Semi-*Pakka*	01 (06.7)	10 (16.9)	03 (23.1)	0	14 (15.9)
Jhopri	02 (13.3)	06 (10.2)	0	0	08 (09.1)
All Households	15 (100.0)	59 (100.0)	13 (100.0)	01 (100.0)	88 (100.0)

Source : Field Survey, 2003.

All the households have bedrooms available in the residential houses. However, the other facilities like kitchen, bathroom, and toilet are not always available for households. Bathroom and toilet are not available for households in STs and BCs. Only one-sixth of the STs have separate space available within the residential house as kitchen, which is 40.0 per cent for *Mallahs*. Nearly three-fifths of the households in general castes have kitchens. Bathroom is available for less than one-fifth of the households in general caste, while only one household in this caste has separate toilet in the residential house. Of all households, thus, toilet is not available as a separate space in the residential houses of the households, while separate bathroom is available for less than one-tenth of all the households (Table 7.12).

Table 7.12 : Facilities Available in Residential Houses of Households by Castes

Facilities	*Availability*	*Households by Castes (%)*			
		Scheduled Tribes	*Backward Classes*	*General*	*All Households*
Rooms	Available	13 (100.0)	30 (100.0)	45 (100.0)	88 (100.0)
	Not Available	0	0	0	0
Kitchen	Available	02 (15.4)	12 (40.0)	26 (57.8)	40 (45.5)
	Not Available	11 (84.6)	18 (60.0)	19 (42.2)	48 (54.5)
Bathroom	Available	0	0	08 (17.8)	08 (09.1)
	Not Available	13 (100.0)	30 (100.0)	37 (82.2)	80 (90.9)
Toilet	Available	0	0	01 (02.2)	01 (01.1)
	Not Available	13 (100.0)	30 (100.0)	44 (97.8)	87 (98.9)
All Households		13 (100.0)	30 (100.0)	45 (100.0)	88 (100.0)

Source : Field Survey, 2003.

Even for the single household in the highest income bracket (Rs. 5,001-Rs. 10,000) in the village, toilet is not available. All the other facilities for comfortable living are available for this household like bedrooms, kitchen, and bathroom. For the lowest income bracket household (less than Rs. 1,000 p.m.) separate bathrooms and toilets are not available. For almost all the households in low income bracket, bathrooms and toilets are not available. Presence of toilet for a single household in income bracket (Rs. 1,001-Rs. 2,500) is an exception to the general absence of toilets for the households in the village. Excepting a few *pakka* houses owned/used generally by households in general caste, all the *katcha,* semi-*pakka,* and *jhopris* show only space as little as possible that accommodate households of average size of 7.7. The idea of having separate bathroom is also rare in the mindset of most of the households in village Bhaganpur, water for bathing being a natural source outside the residential house, like public pond, public well, canal, river etc. Toilet as an urban concept is yet to enter the mindset of people settled in the village (Table 7.13).

Table 7.13 : Facilities Available in Residential Houses of Households by Income

Facilities	*Availability*	*Households by Income (%)*				
		Below 1000	*1001-2500*	*2501-5000*	*5001-10000*	*All Households*
Rooms	Available	15 (100.0)	59 (100.0)	13 (100.0)	01 (100.0)	88 (100.0)
	Not Available	0	0	0	0	0
Kitchen	Available	04 (26.7)	25 (42.4)	10 (76.9)	01 (100.0)	40 (45.5)
	Not Available	11 (73.3)	34 (57.6)	03 (23.1)	0	48 (54.5)
Bathroom	Available	0	03 (05.1)	04 (30.8)	01 (100.0)	08 (09.1)
	Not Available	15 (100.0)	56 (94.9)	09 (69.2)	0	80 (90.9)
Toilet	Available	0	01 (01.7)	0	0	01 (01.1)
	Not Available	15 (100.0)	58 (98.3)	13 (100.0)	01 (100.0)	87 (98.9)
All Households		15 (100.0)	59 (100.0)	13 (100.0)	01 (100.0)	88 (100.0)

Source : Field Survey, 2003.

Only the households in general castes have got legal electricity connections in the village. The households in STs and BCs have no legal electricity connection. As reported by all the households in STs, BCs and general caste, electricity supply per day remains operational for seven hours on average. Among all households, only 15.9 per cent have legal electricity connection, while 44.3 per cent use/avail electricity illegally.

None of the households in STs, BCs, and general castes use gas lamp, generator, emergency light, and candle sticks as alternatives to electricity at night. They use either self-made kerosene light and ordinary lamp at night. Of these again, none of the STs and BCs use ordinary lamp at night. As high as 97.8 per cent of the households use self-made kerosene lamp at night, in addition to only two households in general caste using ordinary lamp. Thus, the households in the village are dependent on availability of kerosene for having any light at night in the village.

Fuel for Cooking in Residential Houses

None of the households by castes like STs, BCs, and general has fuel facilities like kerosene-stove, heater (electricity-run), and smokeless *chulha* for cooking purposes in residential houses in village Bhaganpur. None of the households in STs and BCs use wood/timber, and gas-stove for purposes of cooking food. Gas-stove is used by only one household from the general caste, while wood/timber is used by only 12.5 per cent of households (that too from the general category). 86.4 per cent of all the households use *'kanda'* (cowdung cake) as fuel for cooking in village Bhaganpur. One hundred per cent of the households from STs and BCs are totally dependent on *'kanda'* for cooking, while 73.3 per cent of the households from general caste depend on *'kanda'* for cooking. The rest of the households depend on wood/timber excepting one using gas-stove for cooking (Table 7.14).

Table 7.14 : Fuel for cooking in Residential Houses of Households by Castes

Equipments and Fuel	*Households by Castes (%)*			
	Scheduled Tribes	*Backward Classes*	*General*	*All Households*
*Kanda**	13 (100.0)	30 (100.0)	33 (73.3)	76 (86.4)
Wood/ Timber	0	0	11 (24.4)	11 (12.5)
Gas stove	0	0	01 (02.2)	01 (01.1)
All Households	13 (100.0)	30 (100.0)	45 (100.0)	88 (100.0)

* Cow dung cake
Source : Field Survey, 2003.

Drinking Water Facilities for Households

The major source for most of the households is India Mark-2 for water for drinking purposes. The other sources are well (public/private), general hand pump and pond. Households use multiple sources for having access to drinking water.

Access of People to Food distributed by Public Distribution System

In village Bhaganpur there were 39.8 per cent of the households in BPL and 63.6 per cent in APL, implying some households owning more than one type of cards and/or owning more cards than fixed per household/family. Almost all the households in STs are in BPL while most of the households in general caste are in APL. *Mallahs* are evenly distributed between APL and BPL. The household in the highest income bracket is in APL by cardholding, while some high-income households (Rs. 2,501-Rs. 5,000) enjoy BPL cards (Table 7.15).

Table 7.15 : Ration Cards Owned by Households by Income

Categories of Households	*Households by Income (%)*				
	Below 1,000	*1,001-2,500*	*2,501-5,000*	*5,001-10,000*	*All House-holds*
BPL	04 (26.66)	27 (45.76)	04 (30.76)	0	35 (39.77)
APL	11 (73.33)	34 (57.62)	10 (76.92)	01 (100.0)	56 (63.63)
All Households	15 (100.0)	59 (100.0)	13 (100.0)	01 (100.0)	88 (100.0)

Source : Field Survey, 2003.

Clothing of People

The households buy/use both old and new clothes depending on the necessity, rituals, seasons (climatic conditions) and also gifts. In all these senses, the village life remains accommodative by voluntary participation of households in social non-monetary transactions and mutual dependence.

More than half of the households in the village can afford to buy new clothes. The STs are exceptions who cannot depend only on new clothes. The households in general castes do not buy old clothes. These high caste households also do not take any gift (clothes) from others in the village. The time when the high caste households accept gifts also imply that they offer gifts to their relatives. The BCs buy new clothes, buy and use old clothes, very rarely get clothes as gifts. The STs depend more on 'gift clothes'.

The single household in the highest income bracket (Rs. 5,001-Rs. 10,000) buy/use only new clothes. The households in the medium income bracket (Rs. 2,501-Rs. 5,000) buy new clothes and use both new and old clothes, and do not depend on clothes as gifts from others. The households on the middle income bracket (Rs. 2,501-Rs. 5,000) depend on new clothes but use both new and old clothes. These households do not buy old/second hand clothes and do not depend on or search for any possibility of 'cloth gifts' from others. The dependence of households on both old and new clothes (second hand purchase, new purchase, receiving after being used by elders within the household) is more for households in low income bracket (below Rs. 2,500 p.m.). These are the households also who depend on 'cloth gifts'. Thus, mutual dependence (via purchase/use/exchange) of clothes is more glaring for low-income households.

For STs, festivals do not matter in taking decisions regarding purchase of clothes. 'Necessity' is the single most important reason for all the households behind purchasing clothes. The STs depend more on windfall income to buy new clothes. Marriage is one of the reasons when the households buy new clothes.

Consumer Durable Goods Owned by People

We have included consumer durable items like bicycle, wrist watch, radio, TV, scooter, air cooler, refrigerator, ceiling fan etc. to examine if the households the village Bhaganpur own these.

While three-fourths of the households have bicycles, half of the households have wristwatch and nearly one-third have radio. Around one-tenth of the households have TV, and one-tenth have scooter/motor cycle. Only one household (out of a total of 88 in the village) from the general caste has both cooler and refrigerator. Two households from high (general) caste have jeep/car in the village. In other words, only two households from general caste in the village own high-cost consumer durable items like air cooler, refrigerator, and car/jeep.

None of the households from STs and BCs owns TV, refrigerator, air cooler, scooter/motor cycle, car/jeep, and even ceiling fan/table fan. The households in general caste have these, and that too, all the items enjoyed by a few within the general caste households. The general basket of consumer durable goods, thus, centre on bicycles, wristwatch, radio for half of the households constituted by STs and BCs while for the rest half (general/high caste) the general consumption pattern of consumer durable goods centre on these low cost goods plus TV, ceiling/table fan, and scooter/motor cycle (Table 7.16).

Table 7.16 : Households having Consumer Durable Goods by Castes

Consumer Durable Goods	*Households by Castes (%)*			
	Scheduled Tribes	*Backward Classes*	*General*	*All Households*
Bicycle	08 (09.1)	23 (26.1)	33 (37.5)	64 (72.7)
Scooter/Motor cycle	0	0	08 (09.1)	08 (09.1)
Radio	01 (01.1)	05 (05.7)	20 (22.7)	26 (29.5)
Television	0	0	11 (12.5)	11 (12.5)
Wristwatch	03 (03.4)	12 (13.6)	29 (32.9)	44 (50.0)
Fan (Ceiling/Table)	0	0	15 (17.0)	15 (17.0)
Refrigerator	0	0	01 (01.1)	01 (01.1)
Air-Cooler	0	0	01 (01.1)	01 (01.1)
Car/Jeep	0	0	02 (02.3)	02 (02.3)
All Households	13 (14.8)	30 (34.1)	45 (51.1)	88 (100.0)

Source : Field Survey, 2003.

The households in bottommost income bracket (less than Rs. 1,000 p.m. per household) own only bicycle, radio, and wristwatch. Only one household in high income bracket (Rs. 2,501-Rs. 5,000) and the single household in the topmost income bracket (Rs. 5,001-Rs. 10,000) own a car/jeep. Refrigerator is also owned by the single household in the topmost income bracket. The high-income households (Rs. 2501-Rs. 5,000) have almost all the consumer durable goods, excepting cooler and refrigerator. This does not imply that most of the households in high income bracket have all the consumer durable goods. Even within high-income households in village Bhaganpur, costly consumer durable goods are rarely owned/used by most of the households (Table 7.17).

Table 7.17 : Households having Consumer Durable Goods by Income

Consumer Durable Goods	*Households by Income (%)*				
	Below 1,000	*1,001-2,500*	*2,501-5,000*	*5,001-10,000*	*All Households*
Bicycle	07 (07.9)	44 (50.0)	12 (13.6)	01 (01.1)	64 (72.7)
Scooter/Motor Cycle	0	04 (04.5)	03 (03.4)	01 (01.1)	08 (09.1)
Radio	01 (01.1)	17 (19.3)	07 (07.9)	01 (01.1)	26 (29.5)
Television	0	05 (08.5)	05 (05.7)	01 (01.1)	11 (12.5)
Wristwatch	04 (04.5)	28 (31.8)	11 (12.5)	01 (01.1)	44 (50.0)
Fan (Ceiling/Table)	0	09 (10.2)	05 (05.7)	01 (01.1)	15 (17.0)
Refrigerator	0	0	0	01 (01.1)	01 (01.1)
Air-Cooler	0	01 (01.1)	0	01 (01.1)	01 (01.1)
Car/Jeep	0	0	01 (01.1)	0	02 (02.3)
All Households	15 (17.0)	59 (67.0)	13 (14.8)	01 (01.1)	88 (100.0)

Source : Field Survey, 2003.

IV. Living Condition of People in Village Bhaganpur : Some Lessons

We selected a small village by size of population, number of households, geographic area, on the bank of river 'Tons' that provides water throughout the year.

While *Adivasis* in the village identify themselves as a group separated from the castes, for all practical purposes their behaviour is similar to that of the others. In terms of indicators like production, consumption, habits, culture, mobility and movement, these *Adivasis* have merged into the mainstream of the village Bhaganpur. However, that mainstream itself remains divided between castes. In other words, the village society could not come out from the rigid caste hierarchy. Social immobility also leads to less exposure of people to external world. High illiteracy, particularly female illiteracy, keeps the society tradition-*cum*-custom bound. This makes living condition caste-confined or birth-determined.

No one likes to leave the village permanently. Cash habit or market habit is very rare for the settled people in the village. By being a small village by size of population, and visibility of activities of all, the village life remains accommodative. There is no visible/recorded obstruction for movement of individuals across castes, the most visible social indicator by birth in the village, within the village and outside the village. The villagers are not obstructed to walk on any public road, lift water from any public well/pond, and perform 'puja' (worship) in any temple. The village has not experienced any caste-community linked conflicts in the recent past. The tribes have merged into mainstream life in the village. Thus, operationally, the *Adivasis* in the village, settled over generations, are accommodated in Hindu rituals and practices. The economic activities differ, for example, *Mallahs* in the village are more water-centric, but most of the people in the village are land/agriculture dependent. The ownership and use of land, in addition to other productive assets, make the economic life of people in the village comfortable.

The village is yet far from having adequate infrastructural facilities like motorable road (all seasons), electrification (regular supply), communications (private and public), and irrigation (by durable and assured water supply by public methods). The village is far from development of economic bases of life, like money-based production (market-oriented) and exchange of goods, leasing-in and leasing-out of private assets (like tractors, pump-sets) for public purposes. The village is yet to be exposed to mobility-led improved awareness of individuals. The village women are far from literacy and participation in public places without fear and shame.

The business and commercial activities in the locality adjacent to the village shows a break from caste-dependent activities in rigid-hierarchic frame to freedom of individuals in acquired skill-specific jobs. The occupation pattern, thus, is linked more with economic parameters and less with social (caste) parameters. The point is not that introduction of money-centred trade/business will lead to reducing/eliminating inequality. The point is that the emergence of economic forces introduces impersonal inequality. The point is not that with mobility of individuals, caste as a determinant of activities vanishes. The point is that the introduction of economic forces offers a comparative scenario and hence a choice to people : the choice between mechanical (by birth-caste) solidarity to organic (economic mode) solidarity. In essence, thus, the conversion of the social/non-economic individuals to social-economic individuals shows a path in social progress.

V. Concluding Comments

The study is exploratory to uncover some of the dimensions of living condition of people settled in village Bhaganpur. The possibilities that we talk about here are more indicative, and less strategic.

We suggest necessity-specific intervention of the Government in the transformation of the village Bhaganpur. By transformation, we do not mean here conversion from a rural-type society to an urban society. We believe that even within a rural-type society, the living condition of the people may be transformed. This transformation has to ensure improved physical infrastructure, by connectivity of the village through motorable roads, railways (subject to constraints of national railway network), river/water transport (for which the village is most suitable), river water-led irrigation, communication and electricity. In all these cases, the state has to be interventionist that can promote public space for private operations. The state can also promote health and education facilities in the village, by operationalizing a health centre and school at least up to the secondary level (with all facilities, including mid-day meal), that will promote social infrastructure in the village.

There have to come new institutions that help develop caste-neutral 'cooperation' among people in the village. So far, we found, each caste group is consolidated within. The task is to form village community across castes, and there the visionary/educated/experienced section within the village can take a lead role. One has to take a step ahead of the current time frame to make the people not only aware about the world beyond their own village boundary but also initiate measures by formation and functioning of lead groups that really aim at improving living condition of people settled in village Bhaganpur.

Acknowledgement

This paper is a revised version of the paper presented in the National Seminar on 'Rethinking Villages' organized by the G.B.Pant Social Science Institute, May 24-25, 2004. The author remembers the suggestions of the participants of the seminar while revising the paper. The remaining errors lie with the author.

REFERENCES

Dasgupta, Biplab (1977), *Village and Labour Use,* Oxford Univ. Press, Delhi.

Desai, A.R. (2001), *Rural Sociology in India,* Popular Prakashan, Bombay.

Dreze, Jean (2002), *'Palanpur, 1957-93: Occupational Change, Land Ownership, and Social Inequality'*, in Madan, V. (Ed), The Village in India, Oxford Univ. Press.

Dube, S.C. (2002), *'A Rural Development Project in Action'*, in Madan, V. (Ed.), Oxford Univ. Press.

Fuller, C.J. (2002), *Rituals of the Village,* in Madan, V. (Ed.), Op. Cit.

Jaer, Oyvind (1995), *Karchhana, Lifeworld—Ethnography of an Indian Village,* Scandinavian Univ. Press, Oslo, Norway.

Lambert, Helen (2002), *Caste, Gender and Locality in Rural Rajasthan in Madan,* V. (Ed), Op. Cit. Oxford Univ. Press.

Madan, T.N. (2002), *'The Social Construction of Cultural Identities in Rural Kashmir'*, in Madan, V. (Ed), Op. Cit.

Menchel, Joan P. (2002), *'A Tamil Village: Changing Socio-Economic Structure in Madras State'*, in Madan, V. (Ed), Op. Cit., Oxford Univ. Press.

Patel, M.L. (1982), *'Agro-Economic Problems of Tribals of India'*, in Chaudhuri, B. (Ed), *Tribal Development in India, Problems and Prospects*, Inter-India Pub., Delhi.

Ramachandran, H. (1980), *'Village Clusters and Rural Development'*, Concept Pub. Co., New Delhi.

Rangarajan, L.R. (1992), *'Kautilya, The Artha Shastra'*, Penguin Books, India.

Roy Burman, B.K. (1982), in Chaudhuri (Ed), Op cit., Delhi.

Sinha, Surajit (1982), *'Tribal Solidarity Movements in India, A Review'*, in Chaudhuri, B. (Ed), *Tribal Development in India, Problems and Prospects*, Inter-India Pub., Delhi.

Srinivas, M.N. (1976), *'The Remembered Village'*, Oxford Univ. Press.

Srinivas, M.N. (1996), *'Village, Caste, Gender and Method, Essays in Indian Social Anthropology'*, Oxford Univ. Press, Delhi.

Srinivas, M.N. (2003), *'An Obituary on Caste as a System'*, Economic and Political Weekly, Feb. 1.

8

Selection of Villages for Understanding Social Sciences

K.N. BHATT and BHASKAR MAJUMDER

We can maintain a high growth economy at a high cost at the exclusion of the majority of population. At the beginning of production, historically it was a case of 'natural inclusion' of the population by voluntary participation. With respect to time, particularly in post-private property world, there came want (endless) and accumulation by a minority via appropriation of the fruits of labour of the vast majority of population. The issue is bigger than one of attaining higher and higher economic growth rate, or one of structural changes by industrialization and associated changes in occupational structure. The real issue is inclusive development. Initial economic interdependence has to be carried forward by inclusive development. The participants now engaged in producing socially necessary goods and the participants standing in the queue are to be accommodated in a well thought out product planning through 'bottom up' approach so that no one feels deprived. A process of growth visible to all has to be shared by all.

How can we reach the sections of society that are the most deprived from the changes taking place all around? Of the various options available, one could be to define certain geographical regions as small units on which such experiments could be conducted. A village serves this purpose as a unit for developmental interventions. In any country, there are sharp differences between the quality of life in the city and that in the rural areas. This is specially so in the case of India where differences are compounded by the easy access to so-called 'modernizing influences' that are available to the urban population while the rural people remain blissfully unaware of these. A rural society is characterized by population engaged mainly in cultivation that has a direct relationship with nature. The farms are open, communities small and population density lesser as compared to the city. Also, the population settled in a village is more homogenous in terms of social and psychological parameters and stratification and differentiation are less than an urban society. Social mobility is less intensive being confined to the migration of country folk to the city. In terms of interpersonal relationships, the focus is more on primary contacts and personal and durable relations with comparative simplicity and sincerity of relations.

Village elders are the custodians of local culture and traditions, conventions and moral values. The modernized city very often discards and disowns the age-old traditions. The villages are even today wrapped up in customs and practices, the adherence to which is often considered as a symptom as well as a cause of their backwardness. This is not to justify the extreme poverty and less than human living conditions that prevail in some villages.

The rest of the paper is structured as follows. In section I we take village as a unit of analysis. In section II we present the characteristics of Indian villages. Section III deals with the objectives of the study. In Section IV we pose the problems in village selection. Finally, in section V we offer conclusions.

I. Village as a Unit of Analysis

Villages in India seem to have a timeless quality about them. The village communities are small economically. This has been possible because of the simple, autonomous and self-sufficient nature of the village organization. On the social side, the development of the social structure on the basis of the caste division was responsible for the social as well as the ideological stability with its attendant division of labour and the spiritual sanctions accompanying it (Mukherjee, 1969). One of the salient features of a rural community is its complete dependence on agriculture. The villages are socially organized along kinship, caste and territorial affinities. Caste is the most significant organizing principle in these communities and it determines or at least greatly influences, the kinship pattern as well as the choice of occupations. The village as a unit of social structure cuts across the boundaries of kin and caste and unites a number of unrelated families within an integrated multi-caste community (Dube, 1969).

Generally a village has a more or less stable population that shares common values and past, both oral as well as recorded. Much of this oral history is coloured by the perceptions of the speaker that are influenced by the socio-cultural identity of the speaker. Though the villages maintain their individual identity, since no two villages are the same even though the villages in a particular region might share a common cultural environment, at times the different villages may act as a unit. The economy of the village is based primarily on agriculture. Those engaged in agriculture have a superior position both economically and socially than those doing other kinds of work. One characteristic of the rural society is the great attachment that the people owe to their land to the extent that they derive their identity from it. The village inspires a sense of belongingness and allegiance despite the great diversity and at times even conflicts that are a part of it. This identification with the village is crucial for the identity formation of the individual. The rural society is caste-structured. There are various traditions and rituals that serve to integrate the different sections of the community in terms of economic, socio-religious and administrative aspects of the village.

II. Characteristics of Indian Villages

"A village is not just a physical space or a settlement of a group of people. Social life here is organized along definite ritual and secular principles, such as those of caste, kinship, economy, politics and religion. The physical character of the village is influenced by its dynamic interaction with these principles and patterns of settlement" (Madan,2002, p.13). The social structure of the village in India is often determined by the castes and religious groups that exist within it. A village may have a majority of one caste or ethnic group or it could be multi-religious or multi-ethnic. The political structure of the villages also varies ranging from villages headed by headmen, village panchayats and also some villages that have inter-village councils. However, the village panchayats are the most significant bodies and they govern the caste behaviour and the interactions between different castes. The panchayats are representative bodies and have the power and authority to enforce rules and impose sanctions. Often people belonging to a particular caste have their own customs and traditions that are unique to their group and they may also have their own caste panchayats that enforce the traditional customs and rules specific to their community.

The power structure of the villages may also vary but most often the caste groups that have ritual status, economic prosperity, political influence and numerical preponderance becomes dominant and begin to dominate the affairs of the village (Madan, 2002). Though in most instances this is the case with the upper castes, at times a lower or elsewhere marginalized community can also become dominant if it has economic and numerical strength as has been documented in the study of village Ramapura by Srinivas (1955). Factionalism and local caste associations also influence the political behaviour of the people at the village level.

Traditional marriage and kinship values that prevail in every village govern the pattern of social relations of the village and often these relations extend the interactive network and social space of the village into its neighbouring regions (Marriott, 1955). One such traditional value is that of village exogamy that is practiced. Real or fictive bonds of kinship and marriage govern most interactions in the village. The typical rural family is a joint family adhering to patriarchal values and common property and household. Social values governing family life define the status of women. The kinship terminology reflects social status and inequality. The social hierarchy that exists in the rituals and various customs at a psychological level is also manifested physically in the demarcation of certain parts of the village like the streets and neighbourhoods and reflect the super-ordination and subordination of certain groups and the values accompanying such demarcation (Madan, 2002). However, these patterns of relationships between various communities and caste groups have undergone some, though only minimal, changes in the last few decades due to the modernization process that was set in motion after independence.

Thus, it would seem appropriate to select village as a unit for understanding the development status of a village. In order to study the scenario of human development in some of the western U.P. villages located in Mawana and Hastinapur Blocks of Mawana Tehsil in Meerut district, we accepted the problem of selecting some of these villages (Tripathi, Majumder & Bhatt, 2006). What methodology should be adopted keeping in view the basic objectives of the study? How to shortlist the villages from larger sample? In this paper we examined these questions.

Of all the four administrative regions in UP, the western region is considered to be economically most developed having per capita income almost twice that of the eastern region, which has the lowest per capita income. Industries are located mainly in the western and central regions of the state. The western region is part of the granary of India. Land resources are most abundant (in per capita terms) in the Bundelkhand region, followed by the western region, but the former region also has the lowest irrigation intensity (Planning Department, U.P., 2003).

II. Objectives of the Study

Our study aimed at understanding the linkages between education and development. The attempt here was to ascertain whether educational development actually leads to development on other fronts like economic and social. The specific objectives were to see if (i) economic development leads to educational development and the converse, (ii) whether educational development leads to economic and social development, and (iii) identify the villages that seem to be most suited for external institutional intervention for social development.

IV. Problems in Village Selection

Village studies in India pose a number of problems like obtaining reliable data. The questions often posed make little sense to the villagers because they are based on some theoretical construct, which is too abstract to convey anything in words to the rural people. We approached the problem in two ways. First, we focused on the data already collected by various agencies what are called secondary data and then had Focus Group Discussions (FGDs) on problems the villagers faced, particularly relating to education. This consisted the First Phase of our study. In the Second Phase, we used a structured schedule to collect information on a wide variety of issues. For this purpose we selected respondents randomly from the villages chosen for the study.

First Phase Investigation

The initial objective of this study was to identify 20 villages out of a predetermined list of 40 in block Mawana of Meerut district that are low on economic and social development, and to develop detailed profile of these villages so as to establish a baseline for development. Subsequently, the task was to select 10 villages slow by economic and social development based on certain indicators of development.

After a pilot survey during June-July 2005, 20 villages out of a pool of 40 were drawn. The focus was on gathering information related to the social development of these villages. This information was obtained through detailed discussions with the public administration and interviews with various sections of the people in the villages and also secondary data that were obtained from government officials.

The human development indicators, viz., education, health and economic well-being were in mind while making the selections. On the economic front, most of the villages were free from extreme poverty and deprivation, especially in terms of survival needs, though there did exist inequality with respect to the distribution of productive assets. Basic infrastructure like electricity, roads and communication facilities was observed to exist in most of the villages.

The general health facilities were poor in majority of the villages. Gender development in terms of female participation in the Panchayati Raj system served as a criterion for the assessment of developmental status of the villages.

Major Variables by Total Coverage of the Study

In Table 8.1 we enlist the major variables as indicators for selection or shortlisting of villages.

Table 8.1 : List of Major Indicators and Variables Taken for First Round Survey

Indicators	*S.No.*	*Variables*
Economic Well-being	1.	Overall Work Participation Rate.
	2.	Female Work Participation Rate.
	3.	Percentage of BPL Households.
	4.	Land Ownership by size of Land.
	5.	Land Use Pattern.
	6.	Classification of Workers by Work and Duration.
	7.	Economic Activities of the People except Farming .
	8.	Skill existed in the Different Types of Communities.
	9.	People Facing Livelihood Problems for Their survival.
	10.	Outside Migration of the People by Work and Duration.
	11.	Inside Migration of the People by Work and Duration.
	12.	Suggestions of the People for Enhancing the Employment Opportunities.
	13.	% of Households Having Telephones
Education	1.	Overall Literacy Rate.
	2.	Female Literacy Rate.
	3.	Number of Total 6-11 Years Children and Their Enrolment.
	4.	Number of Total 11-14 Years Children and Their Enrolment.
	5.	Distance of Different Types of Schools.

(contd.)

(Table 8.1 contd.)

Indicators	*S.No.*	*Variables*
	6.	Basic Facilities Available in the Schools.
	7.	Number of Teachers by Gender and Teacher Student Ratio.
	8.	Method of Teaching in Different Types of Schools.
	9.	Enrolment Pattern by Types of Schools (Private and Government).
	10.	Education Problems Existing in Different Types of Schools at Different Levels.
	11.	Suggestions for Betterment (Quality Education).
	12.	Work of Children After the Complication of Different Levels Education.
	13.	Aspiration of Parents Regarding Work Done by Their Children at Different Levels of Education.
Health	1.	Distance of Private and Government Health Services (Including Animal Husbandry).
	2.	Infant Mortality Rate (0-5 Years Age Group).
	3.	Overall Death Rate.
	4.	Birth Rate by Gender.
	5.	Types of Diseases at Different Levels by Age Group and by Gender.
	6.	Priority of the People for Taken Existing Health Services.
Governance	1.	Number of Civil Cases Existed in the Villages.
	2.	Number of Criminal Cases in the Villages.
	3.	Fear of the People in Sending the Female Outside the Village.
	4.	Security Problems of the Girl Child on the Way to Schools.
Functions of Panchayats	1.	Performance of PRI in Term of Development.
	2.	Initiatives Taken by Panchayats for Deprived Persons.
	3.	Nature of Disputes in Panchayats.
	4.	Voting Attitudes of the People.
	5.	People Benefited by Different Development Schemes.
	6.	Households Holding Different Types of Ration Cards under PDS.
	7.	Development Impact on Villages by Regions.
	8.	Working Pattern of Panchayats
	9.	Identity of the Village
	10.	Suggestions of Panchayats.
Social Evils	1.	Reasons for Belief in *Parda* System
	2.	Caste and Class Gap among the People.
General	1.	Sex Ratio
	2.	Caste-wise Population
	3.	Basic Amenities Available in the Villages
	4.	Distance Chart from Village to Village
	5.	Observations on Selected Issues

Variables for SWOT Analysis

The data obtained were then coded (qualitative data coded into categories) and analyzed statistically. After the analysis of the data, 21 indicators were selected on the basis of conventional social-*cum*-human development indicators and the status of 20 villages on these was observed. The villages were ranked from 1 to 20 on each indicator so that a rank of 1 meant high development while a rank of 20 indicated low development on that indicator. Whether a particular village scores above the mean value for the sample or below it, has been included in profiles of the villages. The indicators and the position of the villages on each along with the mean of all the villages on that particular indicator have been combined to form a profile of each village.

Table 8.2 : Indicators Chosen for the SWOT Analysis of the Villages

1. Overall Literacy Rate (%)	12. Distance from Nationalized Bank
2. % of BPL Households	13. Female Infant Mortality Rate
3. Female Literacy Rate (%)	14. % of Households having telephone
4. % of Population Facing Livelihood Problems	15. Overall Infant Mortality Rate
5. Enrolment % of 6-14 Years Children	16. Distance from Primary Health Centre
6. Number of Civil Cases	17. % of Population Affected from Diseases
7. Sex Ratio 0-6 Years Population	18. Distance from School (Primary, Middle & Secondary)
8. Distance from the Main Road	19. Female Work Participation Rate (%)
9. Overall Sex Ratio	20. Overall Work Participation Rate (%)
10. Distance from Bus Stop	21. No. of Criminal Cases
11. Girl Child Born per 100 Boys	

From the 21 listed indicators (Table 8.2), we selected ten that cover literacy, health, economic well-being and governance (Table 8.3).

Table 8.3 : Selected Indicators for Shortlisting of Villages

Sl. No.	*Indicators*	*Sl. No.*	*Indicators*
1.	Female Literacy Rate	6.	Overall Infant Morality Rate
2.	Overall Literacy Rate	7.	Female Work Participation Rate
3.	Sex Ratio 0-6 Years Population	8.	Overall Work Participation Rate
4.	Overall Sex Ratio of Population	9.	Percentage of BPL Households
5.	Female Infant Mortality Rate	10.	Number of Civil Cases

First Phase Data

We selected the Meerut district of the south-western region of India for the study. The purpose of the study was to understand the economic and social development of the region, in turn, to plan interventions for its educational development with a view to improving the overall development status of the region.

The Mawana sub-division has a total population of 8,87,066 with 3,66,141 male and 3,20,925 females belonging to 1,02,839 households. Of the total number of households in the sample villages 19.1% households were BPL. As per the Census 2001, 16.6% of the population was in the 0-6 years age group. The caste composition of the households in the selected villages showed BCs comprising 49.7 per cent of population, SCs 23.5 per cent, followed by minorities 16.8 per cent. Nearly 64.4 per cent of the total sample was landless. In keeping with its comparatively better economic status, all the villages in the Mawana region were well connected by roads, majority of them being linked to the main road by a *pucca* link road. They were all accessible by road all the year round.

Electricity was available in all villages in the sample. All villages had telephone connectivity—mobile phones were available where landlines were non-existent. Only 4 of the sampled villages were without any telephone facility (either a PCO or a telephone in the house). Only in two of these villages the Gram Panchayats had a telephone connection. The average distance of the bus stop for the villages was 1.7 k.m., for the post office 1.8 k.m., 2.9 k.m. for nationalized bank, 3.45 km. for the weekly market and 3.95 km. for the police station.

53.4 per cent of the total population had connectivity through phones or mobiles. Some villages were very far (up to 10 km) away from a PHC.

Literacy rate in the total population in almost all the villages was higher than that for the state of Uttar Pradesh barring one village where it was the lowest. The literacy rate among the females in most of the villages was also higher than that for the state of UP. The work participation rate was below 50 per cent in all the villages except for two villages. Amongst females, it was considerably higher in most villages than that for the state of UP, the highest being 58.3 per cent and the lowest being 8.6 per cent. The gender gap in work participation was lower in most villages than that for the UP.

Majority of the population was non-working (59%). The main workers constituted 27.5 per cent and 13.5 per cent who were marginal workers in the total sample. The percentage of population of the total sample in the main and marginal workers category was higher than that for UP while the percentage of non-working population was less than the percentage for UP. In most of the villages more of their population was engaged in work as compared to the percentage that obtains for the state of UP. The largest percentage of the total sample was engaged in cultivation, which is high as compared to the rest of the state. A very small proportion of the population was engaged in household industries. The net sown area for the entire sample was 85 per cent of the total cultivable area. 39.4 per cent of it was sown more than once and the same was also irrigated more than once.

Of the total births in the sample villages during last one year, almost 53 per cent were boys. The gender gap in birth in terms of percentage was 5.85. The death rate for the sample was 5.19 per 1000. It was higher for males than for females. For the population below 1 year, the death rate was 1.4 and for 1-5 years age it was the lowest at 0.4. The sex-ratio of the Mawana sub-division as per 2001 Census was 877, slightly better than that for Meerut but lower than for the state of U.P. The sex ratio was very low in most villages and in all groups.

An exception to the general trend was one village where the number of females in the 0-6 years age group exceeded the number of males. The sex ratio in the SC category was only 250 per 1000 males. The work participation rate was below 50 per cent in all the villages except for two where it was 61.9 per cent and 54 per cent respectively.

The distance of both government and private educational institutions from the villages was very far up to the secondary level, the average distance being 1.46 km. for government and 1.89 km. for private schools. 50 per cent of the government schools had mats available for the students while almost 60 per cent of the private schools possessed them. 41.4 per cent of the total children in the 6-11 years age range and 62.7 per cent of those in the 11-14 years age range were studying in private schools.

52.85 per cent of the total 6,487 students enrolled in the 6-11 age group were boys. There was no gender enrollment gap in the case of only one village. In the 11-14 age range, of the total enrolled students, 41.8 per cent (2,902) were girls. The lowest number of girls in this age range was enrolled in one village which also had the lowest number of boys enrolled in school. Two villages had no school (upper primary) for the children in this age range. The gender gap in enrollment in the 11-14 years age range was the highest in one village. The gender gap in enrollment in 11-14 age group favoured the girls in seven of the villages and it was the most favourable in one village.

Caste based discrimination that was not experienced by girls at the primary level of education comes up at this stage. Another problem unique to girls was that of lack of parents' desire to educate their girls beyond class 5. Some of the problems common to both boys and girls were that of the teacher charging money, in addition to lack of basic facilities in schools, and admission problems due to poverty.

Villages Included in Second Phase Study

In the second phase of study, we collected data from the villagers living in the selected villages on a large number of issues so that we may get better insights into the development and quality of life related issues. After comparing the status of the village on the selected indicators, ten villages that were relatively underdeveloped in the sample were selected.

Data Collection

Once the villages were selected on the basis of first phase study, three sets of schedules were developed for the second phase of data collection. These schedules were meant to be administered on households and there was one schedule each for the head of the household, a woman from the household and a child (above 6 years) from the household. Thus, while the first phase study focused on getting information at the level of the village and got it both from primary and secondary sources, the second round sampled households level exercise was an in-depth study focusing on primary data. The household schedule sought information on demographic variables and then proceeded to questions around the economic status and aspirations, quality of basic amenities, education, health, and social questions. The schedule for women focused aspirations for their children, child rearing practices they use, health, issues related to female feticide, family responsibilities and role in decision making as well as certain questions relating to their desire to learn skills and participate and contribute in any efforts aimed at providing education. The schedule for children included questions about the various activities they were engaged in and the time spent on each, their aspiration and educational needs, as well as their liking for the school and the teacher.

The respondents were asked questions and the responses were noted. Since most of the questions were open-ended, the respondents were not given the options beforehand. It was only when they had responded that their answers were coded.

Sample Profile

The questionnaires were administered on three groups of participants : heads of the household, women and children. In all, 2114 respondents comprised the study sample out of which 873 were heads of households (660 men and 213 women), 806 were women and 435 were children (236 boys and 199 girls). An attempt was made while sampling to include a cross-section of castes that is representative of the caste composition of the population. Though the attempt was to include women and children in each household, this was not possible in all 873 households. In the case of children's schedule, only those children who could respond to the questions in an informed manner were interviewed.

Comprehensive Human Development Index

Based on the data on the various indicators of development, a Comprehensive Human Development Index (CHDI) was computed for all the villages in the sample in the second phase. The variables that were included in this index included :

Table 8.4 : Variables for Comprehensive Human Development Index

1. Female literacy rate	6. Overall infant mortality rate
2. Overall literacy rate	7. Female WPR
3. Sex ratio for 0-6 years population	8. Overall WPR
4. Overall sex ratio	9. Per cent of BPL households
5. Female infant mortality rate	10. Number of civil cases

The CHDI was computed using the method that has been used in estimating it in the UP Human Development Report (HDI) and the actual scores of the villages on each of the indicators were used for this purpose. The following formula was used :

$$\frac{\text{(Actual value – Minimum Value)}}{\text{Range (Maximum – Minimum)}}$$

Using the above formula for computing the CHDI, a score for all villages on each of the indicators was obtained. This score ranged between 0 and 1, wherein 0 indicated a poor standing on that indicator and 1 showed the best status. The overall CHDI was a summation of the scores on all the indicators in each of the villages. It may be noted that Comprehensive HDI as conceptualized for the purpose of the study in context does not correspond with the HDI since it is based on a number of other indicators.

V. Conclusions

The study began with the purpose of identifying villages in the Mawana and Hastinapur region which were lagging behind on educational development. We set out to assess the educational needs of the people and map out the assets, both human as well as material which can support educational development. The objective was to select those villages where there was a great deal of poverty and which needed educational interventions. The results of this study force us to rethink this approach.

Since the purpose of this paper was to locate the research zone and identify the villages with more backwardness by social development indicators, hence we abstain from delivering any firm conclusion on the outcome of research as such. Our focus was on short-listing a few villages for warranted intervention by institutions for setting up of and promotion of educational institutions in the villages ultimately selected. We developed the comprehensive human development index for selection of such villages and left the question of intervention to the appropriate body that supported the research we carried out.

BACKGROUND DOCUMENTS USED

Backer, G.S. (1964): *Human Capital: A Theoretical Analysis with Special Reference to Education,* New York, Columbia University Press.

Blaug, M.R., Layard and Woolhall (1969): *Causes Of Graduate Unemployment in India,* London, Penguin Press, 1969.

Brickman, P. & Campbell, A. (1971): *Hedonic Relativism and Planning The Good Society.* In M.H. Apley (ed.) *Adaptation Level Theory : A Symposium,* New York: Academic Press, pp. 287-302.

Brunei, L. & Porta, L.P. (2005): *Economics and Happiness,* London, Oxford University Press.

D.C. McClelland, (1961): *The Achieving Society* (New York: Vam Nostrand Reinhold).

Denison, E.F. (1967): *Why Growth Rates Differ: Post-War Experiences in Nine Western Countries,* Washington, D.C., Brookings Institute.

Desai, A.R., (2001): *Rural Sociology in India,* Popular Prakashan, Bombay.

Dreze. J. & Sen, A. (2002): *India Development and Participation,* Oxford University Press.

G. Hofsted, (1980): *Culture's Consequences: International Differences in Work Related Values* (Beverly Hills, CA: Sage).

Madan, V. (2002): *The Village in India,* Oxford University Press.

Mahalanobis P. C., (1985): *Papers on Planning,* in Bose, P.K. and Mukherjee M. (ed.), Statistical Publishing Society, Calcutta, 1985.

Marriott, M. ed. (1955): *Village India: Studies in the Little Community,* Chicago, University of Chicago Press.

Minear, J. (1974): *Schooling, Experience and Earnings,* New York, Columbia University Press.

Myrdal Gunnar, *Asian Drama : An Inquiry into the Poverty of Nations,* Vol. III, Kalyani Publishers, New Delhi, 1982.

Planning Department (2003), *Human Development Report,* Uttar Pradesh, Government of U.P. Lucknow.

Psacharopolous, G. (1995): *Returns to Education: A Further International Update and Implications,* Journal of Human Resources, Vol. 20, No. 4.

S.C. Dube (1969): *"Encyclopedia of Social Sciences",* Vol. 15, *Village Community* by Harold J. Poker.

Schultz. T.W. (1961): *Economic Value and Education,* New York, Columbia University Press.

Tilak, J.B.G. (1987): *The Economic of Inequality in Education,* New Delhi, Sage Publication.

Tripathi, R.C., B. Majumder & K.N. Bhatt (2006): *Education for Development: The Mawana Study,* sponsored by Shriram Memorial Foundation, New Delhi, G.B. Pant Social Science Institute, Allahabad, Mimeo.

UNDP, (2005): *Human Development Report.*

World Bank, (1987): *World Development Report,* Oxford University Press.

9

Rethinking Village

RAMASHRAY ROY

The two key terms in the title refer to two different and distinct aspects of enquiry about villages in India. The first aspect refers to the epistemological question of how one must go about constructing knowledge about Indian village so that the totality of its being, functioning and capability endowment may be fully apprehended. The second aspect of "rethinking village" focuses our attention on the village itself in two modes of its existence. One of these modes refers to its characteristics pertaining to what it has been in the time past. But like everything else, the village too has been inexorably trapped in the "melting pot" of change. As a consequence of this, the village is enmeshed in the process of becoming; we do not have any idea nor can we hazard any idea at this moment as to what it will ultimately become except that it is changing. And if it is changing, it is becoming something else than what it was before.

It is "this something else" that the process of rethinking about village must be concerned with. But how do we catch sufficiently firmly "this something else" so that it can reveal to us with clarity and precision what aspects of the village are undergoing change and in what direction they are tending to move. In order to apprehend these two vital dimensions of the process of change that is going on, the mere identification of changes taking place in the externality of organized village community life is not enough. This is so for the reason that whatever changes may seem to be taking place, they cannot be treated as random. To treat them as random is to impute fragility and brittleness to the organization of social life perhaps because no (sturdy) constitutive principle of organization holds together different dimensions of community life. Similarly, to simply note the changes that are taking place in the village society without specifying the significance of these changes in theoretical terms does not add to our comprehension.

It is enough to suggest that we need to have a theoretical base for projecting and directing the beam of enquiry with a view to uncovering and illuminating underlying principles of both the village society as it was and what it is becoming now. Without a theoretically sound perspective on the village, it will always appear to be something other than what it is. It is against this background that we can appreciate why most of the existent approaches to the study of village life seem partial, incomplete, and, in many cases, distortive. One can understandably appreciate the reasons that seem to impinge heavily on the status of the present knowledge of villages. Looking back on Indian villages historically, what becomes apparent is that most of the accounts of village life and relations are based on insufficient documentation or theoretically exhilarating vision. What should also be added is that many of the village studies are based on a characterization of village life that is true of one region of India but not of other regions. However, there exists the tendency to make it universally applicable to all Indian villages.[1]

Another caveat that must be added to it is that most historical studies of villages in India are impressionistic. The sheer number of villages in India is daunting for all; no one can think of covering all the seven hundred thousands of villages. If a "representative" sample of villages is considered capable of yielding a reliable knowledge of Indian villages, it is plagued by the fact that we generally encounter three broader classes of Indian villages as they have emerged since the early days of British occupation. One can argue that despite the differences supposed to be associated with this classification, there has been a fundamental unity of culture. Indian culture has emanated from what we can for the sake of convenience, call spiritually-oriented perspective on man and his world.[2]

Culture refers in this regard to something inherent in every society signifying the entire complex of all the ways and expressions of life which characterize it and make it distinct, even different, from other societies. And as long as this culture remains robust, the unity of cultural ethos behind the divergent organizations of economic life and relations sustains, supports and reinforces the homogeneity or similarity or identity, understood in a deeper sense. That the rootedness of village life in India, despite external dissimilarities, in one unitary cultural ethos lends it homogeneity must be taken note of. Culture constitutes a common fund of mature social and intellectual forms and ideals. It persists regardless of the manifold variations and interruptions. The fact that culture then stands for resistance to change and destiny cannot be denied.

This understanding of the homogeneity of Indian village life ignores the relationship between the spiritual and the material dimensions of individual as well as existence. Max Scheler views human association always to be a confluence of two factors—material and spiritual. But real efficacy, he insists, lies in material condition whose inner workings are fateful for humanity. He concedes that Marx is correct in saying that it is not the consciousness of men that determines existence but it is their existence that determines their consciousness. But Scheler argues that Marx is only partly correct since he denigrates the spiritual aspect of human existence as compared to economic factors, to conditions of production and reproduction.

As against this, Scheler argues that human existence is also conditioned by geological and political factors which are no less necessary for human life than the economic one. Thus, even while material conditions are necessary for human life, they are not utterly fatal; they may, in fact, be modified. The elements of the spirit also develops independently out of their inner tendencies. However, the development of the spirit, for Scheler, is subject to two factors. In the first place, it constitutes only one of the possibilities that impinge on human existence. He refers particularly to the logical-rationalist development of law and the immanent logic of religious history as examples of this process. People may choose freely among them. In the second place, spiritual developments are not dissimilar to biological drives; unless they are attached to biological drives, they will come to nothing. And since spiritual developments are akin to biological drives, their growth and extension are governed by two limitations, one biological and the other material, both defining the parameters of the possible scope for spiritual developments. "And should spiritual goals exceed the limits of the possible, in contradistinction to biological and the causal laws of matter, they will remain mere utopia that ... bite on granite and disintegrate."[3]

Scheler likens material conditions to sluice gates that release spiritual elements or inhibit their entry into the stream of life. But once released, spiritual elements can grow further, draw energy from the material substrates, and influence their direction.[4] Thus, for Scheler, to reduce human existence to either the merely spiritual or the merely material is equally in error. It is the result of the interplay of the two realms of matter and spirit, of the real and the ideal, that, Scheler asserts, human necessity and human freedom are both modified.[5] What is clear from the account is that Scheler treats the realm of necessity and that of freedom as autonomous centres of energy and drive. It is true that both of them are modified by virtue of their interpenetration. Still they constitute possible alternative realms from which one can choose freely and lay down the pattern of one's life. He fails to see that, despite the fact that even though the realm of spirit is not, cannot be, the source of material conditions, it is certainly the regulator and controller of economic life and relations.

This alerts us to the fact that the traditional understanding of these domains is not as coordinate spheres but as hierarchically organized and structured. It is the spiritual realm that lends organization to the disorganized external world and constitutes the seed-bed of morality; it is moral sensibilities that regulate and control the excesses of the mode of life given primarily to the quest of progressive material well being.[6] Without moral superordination, economic life and relation tend to be affiliated with what traditionally is known as *matsyanyaya* or what Aristotle calls *pleonexia*. This hierarchical ordering undergoes the process of change when man's consciousness differentiates in a way to attribute higher value to the pursuit of the goal of material well being as it has happened in modern times. In the traditional perspective, man's consciousness was grounded in the understanding of the need to maintain a balance among the three poles of reality alternatively characterized as absolutes. These poles are the absolutes of divinity, humanity, and the world.[7] The hierarchy joins the spiritual, the moral and the pragmatic dimensions of man's existence with the spiritual; it is spiritual realm that occupies the apex of the hierarchy; it is sustained as long as the absolute of divinity is treated as primary. Once this balance is upset in favour of either the absolute of humanity or that of the world, the spiritual realm undergoes a process of denigration, even elimination and suppression.

If this happens, the material aspect of life assumes predominance and the life of the community undergoes radical changes both psychologically and materially. And this change did happen in the case of most of the Indian villages after the British rulers consolidated their hold and began, even though hesitatingly in the beginning, to change India socially, culturally, economically and politically. Through a series of transformations or inversions, they succeeded in bringing about a radical change in the orientation first of educated Indians and later the common man too. This radical change was instrumental in making material well being the most preferred objective in life. Colonial history of India testifies to the emergence of land as the most valued economic wealth and the pattern of land ownership and land relationship came to make a heavy impact on village life and relations. What must be added in this regard is the fact that, broadly speaking, three different systems of land ownership prevailed in India. Interested more in creating a reliable source of revenue and ease in its collection, the British rulers "settled" land following usually local conditions. Three general types of settlement—with prominent individuals, joint landlords, or individual shareholders in co-parcenary communities—could very easily be identified. These different types of land settlement had different ramifications for intra-village relationships among different socio-economic interest groups. Whatever consequences land settlement patterns might have had for industrial growth and development, they did certainly have a deeper, even distortive impact in terms of agricultural and rural life.[8]

The three broad types incorporate within them a tremendous amount of variation as a result of greatly differing local traditions and prevailing conditions. Unless all these variations along with certain "stable" characteristics of village life in India are taken into account, we do not have any reliable understanding of village life. Moreover, even if we cast our exploratory net wide and succeed in catching some of the defining characteristics of the Indian village, we still face the challenge of change that goes on modifying these characteristics in a way that makes any historical account stale and therefore inadequate. It is against this background that historical studies of Indian villages, even though they are quite sound, are not enough. It is true that there is extant a body of what we can call "systematic" study of village life in India following social scientific methods and approaches. These studies are confined largely to anthropological and sociological disciplines. Recently, few political scientists, too, have, entered the field. However, these studies suffer from three basic lacunae. These lacunae make such studies quite a feeble base for projecting the identified pattern of community life in one or a few villages on to all villages.

The first lacuna concerns the typical sobriquet in village studies, the sobriquet of "my village". The very fact of the use of the term "my village" in discussion about villages is a silent recognition of the fact that the findings from one village can be generalized for all villages only at the cost of a gargantuan fallacious reasoning. The second lacuna refers to disciplinary biases or commitments in the study of the village. Underlining as well as the most serious of these limitations is the fact that most village studies suffer from one of the most grievous defects, the defect of projecting a perspective that has its origin and is grounded in the western view of man and society. This perspective is broadly defined as an orientation which has passed through two distinct phases, one symptomatized as the White Man's Burden and the other characterized by the arrogance of the superiority of western civilization. Both these phases have one origin but two different historical manifestations in two different historical situations—one colonial and the other post-colonial. The origin of both these phases lies in what Solomon calls "universal ego" or "universal pretense" and its linkage can be traced back to the transmutation of the purely inter-polity relationships among nation-states confined largely to Europe into inter-civilizational relationship when the non-European world was reduced to a romping ground for the White Man. This raised the vital question of the kind of relationship the European nation-states were to establish with the non-White world. The answer came from Fransisco Vitoria[9], who was seized with the problem of the justification of Spanish conquest, of Indian territories in the America. At the core of the problem lies the conflict between the idea of mankind revolving around the Christian man as the model of humanity and the empirical fact that the majority of civilizations do not conform to this model. Specifically, the question that concerned Vitoria was : By what right a Christian state could occupy a non-Christian people?

Vitoria resolved this conflict in favour of conquest over non-Christian people on three grounds. In the first place, he argued that Christians have a right to punish, even conquer, if they are disturbed and obstructed in preaching their religion or if the converts are mistreated. In the second place, the natives must be punished if they mistreated travellers. And, lastly, Christian rulers have, Vitoria argued, the right to intervene in non-Christian societies because they (the Christian states) represent a superior civilization and the non-Christian people lacked civil sense. It is in this regard that inter-civilizational relations partake of a character that finds its expression in colonization and colonial subjugation of non-Christian peoples in large parts of Asia and Africa. At the root of this subjugation is what Robert Solomon calls "the transcendental egoism"[10], the natural consequence of the breakdown of the medieval Christian world-view. It signifies that it is the self, as constituted by the modern western sensibility, that is considered as the bed-rock of experience; it is the self that seeks to understand the world and itself as well as its relation with the world and its diversity. It does so with the help of certain categories of thought immanent in the Mind (*a la* Kant). Its understanding is mediated through what Solomon calls "universal reasoning" that signifies the attitude that "everyone, everywhere ought to believe in the same scientific truths, follow the same moral guidelines, endorse the same God or Gods."[11] By the same token, all societies should also embrace liberal institutions of economic and political life and relations as they exist in the west.

The rise and spread of the "transcendental egoism" so skilfully articulated by Kant had a firm footing in Vitoria's arguments justifying the division of the world between superior and inferior civilizations. The Barbarians may not, for Vitoria, be imbeciles but they are not very far from it. They are hardly fit, Vitoria argues, for establishing and administering a republic that is legitimate by human and civil standards. They have no proper laws or magistrates; they are deficient in arts and letters and are economically backward. Such backward peoples, Vitoria argues, need to be ruled by civilizationally superior power. In the context of the modern age, this attitude attains its apotheosis, as already indicated, in the guise of White Man's Burden; it signifies that people with gadgets have the right and the moral duty to rule peoples without gadgets in the interest of the backward people themselves. This understanding of the relationship between the idea that assumes the Christian man to be the model of humanity and the empirical fact of the world peopled by non-Christian men, who, by definition, are "primitive" if not Barbarian is, it is needless to say, the causative factor for both the centrality of economic factors in man's life and the autonomy of technology from the considerations or discipline of morality.

It is the concatenations of the structurally linked ideas that symbolizes itself and is in the form of White Man's Burden in the colonial period. It is true that the colonial age is over and with it the idea of political domination and rule by one country over any other has been put paid. But this does not signify by any means that the idea that gave rise to colonial expansion by European countries has completely been blanked or blocked. This idea still survives and the mode of its articulation is what we know as orientalism. As Edward Said defines the term, he adds two other dimensions to the term orientalism apart from its ordinary meaning referring to the study of languages, literature and cultures of the orient as a geographical unit. These dimensions are "a style of thought based upon an ontological and epistemological distinctions made "between orient" and the occident (most of the time) and a western style for dominating, restructuring and having authority over the orient."[12]

It is very clear that Said adds a cultural and political dimension to what, seemingly, is for all intent, an innocent characterization of a particular field of study. With these added dimensions, orientalism signifies more a cultural and political situation in which discourse about the Orient as "the other" of Europe dominates; it is symptomatic of Europe's dominant position. As such, the body of European discursive practice in regard to the Orient generates a self-affirmation of account of what is essentially inferior to Europe and so on.[13]

Said's theory has been criticized by scholars mainly on the ground that it constitutes a single discourse. It represents, for example, a lumping together of different types of orientalism. The orientalism of the nineteenth century itself had two sides.[14] Heeh argues that orientalism is a highly differentiated discourse that spans over six styles of orientalist discourse which can be divided by two broad categories, colonial and post-colonial. The colonial style can, Heeh notes, be further divided into three ways—Patronizing-Patronized, Romantic and Nationalist, while the post-colonial style has three sub-divisions—Critical, Reductive and Reactionary.[15]

In identifying these six types of orientalist styles of discourse, Heeh is quite correct in making a distinction between colonial and post-colonial styles. And, as already indicated earlier, this distinction comes about as the result of the termination, especially after World War II, of the colonial era. And yet the fact remains that the sensibility that gave birth to colonialism is still existing with reinforced strength. This reinforcement derives from the act on the part of the backward peoples of embracing the "other", the other symbolized by the ascendant occident and trying eventually to become the other. This in itself is symptomatic of the acknowledgement of the superiority of western civilization; it is the model that almost all the euphemistically called developing countries have accepted as the model representing universal reason alluded to earlier.

Heeh, however, confuses two very essential facts in making his classification as a tool of his critique of Said's theory. In the first place, he is confusing two different historical stages, especially in regard to how the Europeans perceived Indian civilization. These stages can, following Trautman referred to by Bryant[16] be identified as Indophilia and Indophobia. The phase of Indophilia that prevailed in the late eighteenth and early nineteenth centuries was marked by reports by scholars associated with the East India Company about India that pointed to a vast antiquity and superiority of ancient Indian civilization. These reports sent waves of thrill in many influential intellectuals in late eighteenth century and captured the imagination of Romantic Europe. Astronomer Bailly located the earliest human settlement on the banks of the Ganges and claimed that the Brahmans were the teachers of Pythagoras, the instructor of Greek and, through her, the whole of Europe[17] Voltaire too voiced his agreement saying : "In short, sir, I am convinced that everything—astronomy, astrology, metempsychosis, etc. comes to us from the banks of the Ganges."[18] According to Poliakov, Schelling, the famous metaphysician, asserted in 1807: "What is Europe but a sterile trunk which owes everything to oriental graft."[19]

Even the British scholars, such as, John Holwell, Nathaniel Halhead, Alexander Dow and several others, all of whom were associated with the East India Company, relayed back to Europe gleanings from *Puranic* sources that proved the Genesis story of creation of the old Testament wrong. Holwell, for example, argued, on the basis of his knowledge of Sanskrit texts, that they contained higher revelations than the Christian ones.[20] Thus when in the early years of the flood of reports demonstrating the superiority of Indian civilization antidated Europe, it was natural for European intelligentsia and learned men to become exhilirated by what they considered a better alternative than offered by Christian dogma for viewing and doing things. This is evident from the disaffection of a particular section of Christians who were fed up with Christian dogmas. The relays of information about what India signified as a civilizational unit and her immense antiquity reached Europe, they provided the ranks of disaffected Christians such as the vociferous Voltaire with valuable materials with which to attempt to shake off the constraints of Judeo-Christian chronology (of creation) and refute Jewish or Christian claims to exclusive mediation between man and providence.[21]

The euphoria of Indophilia was soon to raise the blinding form of Indophobia, a concerted move to condemn Indian cilization and what it signified. A cacophony of voices was raised by those who feared that "the daring assumptions of certain skeptical French philosophers, with respect to the age of the world,... arguments principally founded on the high assumptions of the Brahmins... (which) have a direct tendency to overturn Mosaic system, and with it Christianity.[22] It fell upon Sir William Jones to stem the tide of Indophilia and lay the firm foundation of Indophobia. Jones' contribution lies in his formulation of linguistic history that destroyed the claim of Sanskrit language as the mother of languages.[23] He injected a uniform system of positive law, and demonstrated the superiority of western civilization reflecting the ethos of Christianity.[24] Other voices joined that of Jones and the downgrading of India as a civilizational unit resulted inevitably in the demise of Indophilia. But Indophilia "did not die of a natural causes, it was killed off and replaced by Indophobia artfully crafted by Evangelism and utilitarianism, epitomized by Charles Grant and James Mill respectively."[25] Well before Max Muller's glorification of India, Grant[26] pursued an aggressive campaign of Anglicizing and Christianizing India with the help of his vituperative assertions that disparaged Indian laws, religion and character. He went to the ridiculous extent of declaring that "in the worst parts of Europe, there are no doubt great numbers of men who are sincere, upright, and conscientious. In Bengal, a man of veracity and integrity is a great phenomenon."[27]

Other Christian leaders joined the chorus and argued, as did Reverend Alexander Duffy, that

> Hindus have no will, no liberty, no conscience, moulded into shape by external influences, mere machines, blindly stimulated at the bidding of another to pursuits most unworthy of immortal creatures. In them reason is in fact laid prostrate. They launch into all the depravities of idol worship. They look like the sports and derision of the Prince of Darkness.[28]

Next in line to attack Indian civilization were the Utilitarians spearheaded by James Mill who considered India as barbarous since the ends she was pursuing were contemptible and mischievous. India, therefore, justified despotic rule until she was capable of self-government. A reflection of the voice of Vitoria can easily be traced in what Mill supposed India to be. And the despotic rule that Mill proposed was to recast Indian society to conform to the universal principle of rationality and utility as visualized by the utilitarians.[29] It is the combined attack on what the Evangelists and James Mill thought about India that came to full flowering as Indophobia for the Evangelists, they found innumerable souls making their painful trek to hell of perdition since or were bereft of the benefits of Christian salvation. The Utilitarians, on the other hand, saw in India a decrepit civilization tottering on the brink of barbarism from which it can be saved only by hitching its destiny with utilitarianism. And Lord William Bentinck, Governor General (1828-1835), was the pilot mainly responsible for trimming the sails of the British Indian State to the wind of change.[30] The overall objectively of the regnant Indophobia was to change Indian society wholly to conform to the dominant ideas prevalent in England.

Thus the intent of Indophobia was not simply to pull Indian civilization down to an inferior, almost primitive position, but also to spread western enlightenment, the dazzling light of "reason" to India and impel her to abandon her old ways of thinking and doing and advance on the path of progress paved by the rapid strides that science and technology had made. But the path of progress did not simply mean improving economic life and relations but, more importantly, the wholesale change of the psychic world of Indians. It is in this context that we can appreciate the approach of the Utilitarians who wanted what they called "universal reason" to dictate the terms of the transformation of Indian society releasing it from its captivity in orthodoxy, superstition and blind faith into a social order ever willing and ready to be exposed to and receive the liberating influence of reason. It is against this background that we can appreciate Viceroy Northbrooke's, observation that "We are modifying, unavoidably modifying. Not harshly, not suddenly, but slowly, greatly and with sympathy, but still modifying the whole collective life and character of the population of the Empire."[31]

The spread of the dazzling light of Enlightenment found its Indian admirers when Bankim Chandra Chattopadhyaya[32] looked to the "benign" presence of English army with relief and an expectation of a happy future under the British Raj. Similarly, Keshab Chandra Sen reconciled himself by the thought that the ancient civilization of India and the modern civilization represented by England would prove beneficial to each other. As he obsorved "in the advent of the English nation in India, we see a reunion of parted cousins, the descendants of two different families of the Aryan race." He however believed that each had a very important role to play. "India in her present fallen condition seems destined to sit at the feet of England for many long years to learn western art and science. And, on the other hand, behold England sit at the feet of hoary headed India to study the ancient literature of this country."[33] Whether England learned a lesson from hoary headed India or not is a moot point. However, the burden of Sen's and Vivekanand's argument seems to suggest that India had lost all those vital inner forces that would have carried Indian civilization forward in a manner suitable for its own genius.

What is important to note is that India did learn a new way of looking at and doing things.[34] And the role of Lord Bentinck was crucial in transplanting western ideas and institutions in the receptive soil of India. He succeeded, during his tenure as Governor-General, to fully transform the tendencies that were present in embryonic stage into a full movement sweeping away most of the distinguishing characteristics of India as a civilizational entity. The several measures that were taken during his rule amounted to planting western ideas and institutions on Indian soil and leaving them to grow as they would.[35]

The floodgates opened by the introduction of English education released a large volume of new ideas, new ways of looking at the world and doing things. The released flood waters introduced a vision of the world whose realization depended upon the extent to which the onslaught of modernization succeeded in inducing the motivation to go on breaking the habitual contexts of thought and action, willingness to experiment and try new ways of doing things, and the preparedness to have new experiences. The process of modernization set in motion went a long way to stir new life into a dormant body. When that body came to be animated with new life, it did embrace the strange, the new and the alien ways of thought-ways and work-ways. There were resistances, to be sure. However, they were easily overcome opening the way for rapid expansion and acceptance of new thought-ways and work-ways first by the growing English educated class and then very slowly, of course, affecting life and relations in Indian villages. Thus, orientalism did not die with the coming of the independence; it only underwent a process of change as a result of the intermingling of the elements of Indophilia and Indophobia. However, the intellectual perspective that made Indophobia so potent survived. It is the combination of the two strands of European views about Indian civilization that makes Heeh speak of six kinds of orientalism. Without, of course, making the necessary distinction and specifying the historical context in which six kinds of orientalism made their appearance.

What is clear then is that most of the village studies reflect a perspective that is not rooted in Indian sensibility or, to put it another way, indigenous view(s) of life. Add to it two other considerations that make village studies in India somewhat partial and incomplete : The first consideration relates to the difficulty caused by the fragmentation of the universe of discourse. This fragmentation was caused by the rise of secularism after the passing out of the Middle Ages. Consequently, the unity of discourse grounded in the universally accepted idea of man inspired by Christianity also broke down. In its place emerged a plethora of perspectives on man and his world. With the abandonment of the idea of a shareable commonality characterizing each person, knowledge construction, both about man and his world, came to rely on what we know as scientific method. Scientific method signifies a process of observation, analysis and classification with the help of projecting on the world a conceptual torch-light to illumine a particular segment of reality. Such a project, it must be emphasized, is undertaken with a particular purpose in mind. However, numerous such projections are possible insofar as the purpose of the projection of a conceptual instrument might differ from one person to the next. Change the purpose, the method of mapping the world changes and with it also changes the nature of reality that is constructed through the artifact of a particular method. And since purposes vary, the picture of reality also varies.

It is clear, then, that each such projection serves a particular purpose, to be true; but the result is the fragmentation of the universe of discourse. What is also interesting to note is that such projections yield only a descriptive account of the segment of reality mapped by a particular projection. However, description is usually transformed into a normative statement claiming the reality as derived from a particular projection to be the only true reality. Thus, the core of social scientific research is the insistence that the structure of the external world, as it is constituted by the projection of a particular conceptual scheme, is ontologically the only real structure of the world.

The second consideration has to do with the prevalence of multiple ideological perspectives as a consequence of the break-down of shareable commonality. The result is that theoretical projections on the factual order comes to be influenced and characterized by a diversity of interests. Since these interests are obstinate and intransigent facts of life, the relevance of a particular theoretical perspective for apprehending reality elevates ideology to a higher terrain where it becomes the dominant referent for evaluating reality and truth. As such opinions and doctrines contend among themselves for recognition as truth. In this contention information about reality does not yield knowledge; it only becomes a weapon in the power game of what counts as the most appropriate way of looking at the external world. Epistemologically speaking, then, three distinct consequences of "scientific" knowledge can be identified here. These are delimitation of the domain of knowledge, proliferation of ideological perspectives on the external world, and loss of unity of knowledge. The application of scientific method severely delimits the domain to that which is sensible and therefore observable. Once observation has revealed certain facts as characteristic of some segment of reality, it provides the touchstone of deciding what is right and what is wrong. Thus truth receives its authenticity and legitimacy from its conformity to facts which are observed through the telescope of concepts.

Add to all this the fact that the status of the village that receives academic attention is never clarified. Is the village under study a world in itself unrelated with the larger socio-cultural context in which it is located and by which it is enveloped? Or alternatively, is a village simply a microcosm reflecting in its pattern of life and relationship the basic features of the macrocosm whatever this microcosm may be. To treat a village and its community life as autonomous and significant in themselves is a travesty of truth. Village life is a part of a larger socio-cultural and political entity and receives most of its characteristics from its relatedness with this larger entity. It is true that variations occur from one village to the next as a result of the variation in time and space. But this does not detract from the fact that as a microcosm, no matter how different one village may be from other villages, remains a microcosm. And if a village is treated as a microcosm, then, the question of its relationship with the macrocosm of which it is not only a part but also a distinctive reflector arises. How is the essential characteristics of the whole the village is a part of reflected in village life and how different it is from the whole? This is a question that must be taken note of; the answer to this question becomes a very important part of village study.

Once the question of the village as a microcosm of a larger entity is raised, another question about India as a civilizational entity at once comes to the fore. What needs to be emphasized here is that at the root of the character of any civilization is the image of man. A civilizational entity may be based on the image of man as a total being combining in him intelligence, energy and appetite, as Plato characterizes it or as *manas, prana, vak,* as the Veda specifies it. In contradistinction to this, a civilization may be said to rest on the image of man as a being with only two faculties—appetites and rationality. In such a case, the substance of civilization gets attenuated and its understanding becomes incomplete. Most of the village studies are based on the basic error of shattering the fundamental unity of the totality of man and rely for their "discovery" on some selected fragments of this fragmented unity. It is ignored that in order to discuss what is relevant in the external world and in society for any science of social order one must develop a philosophy of man and of his place in society and the world at large. Without an "idea of man", Voegelin notes, "we have no frame of reference for the designation of human phenomena as relevant or irrelevant. Man is engaged in the creation of social order physically, biologically, psychologically, intellectually and spiritually" and only some of these engagements admit of "general laws". Accordingly, the criteria of relevance for the constitution of any reliable social science are properly developed on the basis of philosophical anthropology grounded in the philosophy of the phenomenal world in which man is located.

One problem that we face in it is the genuine difficulty that we do not all have the same idea of man and our principles of selection of relevant subject-matter may differ widely. This tripartite division, indicated earlier, or to refer to the Vedic distinction, *manas, prana* and *vak* can easily be collapsed into two important aspects of man's being as well as the external world. As such, man is the conjunction of the spiritual and the material or, to put it differently, of finite and absolute. True, Max Scheler accords primacy to material conditions of life. However, in contradistinction to Scheler, the traditional understanding of these two realms is that they are, or should be, hierarchically organized and structured. It is the spiritual realm that is the seed-bed of morality; it is moral sensibilities that regulate and control the excesses of the mode of life given primarily to what Aristotle calls *apaulistic* life, given to the satisfaction of the senses directed to the quest of progressive economic development. Without moral super-ordination, economic life and relation tend to be afflicted with the decease of *pleonexia*.[36] It is to escape *pleonexia* that culture in the traditional sense becomes central and draws its inspiration from a distinctive world-view that finds its expression in cosmogony. Cosmogony focuses on the relationship of the finite and the absolute.[37] This makes the social order a cosmion, the little world of order.

This cosmion functions as a shelter for man caught in the trials and tribulations of existence, of everydayness, by forging a linkage between the finite and the absolute, the absolute that is the source of truth, meaning and value. This linkage function is based on a distinctive world-view grounded in the attunement of the soul to the divine ground of being. This applies specially to sages, philosophers, or mystics in some primal age. It is this world-view that gives birth to culture that underlines and is often reflected in social order. As a result, society cannot be defined solely by its external aspect or dimension, that is institutional and functional aspects, social practices and procedures. Society has also an internal aspect that shapes society's external form and gives it meaning and relevance. It is this internal aspect that, when embodied in what Heraclitus calls xynon or *Saman-chittata* (likemindedness), endows its members with a deep sense of belongingness to an entity larger than the individual or even society even while they exhibit a large degree of biological, psychological, and social diversity.

As such, society manifests itself in two layers—the external and the internal. The former is constituted by a network of rules and procedures that define what is worthy of man to do and how to go about doing things. This, known by the Greeks as *techne*, refers partly to commandments combining both moral and practical. This combination underlines the intermixture of the prescriptions of external moraliy and the rules of practical wisdom. Partly, it constitutes those professional skills and traditions which are passed from one generation to the next. It defines and regulates thought-ways and work-ways. It is symptomatic of self-knowledge gained during the act of living in a community. The latter, the internal aspect, refers to the development of those elements which when fully operative, controls and directs the way a man must act in the community, not only towards himself, but also towards others. This internal aspect refers again to a network of interests, and work-ways that reflect man's duties to himself and to the collectivity he belongs to. It is the intermingling of and dynamic interaction between these two layers that shapes and informs social consciousness. As Pande notes:

> Social consciousness can be distinguished by the fact that it regulates, as partially manifest order of things, understanding, *Samskaras*, memories and beliefs of its individual members in a relatively longer temporal framework.

In this sense, society can be understood as the deeply embedded soul of all individual members (as reflected in the substratum of their life and life activities), it is because of this that society is capable of making and sustaining the awareness of its members of their identity, ideals, rights and duties and provides them with opportunities (and the means) of living their lives and engaging in action in ways sanctioned by it.

Continuing, Pande adds further:

> Every individual finds himself related with a tradition of knowledge and understanding as well as a network of relationship that are larger than their finite existence. If this tradition of knowledge and understanding can be characterized as culture, the network of relationships can be called society. Man, as a being who is endoweded with consciousness, is in this sense, a resident of a socio-cultural cosmos that has an external form and internal consciousness.[38]

As indicated earlier, it is his residence in two realms that permits him to link his finite existence with the absolute that is the seed-bed of xynon. And because members of particular society share this they constitute a community. This community contains within itself a variety of interests, and opinions each of whom gets the opportunity of articulating, expressing and realizing its purposes. However, this occurs in a context in which every particular member attends to his own needs and aspirations, but he is, at the same time, animated by the spirit of society which expresses itself through its dual structure.

The spirit of the society is reflected in the values shared by many, if not all members, and is infrastructural in regulating both the internal and external activities of each of its members. When these values are stable, the transmission of the way of looking at and doing things continues to take place. It is with the help of this process of transmission that members are initiated and educated in the spirit of society. When these values are displaced or destroyed, social relations are disrupted. The process of change takes over and transforms society from what it was into something else. Once this inner core of society is, for one reason or the other, dissipated, a community is reduced to a multitude losing sight of the spirit of society which is central to its vitality. This situation is brought about and reinforced by what Mahatma Gandhi calls "the constant search for bodily comfort" making man, as Plato puts it, "a slave of many mad masters" or *Kamachar* according to *Chhandogya Unpanishad*. The society that recognizes and builds itself on the primacy of material interest can claim to only what sociologists call "functional integration" symbolizing the exchange of several products and services based on economic mutuality and reciprocity. It is true that the external dimension of society comes to occupy the centre-stage of man's existence. However, it does not totally oust or suppress the spiritual aspect. The spiritual aspect remains but only as dried up shell of a previously luscious fruit; it loses its inner dynamism and does not exist as a living force. It exists only as ritualized routine, only empty rites and rituals. These rites and rituals do remind man's relationship with the divine ground of being. However, they do so only as a hollow obeissance to the unknown without getting translated into action for self-knowledge. The society endures but its social spirit dissolves.

Most of the social scientific studies of villages in India as small *replicas* of society as cosmion suffer from the fact that they do not either take into account the internal dimension of society or, when do take note of it, they do it in a mechanical positivistic manner. What is important is that Indian villages themselves encourage the kind of approaches that animate these kinds of studies. The reasons for this are not far to seek. When the primordial insight into the structure of reality and the social order based on it get caught up in the stream of history, the original insight grows gradually dim and gets lost in the realm of forgetfulness and ignorance which is characterized in the Indian tradition of thinking as *ajnana*. The Indian society organized in thousands of villages was, in the dim past, informed and undergirded by the primordial insight into the structure of order articulated in the Vedic literature, particularly the *Rigveda*. The *Chaturvarnya Vyavastha* (supposed to be derived from the_*Purusha Sukta*) and the system of *purushartha* were the two mighty pillars of a social order based on the notion of *Yajna* (sacrifice). As is well known, sacrifice calls for four essential services making up the totality of the *chaturvarnya* system. In such a society different classes of people cooperate to fulfil its fundamental requirements. As Coommaraswamy observes, "the form of order (*yatharthata*) and impartiality (*samadristi*) will mean that every man shall be enabled to become and by no misdirection prevented from becoming what he has in him to become."[39]

The social order reflecting the way of sacrifice must encompass a hierarchy of sacerdotal, royal, and administrative powers, and of physical organs of sense and action. In this order, as Coomaraswamy notes, "there is need and place for all men's work. And there is no more significant consequence of the principle, work is sacrifice, than the fact that under these conditions, every function from that of the priest and the king down to that of the potter and scavenger, is literally a priesthood and every operation a rite."[40]

The complementary aspect of the *chaturvarnya* system is the classification of *Purushartha* into *kama, artha, dharma* and *moksha*. The inner purport of the system of *Purushartha* is the progress in ascending order towards the ultimate goal, that is liberation. It is the combination of these two components that constituted society in India. This perspective does not deny the claim of everydayness and the need of fulfilling ordinary life needs. While giving due importance to the fulfilment of life purposes, this requires that the *artha-tantra* must be subordinated to *dharma-tantra.* To pursue all life activities in accordance with *dharma* is to link the finite existence of man with the absolute which alone is the source of truth, value and meaning.[41]

Structured on this perspective, village society in India gave due attention to the pursuit of both the fulfilment of ordinary life needs and that of a higher life purpose. This combination was never stable; it received in the moving scale of history, several severe jolts. However, it held its own and escaped destruction by preserving itself in one form or the other. The social order continued to be usually characterized by interdependence, cooperation and harmony despite the diversity of orientations and interests. However, the social system based on this perspective began gradually to be corrupted under the pressures of historical changes in thought-ways and work-ways.[42] The social order in the villages became so corrupted that it dissociated itself comprehensively from its internal aspect of traditional culture. It emerged only as a power structure focusing principally on safeguarding and protecting privileged access to scarce societal resources, such as, wealth, power and prestige, by the powerful. The power hierarchy was most competitive and unstable at the upper ranks but lower strata were passive and highly dependent for economic resources on the powerful and the wealthy; they lacked any sense of collectivity or the awareness of collective interest different from and antagonistic to the interest of the powerful and the wealthy. However, their socio-economic condition made them an integral part of the system whether they liked it or not. Thus, while the system might have lost its moral justification, the difficulty in organizing and sustaining collective action to jettison the system prevented any concerted action to overthrow the system either peacefully or violently.

Then came the Muslim rule which proved to be oppressive and posed danger to the continuance of Indian civilization pushing Indian society to a defensive position; this promoted further ossification of its social system. The system survived with numerous bruises in the skirmishes of the mortal struggle between two antagonistic world-views. But its very survival killed its dynamic innovative elements and denuded it of its dynamism. The process of fateful changes began with the advent of the British Rule, especially after the failed 1857 revolt to dislodge the British rulers; these changes vitally affected the central core of the ethos of Indian civilization. These changes were induced and reinforced through a process of inversion or transposition of certain key and strategic elements of the traditional Indian (Hindu world-view) that held sway in India for centuries. The process of inversion began because the alien rulers were endowed deeply with an entirely different and incompatible civilizational ethos; this ethos prompted them to view Indian society from their own culture-specific perspective.

Looking down on India from this perspective, its social, political and economic aspects gave them the strong impression that these different aspects of Indian society needed radical changes if India was to move forward on the path of progress as defined by the West, on the one hand, and adequately serve British interests, on the other.

Impelled by this motivation, the British ruler undertook the task of reshaping Indian society in the mould of their own national experience.[43] Thus began the process of inversions some of which need to be noted here. The first of these inversions was to seek and achieve the unity of Indian society through political and administrative means.[44] The alien rulers failed to appreciate the fact that the unity of Indian society was grounded in its cultural ethos, the state has never been the instrument of unity through political means. India never sought to establish, as Rabindranath Tagore points out, Universal Empire since it preferred Universal Society instead.[45] The quest for unity through political and administrative means signified the superimposition on Indian society, although gradually but definitely, the fundamental political ideas, institutions and practices that prevailed in Britain. Second, this superimposition brought the alien pattern of politics to the villages. As a result, the local communities that were so far removed from the political vortex were gradually brought in the midst of this vortex shattering their isolation from the provincial and trans-provincial centres of power.[46] Third, the spread of English education created an English educated middle class that had soaked deeply the liberal perspective on man and his world. The swelling middle class provided leadership to national struggle for freedom and set off in motion a force that was to alter Indian society scattered in thousands of villages in many radical ways. Add to it the radical alterations in economic life and relations as a result of the introduction and gradual expansion of industrial mode of production. As a result, the material aspect of human existence moved to the centre-stage of man's existence pushing the spiritual aspect to the extreme periphery. And, finally, all these inversions were coupled with a new mode of knowledge construction inspired by the materialization of human world creating in the process a world of mere objects to be studied by someone standing outside it.

The cumulative result of all these inversions was that the social unity was shattered pitting different socio-economic interests against each other. The primacy of the material aspects induced an intense competition among these interests. This led to the politicization of traditional referents of identity formation affecting ultimately village life and relations. It is the combination of these changes that have progressively made their impact on Indian villages altering them in certain vital, even unrecognizable ways. The reconstruction of the life in Indian villages through the lens of the western modes of knowledge construction has come to be dependent on different manifestations of what is called orientalism described earlier. In these manifestations the long and varied course of historical changes, spilling over in three different worlds grounded in different world-views and cultural systems, somehow got collapsed into one but highly diversified field. And what is usually projected as truly the life in Indian villages is just one of the pieces of this diversified field. As a result, most of the recent studies of Indian villages present often only a fragmentary picture, often partial presenting only a particular or partial dimensions of village reality.

As such, to initiate a process of rethinking about villages in India, involves essentially a self-conscious transcendence of the contemporarily regnant modes of knowledge construction. This task is, therefore, something that cannot be completed by our remaining, either willingly or unwillingly, a prisoner of the modern paradigms of knowledge. This is so for the simple reason that it cuts up the totality of man's being into numerous segments and treats these segments as if they are not organically and ontologically linked. As such, the challenge today confronting us in the process of rethinking about Indian villages is both ontological and epistemological. What this signifies is the need to move away from the dominant (especially the western) mode of exploring man and his world. This mode concentrates on knowledge construction involving the quest for an appropriate solution to the problems of language by ignoring the problems of life. But problems of language persist to remain insoluble because they ignore problems of life.

This is symptomatic of breaking the totality of man's being resulting in rendering man as what Iris Murdoch calls "a broken totality". The mending of this broken totality depends on restoring man's ontological wholeness and developing a proper epistemological strategy to deal with the existential problems confronting man today. This requires, in a great part, to move away from the strategy of knowledge construction that fails to grasp the central problem. This problem persists because of the continuing tension and conflict between the private *(idion)* and the public (*koinon*). This is also necessary because villages in India are neither modern nor traditional. Even if modernization seems to be ascendant, tradition still retains its hold even if only in a limited sphere. Thus, villages in India are experiencing a tug of war or a tension between the new and the old. This tension is rooted in self-love as the basis of social life and relations. Further, self-love is the enemy of love for fellow beings. In the ascendance of self-love lies the "self-ish" motivation of the people who relate with each other only on the basis of compatibility of interest. This paves the way for the genesis of politics inspired by reciprocal resistance and erosion of love of beings. The restoration of love as a dominant element of social life depends on the appreciation of the fact that love for man is possible only through the love of God. Accordingly, what needs to be done is, first, to develop an ontological perspective on who man is in the totality of his being[47] and an epistemologically suitable method studying man in totality of his being who nurtures social bond and, in return, receives nurturance from society at large.

A proper approach to this problem is to develop a critical theory about man and his world that permits us to do three things at once. In the first place, it allows us to develop a paradigmatic reconstruction of the wholeness of man that provides appropriate guidelines for the building of a salubrious and beneficial structure of order. In the second place, such a paradigm offers a set of standards against which the contemporary empirical situation obtaining in Indian villages could be judged and evaluated. And, lastly, the paradigm should lead to actions appropriate for correcting existential imbalances in village life. This calls for establishing a relationship between theory and history that allows us to modify reality with the help of theoretical consciousness and revise and reformulate theory in the light of obtaining reality on a time scale but within the limits set by the paradigmatic approach itself. This will facilitate what Martin Buber calls "revolutionary continuity" obviating the need for "revolutionary leap". If this transformation is somehow made, theory will not ever become the master of history, nor will it become the witness of history, it will instead become the accomplice of history.

Such a paradigmatic perspectives was developed in recent times by Mahatma Gandhi.[48] It is this paradigmatic perspective that he applied to the conception of what he called oceanic circle focusing around the primacy of micro-communities inhabited by free individuals. He was not describing village life as it existed. Both Nehru and Ambedkar misunderstood Gandhi as describing a real village despite Gandhi's clarification. This misunderstanding haunts us even today forcing us to continue to misinterpret Gandhi's perspective. It is time to re-examine this perspective and explore how fruitful it is for our own rethinking about villages in India.

END NOTES

1. Two examples should suffice. The first example is that which identifies village life as based on *Yajamani* system, a system that underlined, on the one hand, interdependence among different castes and traditional professions and, on the other, marked by a barter system of exchange. What is interesting to note is that it was the early British views on the Indian village that popularized this characterization. The *Yajamani* system has tended to be seen partly by the British administrators and partly by Indian nationalists, in normative terms as a system that made the village society integrated, self-sufficient, non-commercial, unchanging;

and egalitarian. However, this normative view is based on romanticism rather than a close study of the obtaining reality in Indian villages. It is this characterization that is, nonetheless, still applied to Indian villages.

The second example is provided by the tendency of most students of Indian village life to treat these villages as examples of village republics. As a matter of fact, it was only in the upper Doab and Rohilkhand that *Talukdars,* who earlier dominated village life, were suppressed and the "village republics" were recognized as the proprietary body owning village land. The joint landlords were collectively responsible for the revenue. This system of landownership has, again, been normatively viewed to suggest that Indian villages at large symbolized a democratic system at the grass-roots. Again, nothing can be further from truth.

For a fruitful study, see Tirthankar Roy *The Economic History of India,* (New Delhi: Oxford University Press, 2000, pp. 36-42.

2. P. Sorokin characterizes Indian society as mainly a "closed" society, not a static one. When it remained closed for long, it developed the "identical" traits of culture with more or less defined views on nature of needs and ends and the means of their satisfaction, i.e., of social activity, with specific aesthetic, moral and social values and system. Quoted in B.K. Gopalkrishnan, *Development of Economic Ideas in India* 1890-1950, New Delhi: People Publishing House, 1959, p. 20.
3. Max Scheler, quoted in Harold J. Bershady, ed. *Max Scheler on Knowing and Feeling,* Chicago: University of Chicago Press, 1992, p. 29.
4. *Ibid.*
5. *Ibid.*, p. 30.
6. The hierarchical nature of philosophy, morality and technology is well reflected in Plato's writings. See, for example, Stanley Rosen "Man's Hope", *Social Research.*
7. For a very useful discussion, see Eric Voegelin. *The Spiritual and Political Future of the Western World,* in The ... of Humanity and other Miscellaneous Papers, 1939-1985, ed. William Petropulos and Gilbert Weiss, Columbia University of Missouri Press, 2004, pp. 78-79.
8. For a useful discussion relating to Bihar, see Peter Robb, *In Search of Dominant Peasants : Notes on the Implementation in Bihar of the Bengal Tenancy Act of 1885,* in Clive Dewey, ed. *Arrested Development in India : the Historical Dimension,* New Delhi: Manohar Publications, 1988, pp. 188-222.
9. See his *De Indis de Jure Belli Relectiones* (1532), ed. Ernest Nye, Washington D.C.: Carnegie Institution, 1977.

10. Robert Soloman, *The Rise and Fall of the Ego*, Oxford: Oxford University Press, 1989, p. 9; See also J. L. Mehta, *Philosophy and Religion: Essays in Understanding*, New Delhi: ICPR, 1990, p. 229.
11. Solomon, *Ibid.*
12. Edward E. Said, *Western Conceptions of Orient*, London: Penguin Books, 1991, pp. 3-4.
13. *Ibid.*, p. 94.
14. See, for example, Dennis Vidal, *Max Muller and the Theosophists: the Other Half of Victorian Orientalism*, in Jackey Asayog, *et al. Orientalism and Anthropology: From Max Muller to Louis Dumont* Pondicherry : Institute Frances de Pondicherry, 1997, pp. 14-15.
15. Peter Heels, *Shades of Orientalism: Paradoxes and Problems in Indian Historiography, History and Theory*, 42 (May 2003), p. 170. He provides a classificatory theory on p. 172.
16. Thomas R. Trautman, *Aryans and British India* (New Delhi: Yoda Press, 2004), first published by the University of California Press, Berkeley in 1997: See also Edwin Bryant, *The Quest for the Origin of Vedic Culture: The Indo-Aryan Migration Debate*, New Delhi: Oxford University Press, 2001, p. 14.
17. Jean-Sylvain Bailly, *Lettre sur Lorgine des sciences et.sur celle des peoples de l' Asia*, Paris: Freres Debure, 1977, p. 51.
18. *Ibid.*, p. 4.
19. L. Poliakov, *The Aryan Myth* (London: Sussex University Press, 1971), p. 11; See also Lord Curzon, *On the Original Expansion of Sanskrit Language Over Certain Parts of Asia and Europe*, Journal of Royal Asiatic Society, 16, 1855, pp. 72-73.
20. For a useful collection of the Indian source materials transmitted to Europe by British scholars at that time, see P. J. Marshall, *The British Discovery of Hinduism in the Eighteenth Century*, Cambridge: Cambridge University Press, 1970.
21. Bryant, op. cit., p. 14.
22. Thomas Maurice, *Indian Antiquities*, 1812, Reprint (New Delhi: Navrang Rai, 1984), pp. 22-23. For details, see Ramashray Roy, *Gandhi and Ambedkar: A Study in Contrast*, Delhi: Shipra Publications, 2006, pp. 24-56.
23. Sir William Jones, *On the Gods of Greece, Italy and India*, Asiatic Society Researches, 1788, pp. 422-23.
24. See Roy, op. cit., Bryant, op. cit. and Javed Majeed, *Ungoverned Imaginings: James Mill's History of India and Orientalism*, Oxford: Clarendon Press, 1992.
25. Thomas R. Trautman, *Aryans and British India* (Berkeley: University of California Press, 1997), p. 99.
26. Grant was an influential person in East India Company circles. His vituperative statements are to be found in *Observation on the*

State of Society Among the Asiatic Subjects of Great Britain, Particularly in the year 1772, *Report of the Select Committee on the Affairs of the East India Company*, 1831-32, Reprinted as Irish University Press series of *British Parliamentary Papers Colonies: East India*, 5 vols., Shannon: Irish University Press, 1970, p. 21.

27. *Observations on the State of Society among Asiatic Subjects of Great Britain*, Particularly with Respect to Morals; and the Means of Improving it, in 1792, in Parliamentary Papers, 10, (1812-13), Paper 282, p. 23.
28. The Reverend made the remark in 1840. Quoted in Trautman, op. cit., p. 107. And in 1842 William Hastie, Principal of the General Assembly of the Church of Scotland's institution in Calcutta, in letters he addressed to "educated Indians" about their religion, asserted that "no pen has yet adequately depicted all the hideousness and grossness of the monstrous system." Quoted in Trautman, op. cit., pp. 24-33.
29. James Mill, *The History of British India* (1817) 10 Vols. ed. H. A. Wilson, (London: James Maddens, Piper, Stephenson, and Spence, 1858), Vol. 2, p. 105.
30. Percival Spear, *A History of India* (Harmondsworth: Penguin Books, 1986), p. 123. It is interesting to note that before Lord Bentinck left for India, he met James Mill and assured him that while he would be Governor-General, it would be Mill's idea that would rule India.
31. See the Welcome address of Lord Northbrooke on the occasion of the visit to India of the Prince of Wales in 1875. Spear, op.cit., p. 17.
32. *Anandmath*, a Novel.
33. Keshab Chandra Sen, *Lectures in India* (Calcutta. Navavidhan, 1950), p. 325: (first edition London Cassel, 1901-04). Earlier Swami Vivekanand had admitted that the ancient Greek (In the shape of the British ruler) was meeting the ancient Hindu on the soil of India and recommended that "we must be always ready to sit at the feet of all. At the same time we must not forget that we have also to teach a great lesson to the world... we must go out, conquer the world through our spirituality and philosophy. *The Complete Works of Swami Vivekanand*, 5 vols. Calcutta: Advait Ashrama, 1970-73, Vol. III, pp. 269-73.
34. It was in 1800 that Wellesly, the then Governor-General proclaimed the establishment of a college at Fort William. Originally, the objective of the college was to transform untrained novices arriving fresh from Great Britain into experienced civil servants of the Crown, well-groomed in local languages and culture. In addition, it also aimed at disseminating European knowledge to the Bengali intelligentsia. Fort William College was the first institutional

environment where Bengalis were exposed to western knowledge and sciences. It also provided a nucleus around which a host of other institutions—printing presses, libraries, academic institutions, etc. sprang and radiated the light that made possible the appearance of renaissance in Bengal and later in the rest of India.

When Bentinck came to India, he became instrumental in introducing, through Macaulay, the Law Member, English education which became the conveyor of western knowledge and ways of thinking and doing things. What also needs to be mentioned in this connection is the fact that, as C. H. Philips points out, it is said that Bentinck assured Mill... "I am going to British India but I shall not be Governor-General. It is you that will be Governor General" C. H. Philips, ed. *The Correspondence of Lord William Cavendish Bentinck,* Oxford: Oxford University Press, 1977, 2 Vols. I, Introduction, p. XV.

35. Spear, op. cit, pp. 125-26.
36. It signifies, on the one hand, to a tendency to acquire even those things of life, even if not merited for them (self-aggrandizement and other toleration of injustice voluntarily) Aristotle, *Nochomachean Ethics 1229: b.9.*
37. For a useful discussion on this theme, See Eric Voegelin, *History of Political Ideas: Hellenism, Rome and Early Christianity*, ed. Attanasios Moulakis, Columbia, University of Missouri Press, 1997, I, Appendix A, p. 226.
38. Govind Chandra Pande, *Bharatiya Samaj: Tatwika Our Aitihasik Vivechan*, New Delhi: National Publishing House, 1994.
39. Anand K. Coomaraswany, *Hinduism and Buddhism*, Delhi: Munshiram Manoharlal, 1986, p. 26.
40. *Ibid.*, p. 27. It must be noted here that the four-fold division of person on the basis of *guna* attribute (not on caste or class ranking). It was originally a horizontal system which later became vertical based on sociologically defined considerations.
41. The briefest but succinct articulation of the idea of *Purushartha* is expressed in the saying : *Yamadhikritya Purushah Pravartate.* This answers the question: What is within my right to do? In the modern times, this question relates to agency of the individual, the central concern of the contemporary times. In contrast, the traditional Indian thinking has been concerned with the ultimate end of the self, that is liberation. As such, to ascend in a progressive manner, from tone stage to another till one merges; one's self in the *Purusha* is the true significance of *Pursushartha.*
42. For a brief but useful account, see Pande, op. cit. pp. 80-87.
43. Earlier, Edmund Burke an influential member of the ruling party had clearly stated that the British Government was not in favour

of changing cultural identity of its colonies. William Jones, too, had assured Burke that, as a judge of the Calcutta High Court, he would leave untouched the cultural ethos of Indian society. However, he soon proceeded to change subtly but decisively the judicial system. For details see Ramashray Roy, *Gandhi and Ambedkar: A Study in Contrast*, Delhi: Shipra Publications, 2006, Chap. 2.

44. Viceroy North Brooke, welcoming Prince of Wales promised to work for the unity of India which, to him, like other English men, was infinite in its inhabitants, almost infinite in variety of races... and creeds which have shaped its character involving infinite administrative and political problems. See Ramashray Roy, *Gandhi and Ambedkar: A Study in Contrast*, Manuscript, p. 47.
45. As Selig Harrison notes, India presents "a splotchy tableau of sudden imperial brilliance followed invariably by the dim obscurities of collapse and disintegration." However, as he recognizes, the primary concern in India has been the creation of a durable social order. As he further observes, the creation of a social order out of the influx of diverse tribal and racial groups which it had been Indian's fate to experience was compensation enough for the omission of a lasting political order. Rabindranath Tagore, in particular, pointed that if the Hindus had not achieved a Universal Empire, it was because they were concerned to establish a Universal Society, pervaded by universally acknowledged religious values, *Ibid.*, p. 49.
46. With the rise of the state and empire after the fall of the Athenian democracy, local communities were robbed of their power as political decision-making bodies. Politics moved upwards to the king and his court. In India, the local communities, though removed from power centres retained their power of decision-making in many areas of life. This, however, changed under the British Rule.
47. For a forceful argument about it, see Abraham Heschel, *Who Man Is*? Stanford: Stanford University, 1965.
48. For a useful discussion on this subject, see Ramashray Roy, *Self and Society: A Study in Gandhi's Thought* (New Delhi: Sage Publications, 1985), *Gandhi: Soundings in Political Philosophy*, Delhi: Chanakya Publications, 1984 and Delhi: Ajanta Publications, 1995, *Understanding Gandhi*.

10

Globalization and Linguistic Diversity*

YOGESH ATAL

In the 1930s, Ralph Linton published an article titled "One Hundred Per cent American." The purpose of the article was to demonstrate the phenomenon of diffusion through which cultures add to their material repertory and thereby change and develop. The imaginatively crafted article describes an average American's daily routine from the time he wakes up till he catches the train to go to his place of work. The author told the reader that right from the morning coffee—the brew and the bowl—through the newspaper and cigar to the sleeping bed, most of the items used by the Americans have their origins elsewhere. And yet they have become an integral part of the way of life of an American. The hundred per cent American is the one who leads his life on almost one hundred per cent borrowed material cultural elements. This is how Linton concludes his essay: "As he scans the latest editorial pointing out the dire results to our institutions of accepting foreign ideas, he will not fail to thank a Hebrew God in an Indo-European language that he is one hundred per cent (decimal system invented by the Greeks) American (from Amerigo Vespucci, Italian geographer)".

The point he makes is that the arrival of elements from abroad did not erode the identity of American culture; on the contrary, they enriched it. The case of the American is particularly instructive because America is a society of migrants, and many have described her as a melting pot; and yet American culture has a distinct identity of its own. What was true in 1937 is true in 2001 though over the years America has added to its cultural diversity and its material culture with increasing globalization.

The message of that article was clear: cultures grow through diffusion—they receive traits and complexes from a wide variety of sources—and still their incorporation is so managed that the identity of the recipient culture does not get blurred. The process of cultural screening operates in each recipient culture that determines the receptivity of external traits. Their location within the host culture is governed by the previously established norms and patterns. Every society need not invent the wheel.

That essay was a landmark in American anthropology in the sense that it focused on culture change. The primitive societies that the anthropologists studied were, for long, viewed as "closed" societies—closed from outside influence and closed to any invention, thus remaining as non-changing societies. That is the reason that very little by way of cultural change was attempted in the earlier phases of the development of anthropology. All that anthropologists talked of change was in the evolutionary perspective at the grand civilizational level. So strong was the motivation of anthropologists to describe the way of life of the primitives in its pristine form that the anthropologists were charged for keeping the tribals in a "zoo"—as advocates of a policy of no-change. It is, of course, true that the anthropologists were the first to highlight the adverse effects of outside contacts on the culture of the primitive societies. We have accounts of how the spread of imperialism and colonialism had affected the traditional cultures, and caused disappearance of many traits. There are several reports on the impact of tourism on the cultures of Southeast Asia, which have focused on the "undesirable" influences, particularly on the vanishing traits due to which the authors felt that the uniqueness of these cultures was in danger. In such a milieu, Linton's article, written in common parlance, brought in a fresh perspective—that of viewing cultures as constantly changing as a result of interaction with other cultures. Obliquely, he also told his readers that his discipline was not an advocate of tribal zoos.

It must, however, be admitted that the study of change in sociological and anthropological literature is of a relatively recent origin. Initially, change was studied at the level of human society as a whole. The efforts were to see how humans came into being and how did they evolve a culture of their own which distinguished them from the lower level animals. Later, attempts were made to put different human societies on a single evolutionary ladder, identifying the different stages of evolutionary development. When the West began its journey towards colonialism, it found evolutionary theory helpful in asserting its dominant status by claiming to be on a high pedestal of evolutionary ladder. Change in their own context was "defined by an orientation to the past and postulated an origin from which the present was both a derivation and a distanciation... Modernity was ... defined in opposition to the pagan period, which had been overcome" (Delanty, 2000:9). They compared the present of the primitive world with their past and made forays into the cultures of these societies to bring about change by introducing elements from their own culture. Not exposed to the outside world of the "relatively" developed societies, the primitives first resisted exogenous change and showed adherence to their tradition. Later, as a consequence of constant interactions with the outside world, the primitives began treating the present of the "developed" world as their preferred future. But this was not so simple. Ambivalence reigned on both the sides. The native leaders as well as the expatriate friends of the natives expressed the fear of the loss of the traditional cultures by the winds of change. The instinct to preserve the culture provided stimulus for resisting change brought in *from* the external agents of change—defined change as a move from tradition to modernity. Change became almost a synonym of the death of tradition.

The post-colonial era can be described as an era of change and development. The euphoria of independence brought in a new perspective to view societies. The developed world became the positive reference group, and the newly independent societies of the so-called non-West (which is, of late, re-christened as the South) became "nations in a hurry". The new leadership in these countries took the steps to adopt the alien models, either of capitalism or communism, to bring about radical changes in all spheres, but more particularly in the economic and political spheres. Like the West, these societies also got divided between the radicals and the conservatives. Opposition to governmental efforts to bring about change by emulating the external reference models caused revival of traditions and expressions of fear about the collapse of cultures. Even the modernists in these societies took sufficient care to halt the intrusion of external influences by insisting on accepting the outside elements "on their own terms". A good instance is that of China which claims of its own brand of socialism while changing its path towards capitalism through liberalization of its economy and globalization of its orientation. Earlier, it brought in communism from the outside but pampered it within close door—installing insulators and shutting all apertures.

The current slogan of "think globally but act locally" clearly brings out the prevailing "ambivalence"; in fact, it suggests that the two are not polar opposites and can remain in symbiosis.

This is not to say that culture contacts do not cause damage to tradition. The history of mankind does suggest death of several cultures. The entire science of Prehistoric Archeology is predominantly about dead cultures. There is thus, no denying the fact of the death of cultures, or the death or disappearance, or hibernation of traditions of individual cultures. The factors that cause this are, however, varied and numerous.

Culture contact manifests in several ways. More and more features have been added to this phenomenon with the advances in science and technology. Modern vehicles of transportation easily cross the old impediments of physical geography. And, developments in communication technologies have shortened social and cultural distances by creating conditions for mental motilities without stirring out of one's residence. In today's world, there is no culture—primitive or modern—that can claim to be one hundred per cent original. We live in a world of pluralities. No culture could escape miscegenation. Hybridity is the strength of living culture.

II

A new era of change began as we completed the second millennium. The vocabulary of westernization-modernization gave way to globalization. But just as modernization evoked resistances among the so-called traditional cultures, the newer processes of globalization are also seen as threatening to individual cultures. The threat is viewed in terms of the continued dominance of the North—with the East's collapse, North's monopoly has strengthened. And this dominance is seen not only in terms of the exploitation of the markets of the South, but as invasion of western culture through the media. The most commonly heard complaint is about the erosion of specificities of individual cultures. The homogenization hypothesis that was advanced some fifty years ago with the onset of development era continues to guide those who are opposed to change. It is claimed that the forces of globalization will homogenize the world by destroying the cultural diversities. The argument runs like this: just as bio-diversity needs to be preserved, there is a need to ensure preservation of cultural diversity. The same fear is expressed in the Note that AMIC has circulated. It says that in "recent years, the process of local adaptation is being threatened by the imposition of cultural systems of the advanced industrialized countries... This cultural imposition is partly the result of globalization brought about by advanced communication technologies."

The concern over the disappearance of linguistic diversity is part of the same response against spreading globalization.

The message that I get from reading such statements can be broken down into following statements:

- Cultures of the developing world continue to be at the receiving end;

- There is some identifiable entity that is "imposing" its "cultural system" on "helpless cultures" of the Third World.
- Globalization is a one-way traffic in which things flow from the North to the South.
- Disappearance of cultural traits and complexes herald the death of cultures.

I wish to argue that all these assumptions, or generalizations are false. They are based on wrong notions of globalization, and poorer understanding of the vitality and resilience of cultures.

Years of oppression and colonial rule has certainly brought about radical changes in the cultures of the colonies, but has not succeeded in erasing their identities as distinct cultures. During the modernization phase—that preceded the current globalization—culture was always equated with tradition, and regarded as an obstacle to innovations brought from the outside. At that time, death of tradition was considered desirable for the birth of modernity. But we became wiser as we moved ahead with our agenda for change and modernization. Social scientists began talking of co-existence of tradition and modernity; some even went as far as to discover modernity in tradition. In one of my earlier papers I have said: "All Asian societies and cultures are simultaneously experiencing the twin processes of globalization and indigenization. The universal desire for change notwithstanding, societies are making an equally emphatic assertion of their respective cultural identities. The forces of change have not transformed cultures into look-alike societies. Industrializing Thailand cannot be mistaken for Taiwan, or the roaring tiger of South Korea for Japan" (Atal, 1993:19).

The resurgence and revival of tradition leading to the rejection, or selective acceptance of innovations coming from the outside, puts a big question mark on the conspiracy theory that alleges that the West (or the North) is imposing its culture, and that the recipient cultures are getting eroded. Just as the South is not a single homogeneous entity so is the North. And in any case, North cannot be treated as a synonym of the USA. In today's world there are multiple apertures that link a given society's culture with other cultures of the world.

It is also important to understand the salient features of the process of globalization. This is not the same thing as colonization. Not even the developmental phase that followed it could be termed globalization; during that phase the developing world welcomed all kinds of aid—materials, men, money, and management—from the developed world in its eagerness to change and develop. It will be tautological if globalization were to be defined as merely disappearance of indigenous traditions. The distinctive feature of globalization is its departure from a unilateral flow. It has created such interdependencies that each society is both receiving and supplying. The new phenomenon of international migration is transporting manpower from the developing countires to the developed countries; and this migration is not of unskilled labour alone. As a consequence of this, today all societies of the world have become multi-cultural. In terms of technology, there is a speedy bridging of the gap, and some new technologies are simultaneously arriving everywhere, discarding the earlier patterns of developmental stages, and demonstrating leap-frogging. This spreading multiculturalism—of representatives of different cultures sharing a common habitat and fusion of technologies enriching material cultures and making them hetero-technological—is the key characteristic of globalization, be it of the economy or of the media of communication. Understood in this fashion, globalization is affecting all cultures—and all aspects of each culture. The totality of these effects, of course, varies from culture to culture, but today there is no culture that can claim to have remained untouched by the forces of globalization.

It is also wrong to think that the processes of attrition and addition kill a culture. A living culture continually renovates itself by discarding the obsolete and admitting the desirable—either invented within or innovated from abroad. Cultures that disallow such processes face the crisis of obsolescence and become moribund.

III

With these prefatory remarks, let me now turn to the question of language and the concern about the extinction of world's languages.

Let me first acknowledge the fact that human society has witnessed death or disappearance of several languages, and also birth of new languages. Many fear that of the 6000 and odd languages that are currently spoken in the world, several are likely to disappear in the next 20-25 years. In view of this impending tragedy, already an International Clearing House has been set up for the world's "Endangered Languages" (ICHEL in Tokyo). There is a UNESCO Red Book on Endangered Languages (published in December 1995). Several seminars and meetings have been held to discuss this problem. Not only this, a Foundation for Endangered Languages has been set up (visit the site: *www.orgmios.org)*. People are raising the question: Can the threatened Languages be saved?

The concern about language death has led linguists to compute the number of existing languages. Most of these figures are guesstimates, but the most reliable are the figures provided by *Ethnologue*, which attempted a world review of languages in 1974 and identified a total of 5,687 languages. This figure was later modified, in 1996, to 6,703 language headings. *The Atlas of the world's languages* lists 6,796 languages. To be sure, this number is far smaller than the number of languages spoken 10,000 years ago. According to Michael Krauss' calculation, assuming a world population of 5 to 10 million some 10,000 years ago, and an average community size of 500-1000, there were then about 5,000 to 20,000 languages. To make his estimates conservative, he reduced the figure to a median value of 12,000. And he predicts that "during the next 150 years it will decline to between something like 3,000, for the best scenario I can imagine, to about 300, a scenario I fear is more likely. One can visualize the language curve as the inverse of the population curve, the language curve now turning the corner to dive downward with but slight delay after the population curve turned the corner to shoot upward" (Krauss, 1998:105).

The language statistics reveal that 96 per cent of the currently live languages are spoken by only four per cent of the world's population, and 80 per cent of these languages are confined to single countries. Of the 6,000 languages, there are only 20 languages that have their speakers in millions and spread over in several countries. Given such a scenario, the fear is expressed that majority of the languages that have few speakers—and these languages have their high concentration in the Asia-Pacific region—are likely to disappear in the next century. UNESCO Courier of April 2000 has recounted the following forecasts made by the specialists:

- In Africa, more than 200 languages have fewer than 500 speakers each and may soon die out.
- In North America, the biggest threats are to indigenous and Creole languages. With the exception of Navajo, Cree and Ojibwa, the 200 Amerindian languages of USA and Canada are endangered.
- In Latin America, nearly 50 per cent of the 500 Amerindian languages are in danger.
- In Southeast Asia the future of 40 of the 600 to 700 languages depends on government policies. On the other hand, only six languages out of Northeast Asia's 47 have any real chance of survival in the face of the Russian.
- In Europe, of the 123 languages spoken, nine are nearly extinct, 26 are seriously endangered, and 38 are endangered.

According to Millennium Family Encyclopaedia (Dorling Kindersley, London 1997), half of the world uses in everyday life one of the planet's eight most widespread languages that includes Chinese (1.2 billion), English (478 million), Hindi (437 million), Spanish (392 million), Russian (284 million), Arabic (225 million), Portuguese (184 million), and French (125 million). If we were to combine the figures of those for whom a particular language is second language with the mother tongue statistics, then the figure for English goes up to 1000 million, and for Hindi-Urdu to 900 million, according to the estimates made by the Summer Institute of Linguistics (SIL).

The above statistics give a clear trend of an increasingly decreasing number of languages in daily use, and the spread of some of the major languages across countries. The concern for endangerment should be seen in this context. Taken objectively, one can argue that since the process of disappearance of languages that are spoken by less than 10,000 people is irreversible efforts should be made to "preserve" this heritage. But preservation need not be understood as promotion of the use of the language. To be sure, the linguists should take effective steps to develop a priority agenda, as the anthropologists did by developing what they called *Urgent Anthropology* in the 1960s. Realizing that they will not be able to stop the process of culture change among the tribal communities, the anthropologists stopped talking about the preservation of tribal cultures (to answer the critics that they do not want tribal communities to be the anthropological zoos) and focused on studying the "dying cultures" before they were dead. The project on the Endangered Languages should, in my view, be oriented to accomplish this task. The language of the unlettered dies with its last speaker and cannot be heard if it has not been recorded. Unlike prehistoric archeology, there cannot be a prehistoric linguistics in the sense that unwritten languages cannot be researched if their speakers are gone. An *Urgent Linguistics* is needed to record the languages that are at various stages of disappearance.[1]

But this is not the same thing as "saving the languages." What should be saved? What can be saved? How can we save? are different sets of questions. A scientist may be in a position to answer the last two questions in terms of available expertise, but the decision to save (or otherwise) is basically a question in the realm of values. Even when the client wants to save, the expert might express his inability to do so. Since the metaphor or death is being used in the context of endangered languages—language death, linguicide, language murder, language suicide etc.—the parallel can be drawn from the field of medicine. A dying patient is taken to the hospital because everyone wants the patient to be saved, but the doctor knows whether he/she can be saved depending on his diagnosis of the malady and the stage of body's deterioration. Even when the doctor shares the feeling of the client, he may be helpless in saving the hopeless cases. Similarly, a linguist with all his paraphernalia may be helpless in saving all the endangered languages; the question of giving a new lease of life to extinct languages is beyond the brief of a linguist. To use the medical simile, a linguist is like a physiologist or an anatomist, not a doctor!!

It is interesting to note that generally the outsiders raise the question of saving the tribal cultures or primitive languages. The points raised regarding the ill-effects of tourism on Bali and Thailand were raised mostly by the non-natives. The natives, in fact, wanted tourism to flourish as it gave them new avenues for economic activities. Not only this, some of the articulate members of these communities saw a sort of conspiracy in keeping them backward—"keeping them in a zoo"—and opposed vehemently all attempts to curb tourism. It is interesting that while the arrival of the tourists changed the economies of the visiting communities and also brought about changes in their world-views, such contacts also helped revive and rejuvenate native cultures. Marketing of cultures meant their continued existence and their spread in all corners of the world. Not only the Thais or the Balinese learnt the languages of the countries that sent tourists in large numbers, the tourists also picked up words and phrases of the indigenous languages, and took back souvenirs to adorn their drawing rooms and thus spread awareness about the distant cultures amongst their compatriots. True, that is museumization of their cultures, but museums do serve an important function.

We know that tourism cannot be curbed with revolutions in transportation technology, and we also know that tourist-native interactions mutually influence each other, and help in developing better appreciation of other cultures, so essential in the interdependent world being created by the forces of globalization.

I know that this Seminar is interested in examining the question of language in the specific context of globalization and revolution in the area of Information Technology. The allusion to the shrinking number of world languages should serve as a reminder that language death is an age-old phenomenon and is not all attributable to globalization trends of recent years. If, however, we regard the entire course of human history as a process of globalization then we can justly attribute death of languages to this process.

While we may acknowledge the fact of death of several cultures and their specific products over the years, there is enough evidence to suggest that the forces of modernization failed to homogenize the world. If at all, heterogeneity of the world has greatly enhanced. Earlier, the world was heterogeneous in the sense that it consisted of large number of *insulated* societies; in the modern context, each society has become a culture that has a mix of indigenous with the exogenous. Societies have become pluricultural, and people have become, at least bilingual. Increasingly, the mother-tongue statistics is becoming irrelevant; there are more speakers of a language than those who claim it to be their mother tongue, and there are many who are unable to speak their mother tongue with proficiency. It is important to collect statistics about the number of languages a given individual speaks rather than just enquiring about her or his mother tongue.

IV

Three features characterize the present phase of globalization: accelerated movement of men, messages, and materials across countires. The phenomenon of international migration has changed its character in terms of the size of the migrant population, sources of migration and the destinations. It is the migration to the North in large numbers from South that has altered the cultural composition of the receiving societies. They have now a sizable number of, what I call *Sandwich Cultures*—constituted by the people migrating from a common departure point and sandwiched between the twin pressures of the parent and host cultures. Rapid advances in information technology have changed the character of communication, allowing speedy and simultaneous relay of messages in several languages. And improved transportation has facilitated material transactions through improved import and export of goods.

Changes in the media culture are producing diverse effects. Mass media of the past, in the absence of radio, cinema, and later television, were the print media. To be exposed to them required literacy—understood in terms of three Rs—Reading, Writing, and Arithmetic. Spread of books and circulation of newspapers provided useful indices for assessing modernization, and diffusion of knowledge and information.

With the advance of literacy, what one notices today is the death of the newspaper and relative insignificance of the book. Literates have become new illiterates because of lack of *computeracy*. And illiterates have found different ways through which to acquire information without going through the ordeal of learning the alphabet.

The lessons of the modernization phase are quite instructive. The agents of modernization have resulted in several unanticipated consequences. For example, contrary to general expectation, mass media have served the function of reinforcing the tradition rather than eliminating it. The rise of religious fundamentalism, the assertion of cultural identity, popular appeal of the mythological serials, and use of chaste vernacular has increased over the years that experienced modernization. At one time, text-books on Mass Communication suggested that mass media "seek to reduce the variety of subcultures and help augment mass society". That people will more and more speak the same language, dress the same way, share the same values, and think and act the same way. In other words, mass media will generate a homogenized culture and impede cultural growth—almost the same premise that the organizers of this Seminar have adopted. With the availability of the various channels competing for audience attention, the monopoly of a single source has been threatened. In India, when STAR TV came with its canned programmes in English, it was thought that it would overwhelm all other channels. The fact of the matter is that it is the Star Channel that had to change its policy and introduce programmes in Hindi alongside of English. On the other hand,

ZEE TV of Indian origin is now being watched by large audiences in more than twenty countries. Not only NRIs (non-resident Indians), but also Pakistanis, Nepalese, and Bangladeshis settled in distant lands prefer to watch Zee TV shows in Hindi, Gujarati, Bengali, Marathi, and Tamil. Even Star TV is following suit to capture this vast Indian audience out of India. The multiplicity of media sources and plurality of audiences, and internationalization of communication have changed the scenario, and it will be too simplistic to lift older generalizations and describe the emerging reality that is very complex.

While it is true that English is spreading, with the increase in literacy rate and opening of the apertures to the wider world, this cannot be regarded as an "imposition"; nor can the use of English be regarded as replacement of the mother language. In fact, some scholars are worried about the changing character of English with the addition of its users from different linguistic groups as a second language. In India, for example, the new type of English that is becoming quite common is called *Hinglish*. You lift any English language newspaper and you will notice the many innovative ways in which the writers and the advertisers are freely fusing vernacular words—nouns and verbs—in their texts. Similarly, local languages are freely employing English words rather than bothering to find their equivalents in their own vocabulary, or creating new words. The French may insist in calling a computer *ordinateur*, but in India a computer is computer whether you write in roman or in *devnagri*. Of course, a Hindi equivalent of the computer (*Sanganak*) is coined but is not so much in use.

I recall my visit in 1973 to England to deliver the Mahatma Gandhi Memorial Lecture at the University of London. I received an invitation to speak at the University of Sussex to a group of trainees of the British Council ready to be sent to various Commonwealth countries as English tutors. I argued with them the need to appreciate the fact that more and more people are adopting English as a second language. This is because English is not as rigid as French in regard to grammar and idiomatic expressions. In fact, I said that rather than repairing their wrong English (from British standards) they should engage in preparing grammars of different versions of English as they are spoken (and written) in different countries. A language should be the slave of its speakers, not its master. When one looks at the evolution of different types of English in vogue one would reach the conclusion that such flexibility offered by English has helped it attain the status of a world language.

Commenting with grief on the English language getting "degraded", Sagarika Ghose says that the English language is more vulnerable to oversimplification and "brazen disregard for the rules of correct or expressive English". Her argument is that "although the 'chutney' languages fulfil an important role, they are as yet not developed enough to become an entire lexicon unto themselves". Her fear is that *chutneyfied* (also a coinage from India for a mixing to blur the identity of individual ingredients) phraseology is "hardly adequate and have the potential to trap users in intellectual sloth" (Ghose, 2001:21). To quote her further: "Today, to speak well might be regarded as 'pseudo', to use words other than monosyllabic rhetoric might be regarded as 'pretentious', and to express oneself with subtlety and nuance might invite the accusation of being old-fashioned. *'My papa loves to tango', let's boogie-woogie'*, and four letter words are bizarre in a context where the young appear to be earning the slang before they actually learn the language. Slang is only slang when there is a mother language to deviate from. But if slang becomes the only means of communication then complex thought might become impossible." Sagarika Ghose assigns "a fair share of blame" for the degradation of the English language to technology, "namely television, internet and the mobile telephone". She blames English language broadcasters, leading English dailies, glossy magazines, and the bureaucracy for contribution to a deadening of language. One may agree or disagree with Sagarika Ghose, her paper makes one point clear: the users of the English language in India, as an example, are taking liberties with it and changing its very texture. This point should alert us to the fact that such a situation is not possible when there is an imposition. The media of today have begun using the language of the street to be closer to the reality. In the Indian context what worries me is not the spread of Hinglish, but an overall decline in readership, more so in case of the prominent national language. It is significant to note that India had two very widely read Hindi weeklies—*Saptahik Hindustan* and *Dharmayug*—and an English Weekly (*Illustrated Weekly of India*) but somewhere in the mid-1970s (long before the talk of globalization) they stopped their publications. While substitutes for English came up, no weekly in Hindi of that reputation came to replace the old. This despite the fact that over the years literacy rate has touched the figure of 70s (for men; for women also it is around 65% according to the recent Census) and a large number of these literates are poor in their knowledge of English. Not only this, the print order for Hindi books in a country of now one billion people is as low as 500, half that of the English books. I regard this as an index of decline in reading, heralding the death of newspapers and books rather than the spread of an international language.

While discussing the Indian case, Sagarika Ghose alludes to an interesting publication by Morris Berman, titled *The Twilight of American Culture* in which the author makes a prophetic examination of western decline through a "dumbing down" process. The reference to that book is to indicate that the crisis is not only limited to the developing world. Berman has provided ample evidence of the collapse of American intelligence in his book. He makes the startling revelation that the number of people reading a daily newspaper in the US has halved since 1965. I am personal witness to the fact that many people do not even open the bulkier dailies and deposit them to the dustbin. For an outsider visiting that country, there is very little by way of news in them; the only purpose they serve is to tell the reader about the places where goods are on sale, or to compare prices. The news of the Royal massacre in Nepal was covered only in one issue of the *Time* magazine, and it was already stale when it came out. Subsequent editions did not follow the story. It appeared that the communication media in that country have insulated the people from the wider world whereas in the developing countries, such as India, the media have served the function of opening the apertures to expose people to the outside world and to broaden their cognitive horizons.

How insulated are the American children can be guessed from Berman's book? He quotes his experience at the Charter High School for Black Teenagers in Washington D.C.: "...some of them, at age sixteen or seventeen, had never heard of the Atlantic Ocean, did not know what 1999 meant, historically speaking, or thought the Civil War had taken place in the 1960s. One student thought that Washington, D.C. was in the Midwest, and was not able to locate New York, Florida, or Texas on a sketchy map." Berman does not regard this as mere "cultural deprivation; it is cultural massacre" (2000:11).

To further cement his argument, quoting other sources, he reports that:

- Forty-two per cent of American adults cannot locate Japan on a world map, and according to Garrison Keillor (National Public Ratio, 22 March 1996), another survey revealed that nearly 15 per cent couldn't locate the United States!
- A survey taken in the October 1996 revealed that one in ten voters did not know who the Republican or Democratic nominees for President were.
- 1995 article in the *New York Times* reported a survey result that said "40 per cent of American adults (this could be upward of 70 million people) did not know that Germany was our enemy in World War II." A Roper survey (1996): 84 per cent of American college seniors couldn't say who was President at the start of the Korean War (Harry Truman). Fifty-eight per cent of American high school seniors cannot understand a newspaper editorial in *any* newspaper, and a US Department of Education survey of 22,000 students in 1995 revealed that 50 per cent were unaware of the Cold War, and that 60 per cent had no idea of how the United States came into existence. (*Ibid.*, 34-35).

He feels that all this is an evidence of "steady lobotomizing' of American culture.

Such lobotomization, making people sluggish seems to be a real danger not only for American culture but everywhere. Recently, in 12 August 2001 issue of *Times of India* reported on its front page some of the answers given by "men and women armed with postgraduate degrees" who appeared for interview for the job of teachers in government schools in Madhya Pradesh. The Paper said that "General Knowledge is not that general" as is clear from the answers to simple questions relative to their own state and district. Here is the sample :

Q: Who is the President of India?

A: Digvijay Singh (who is the Chief Minister of the State)

Q: Name some of the major rivers of Madhya Pradesh.

A: Kshipra, Chambal, hmm, maybe even Vidhyachal (the last is a mountain, and the suffix Achal means in Hindi a mountain).

Q: Where is Madhya Pradesh?

A: Er..... I think in Bhopal (which is the capital of Madhya Pradesh).

Q: Who is the District Collector of Indore? (Indore is the city where interviews were held)

A: Someone whose name sounds like a film star's. I think it is Suleman Khan. (The actual name is Mohammed Suleman)

The point that both the stories make is that there seems to be global trend of dumbing down, exposing low levels of intelligence quotients. Citing titles such as Lewis Lapham's Waiting *for the Barbarians* or Robert Kaplan's *An Empire Wilderness* Berman remarks: "the documentation that they provide—of crumbling school systems and widespread functional illiteracy, of violent crime and gross economic inequality, of apathy, cynicism, and what might be called 'spiritual death'—is quite overwhelming... [The] system has lost its moorings, and, like ancient Rome, is drifting into an increasingly dysfunctional situation" (*Ibid*: 2). This phase has been called by political scientist Benjamin Barber as "McWorld"—commercial corporate consumerism for its own sake. "Check out any TV ad for Nike or Pepsi and you'll see that McWorld has tremendous vitality; it appears energetic and upbeat. The problem is that since this vitality celebrates nothing substantive beyond buying and owning things, it itself is the cultural decline... The United States, as Robert Kaplan suggests, is evolving into a corporate oligarchy that merely wears the trappings of a democracy" (*Ibid*: 3).

The above formulations appear familiar to an analyst of development focusing on the developing countries. But that these relate to the world's number one democracy, and a highly developed society make one realize that the problem is global, experienced by both the South and the North. In fact, the World Summit for Social Development that took place in Copenhagen in 1995 brought home the point that deficit in social development is worldwide and that it has occurred despite progress made on the economic front. Poverty, unemployment, and other indicators of social disintegration are commonly shared problems. What the Summit, however, emphasized was the point that these common problems do not have common solutions. Solutions will have to be found differently for different cultural contexts.

It may be recalled that the students of industrialization and modernization believed that these processes would lead to a certain homogenization of cultures killing their heterogeneity. Five decades later, when we now review the achievements of the past development decades we notice that the one world we live in consists of many voices. That cultures have shown their remarkable resilience is the fact of change. They have changed through adoption and adaptation of several traits and practices that arrived through diffusion from other cultures—both proximate and remote—and yet they have survived the onslaught of domineering cultures by not only maintaining but also asserting their individual identities. Modernity did not kill all the traditions; societies developed a veritable symbiosis of tradition and modernity. The emerging profile is a changed profile and the twin processes of attrition and accretion are causing change. The interesting part is that change is now recognized as a universal phenomenon, and certain kinds of change brought out by rapid advances in technology, particularly in IT, are simultaneously affecting all societies. The crises created by these changes are making all societies cautious of the danger of degeneration of their cultures, and all are exhibiting concerns to prevent the ill-effects of growing consumerism and decline on the intellectual front.

When the West, or the North itself is confronting the crisis of arriving twilight, *a la* Berman, it cannot serve as a reference group for the rest of the world. We today live in a world of multiple apertures. But these openings have not demolished the walls of our individual cultures; only that they have been painted differently making them multicoloured. As long as there are walls, and a defined territory, cultures will have their identities. Globalization has meant the arrival of the globe in each individual culture and the presence of each culture in an interactive mode in the globe as a whole. There is globe in India, and India in the globe. Such a scenario defies any imposition, but anticipates radical transformation of societies and cultures. What is needed is effective management of such a transformation, rather than futile attempts to halt it.

ENDNOTES

1. David Crystal (2000:20) has given the classification of languages provided by Kincade (1991:160-3) and Wurm (1998:192). According to Kincade languages can be classified into five categories:

- Viable languages: have population based that are sufficiently large and thriving to mean that no threat to long-term survival is likely;
- Viable but small languages: have more than 1,000 speakers, and are spoken in communities that are isolated or with a strong internal organization, and aware of the way their language is a marker of identity;
- Endangered languages: are spoken by enough people to make survival a possibility, but only in favourable circumstances and with a growth in community support;
- Nearly extinct languages: are thought to be beyond the possibility of survival, usually because they are spoken by just a few elderly people;
- Extinct languages: are those where the last fluent speaker has died, and there is no sign of any revival.

Wurm has further refined the concept of endangered languages by distinguishing between potentially endangered, endangered, seriously endangered, moribund, and extinct languages.

REFERENCES

Atal, Yogesh (1993) *Asian Cultures : What Destination?* in The Future of Asian Cultures (ed. Yogesh Atal and E. Masini), UNESCO, Bangkok.

Berman, Morris (2000), *The Twilight of American Culture.* New York, W.W. Norton & Co.

Crystal, David (2000), *Language Death.* Cambridge, Cambridge University Press.

Delanty, Gerard (2000), *Modernity and Postmodernity,* New Delhi, Sage Publications.

Ghose, Sagarika (2001), *Degraded Language.* Seminar 501: Culturescape, May Issue. New Delhi

Grenoble, Lenore A. and Lindsay I. Whaley (eds.) (1998), *Endangered Languages: Current issues and future prospects.* Cambridge, Cambridge University Press.

Kincade, M. Dale (1991), *The decline of native languages in Canada,* in R.H. Robins and E.M. Uhlenbeck (eds.) *Endangered Languages.* Oxford and New York, Berg

Krauss, Michael (1998), *The scope of the Language Endangerment Crisis and Recent Response to it,* in Studies in Endangered Languages (ed. Kazuto Matsumura), ICHEL Linguistic Studies Vol. 1, Tokyo, Hituzi Syobo.

Linton, Ralph (1937), *One Hundred Per cent American,* in the American Century, Vol. 40

Matsumura, Kazuto (ed) (1998), *Studies in Endangered Languages,* ICHEL Linguistic Studies Vol. 1, Tokyo, Hituzi Syobo.

Nettle, Daniel and Suzanne Romaine (2000), *Vanishing Voices: The extinction of the World's Languages.* Yew York, Oxford University Press.

Robins, R.H. and E.M. Uhlenbeck (eds.) (1991), *Endangered Languages.* Oxford and New York, Berg

Wurm, Stephen A. (1998), *Methods of language maintenance and revival, with selected cases of language endangerment in the world,* in Matsumura (ed.).

11

The Rural Scene

KRIPA SHANKAR

Rural India is in distress. Introduction of new agricultural technology resulted in a growth process which has petered out. Per capita foodgrains production is falling. Per capita sown area is now 0.13 ha and yield is stagnating. Bulk of rural population is condemned to live in poverty. According to NSS report on Income, Expenditure and Productive Assets of Farmer Households, 2003 there are roughly 90 million farmer households in the country and the total annual income from all sources per farmer is Rs. 25,380.00. The picture is summarized below:

Table 11.1: Average net income per farmer per annum from cultivation and from all sources for different sizes of holding

Size of holding (ha)	*Net Income for Cultivation*	*Net Income from all Sources*	*Annual Consumption Exp.*
< 0.0	132	16,560	27,564
0.01-0.40	3,552	19,596	28,680
0.41-1.00	9,408	21,708	32,064
1.01-2.00	18,936	29,916	37,776
2.01-4.00	32,220	43,068	44,220
4.01-10.00	56,112	68,172	55,512
>10.00	99,852	1,16,004	77,016
All Sizes	11,628	25,380	33,240

Cultivation has become unremunerative as 80 per cent of the farmers having less than 1 ha. have an average annual income of Rs. 5,000.00. They survive by undertaking animal husbandry and wage labour but cultivation by itself is not viable as they live below the poverty line.

This shows the enormity of unemployment and under-employment and surplus manpower in rural areas. The inability of the system to gainfully employ this vast manpower explains the factor behind overendemic poverty and backwardness. More intensive agriculture can no doubt absorb a part of this surplus labour but the basic question is to create gainful employment opportunities for the vast landless and marginal farmers outside crop production syndrome. Obviously, it requires very massive resource mobilisation to increase public investment in those activates which are highly labour intensive and equally productive. Now what are the areas where jobs can be created without much investment which are simultaneously highly productive? One such area is rejuvenation and conservation of natural resources. Our land and water resources are not being optionally utilized. The degraded land in the country is about 340 lakh hectare. Roughly 150 lakh hectare is cultivable wasteland. Another 10 lakh hectare is permanent fallow while current fallow land is roughly 140 lakh hectare. Net area sown in the country is stagnating at 142 million hectare. This is the consequence of a highly unskewed distribution of land where top landowners have no imperative to put all their land under the plough and neither have any imperative to make any investment in regenerating the degraded land. In a situation where there is vast-landlessness as nearly 70 per cent of agricultural workers are either landless or own holdings of less than 0.4 hectare, all culturable waste and permanent fallow land totalling about 160 lakh land should be acquired at market prices which subsequently can be sold/leased out or distributed among poorest households who because of their larger family labour, can make productive use of the land. The more inferior part of such land can be fruitfully planted with trees and shrubs to increase fodder and fuel supply. The worst part can be converted into ponds and other natural bodies to augment irrigation facility.

Irrigation is *sine qua non* for any growth in rural area. As rainfall is concentrated in less than 10 weeks and it generally rains in torrents washing away the top fertile soil and also causing floods in many areas, rainwater conservation holds the key for rural resurgence in the first instance. On account of overexploitation of ground water, the ground water table is falling at an alarming rate and 15 per cent of the blocks have gone 'dark'. The remedy lies in conserving rain water at the village land through contour bonding, check dams, gully, plugging, construction of tanks, ponds and other water-bodies, construction of dug wells etc, on a war footing. Gram Panchayats have to undertake this activity, which will also provide vast job opportunities within the rural areas itself. But Panchayats get very insignificant grant and the programme goes by default. This will be a very cheap and assured means of irrigation with very little operational cost where farmers will not have to depend on an outside agency for water which may not be available when it is required most.[1] It costs the Government Rs. 10,000 to irrigate one hectare of land while irrigation cost from water storages may cost less than Rs. 1,000 per ha. The current year's central budget has provided Rs. 10,000 crore to watershed development out of a total budgetary expenditure of Rs. 7 lakh crore. This shows the apathy of Government to increase irrigation facilities. Irrigated area in the country is stagnating around 550 lakh hectares and only watershed development can be effective in this direction. The Budget for rural development in the current year is Rs. 28,000 crore and another Rs. 1,500 crore has been allotted for land resources out of which only Rs. 1,000 crore has been provided for integrated watershed development programme. As a matter of fact latter should form the core activity under rural development. Various rural employment programmes should also be dovetailed towards it as it is no less employment generating than say, construction of rural roads. Central Government expenditure on irrigation in current years Budget is Rs. 872 crore which constitutes 0.1 per cent of the total budgetary expenditure. State governments spend larger amount on irrigation but their resources are quite limited. This does not auger well for agricultural growth.

It is through price mechanism that peasantry is exploited as the price of their commodities is fixed not by the farmers but is manipulated by traders. There is no storage network for them to store their produce and they have no alternative but to sell the product immediately after the harvest at a price which may not cover even the cost of production. Had there been a network of co-operative marketing societies with their own godowns they could store their produce in such godowns, could get advance from the banks on the hypothecation of their produce to meet their immediate requirements and thus it would obviate the necessity to sell to the trader immediately after the harvest. The ruling urban bourgeoisie would not countenance such a situation as it wants to be readily party to finance urban-industrial growth which can be ensured if agricultural process remains subsumed. This will also put down wage cost to make industrial goods competitive in a globalizing world.

Thus, callousness towards the agricultural sector is distressingly visible in the context of farmers' suicide because of their inability to replay the debts due to crop failure. A comprehensive crop insurance scheme with a very nominal premium could have obviated these suicides which have crossed a figure of Rs. 1 lakh during the last 10 years. Every four-wheeler in the country is insured but not agricultural crops. A highly subsidised crop insurance scheme should be launched. The subsidy enjoyed by car owners in the country is over Rs. 10,000 crore. One should not grudge if peasant producer is also subsidised through very cheap crop insurance as bulk of farmers are dissavers. This is equally true about making bank funds available to them for making producer investments as well as to meet medical and educational expenses. The credit deposit ratio of rural bank branches is 44 per cent and over Rs. 1,00,000 crores is siphoned off from rural banks to metropolitan centres. Likewise, the outflow from semi-urban branches is Rs. 1,70,000. These funds are not utilised in the rural and semi-urban centres because to get bank loan is not hassle free. The poor cannot provide surety nor collateral. All loans to farmers should be provided at a rate of interest of a per cent as recommended by Swaminathan Committee. The loss to banks should be reimbursed by way of interest subsidy. Assuming the difference at 10 per cent, an interest subsidy of Rs. 5,000 crore can lead to a flow of additional Rs. 50,000 crores to rural households. This amount is only one twentieth of what goes to relatively better off sections by way of petroleum and electricity subsidy. The Government can guarantee such loan as is the case with many huge loans to various entities.

Developmental process has not led to any significant diversification of the economy. According to NSS report, organised sector employment in India was 33.7 million in 1999-2000 which marginally deduced to 33.4 million in 2004-05. Unorganised employment increased from 341.5 million to 393.5 million during the same period. Employment growth rate in agriculture decelerated sharply from 1.4 per cent during 1983/1993-94 to 0.8 per cent during 1993-94/2004-05. The fact that at the present rate of investment, organised employment is not increasing and employment growth rate in agriculture is falling suggests that what the country needs is a very massive increase in investment to provide jobs within the rural sector as well as outside the agricultural sector. This calls for massive resource mobilization on the part of Government and no less important, in its productive utilization. Saving and investment have likewise to be raised by cutting ostentatious and wasteful expenditure. The tax-GDP ratio in India at 11 per cent is lowest in the world except a few small unimportant countries. In USA, it is twice and in many European countries it is thrice that of India. In India not only taxation rate is low but on account of various exemptions the effective tax rate is considerably lower. According to the *Receipt Budget* 2007-08, the revenue foregone through these exemptions amounted to Rs. 2,06,700 crore in 2005-06 and Rs. 2,35,191 crore in 2006-07. If these exemptions are withdrawn, Central Government expenditure on agriculture and allied activities, irrigation, rural employment and rural development as power can be raised four-fold.

No less important is the issue of popular participation, control, transparency and accountability of what is being spent. There are vast leakages as the colonial bureaucracy has absolute power over execution with absolutely no popular control, transparency and accountability. The 73rd amendment of the constitution pledges that all developmental activities at the village level will be executed by the village Panchayat which will "function as local institutions of self-government" but the nexus of political leadership and bureaucracy is so entrenched that it cannot countenance any devolution of power to the local institution as it will herald the beginning of loss of power on their part. The Central and State Governments annual expenditure is roughly Rs. 15,000 per capita but if it is not reflected in living condition of vast masses it is precisely because of largely the unproductive use of the resource which goes to enrich a small coterie at the top.

END NOTE

1. Water from state irrigation sources is generally not available in peak days. Where available the poor are at the receiving end.

Index

Accountability, 26, 257
Acculturation, 19-20, 82-85, 105-06
  attitude scale, 89-90, 96
  course of, 94
  groups, 85
  mean scores in, 91-92
  modes of, 85
Adivasis, 66, 121-22, 133-35, 168, 178-79
Administrative classification, 28-29
Advanced communication, 234-35
Agarwal, G., 36
Agra Tenancy Act, 65
Agrarian changes, debates on, 57-58
  internal dynamics of, 54-55
Agrarian reforms, 65
Agrarian structure, classification of, 61-62
Agribusiness companies, 70
Agricultural crops, protection of, 33-35
Agricultural labourers, 58-62, 164-65
  commodification of, 77
Agricultural landholdings, 166-67
Agricultural production, 72, 75-76, 130-32, 149-50
Agriculture, 31-32, 130-32
  development of, 55-56
  growth performance, 71-74
Ajnana, 219
Akhara bandhna, 109-10
Alfred, Mahan, 19
Allauddin Khilji, 48
Almayajna, 14
Ambedkar, B.R., 225
American culture, 19-20, 248-49
  identity of, 231
Amerindian languages, 239
Andhra Pradesh, 35
Anganwadi workers, 128
Ani-e-Akbari, 48
Animal sacrifice, 142
Animal husbandry, 253
Anthropology, development of, 232
Antyodaya schemes, 126
Apaulistic life, 216
Aristotle, 203, 216
Artha (resources), 13
Assets, types of, 168-69
Assimilation, 83-86
  scores of, 94-95
Astronomy, 208
Atal, Yogesh, 25, 231, 236
Atlantic Ocean, 247
Atharva Veda, 17

Baiga Dongri, 121
Baigapada village, 24, 118-145
  agriculture of, 130-31
  caste characteristics of, 121-22
  culture of, 132-37
  housing patterns, 136-37
  liberalised economy, 120, 130-32
  political economy of, 134
  school education of, 128-29
  settlement pattern, 121-22
  zamindari system, 122-23
Bailly Astronomer, 208
Bangladesh, 159
Barber, Benjamin, 248
Beenapani Yuvaka Sangha, 130

Bentinck, William, 210
Berman, Morris, 246
Berry, J.W., 83, 84, 88-90, 93-95
Bhaganpur village, caste-cum tribe composition of, 162-63
infrastructural facilities, 179-80
living condition of people, 148-50, 162-63, 178-80
residential houses, types of, 170-71
Bhatt, K.N., 25, 183
Bhaichara land, 65
Bhumidar, 66, 163
Brahmins, 163
Breman, J., 55
British rule, 221
Byres, T.J., 54

Capitalism, 59, 234
Capitalist mode of production, identification of, 58-60
Cash crop growing area, 60-61
Caste based discrimination, 194
Caste hierarchy, 99-100, 149-55, 158
Caste settlement, age groups of, 99-100
Caste structure, 50
Challenges, 82
Chamaraundha, 112
Chandauli, villagers of Naugarh region, 81-96
Changing Indian Agrarian village economy, 53-60
Chaturvarnya Vyavastha, 219-20
Chauhan, Brij Raj, 23, 40
Chemical fertilizer, 69-72
Chandogya Upanishad, 219
Chattopadhyaya, Bankin Chandra, 211
Christian rulers, 205, 209
Christian World View, 18
Christianity, 19-20, 209-10
Civilization entities, 14, 20
Clans, 42-43
Class formation, problems of, 60-61
Clustered villages, 30
Cohn, Bernard S., 43
Colonial bureaucracy, 26, 203
Colonization, 203, 236-37
Collective action, theory of, 27-30, 32-34
Common land, 28
Commercial activities, 180
Commercialization, 77, 105
Commonwealth countries, 244
Common Property Resources, 32-34
Community and social organization, 36
Communication, internationalization of, 244
Congress Agrarian Reform Committee, 65
Consumer durable items, 176-78
Consumerism, 26, 135-36
Constraints, 62
Contact acculturation, 89-92
Contact farming, 59, 70
Cooley, Charles H., 40
Coomaraswamy, 220
Cooperative market societies, 255
Co-parcenary communities, 203
Corporate Bodies, 71
Corporate farming, 77
Corruption, proportion of, 135
Cosmion functions, 216
Cosmos, natural dimensions of, 12-15
Cost sharing, 67-70
Creole languages, 239
Crop insurance, 255
Cropping pattern, 67-68, 71-72
Cultural artifacts, 98, 116
Cultural existence, 157-58
Cultural homogeneity, 117
Cultural deprivation, 247
Cultural transformation, 20

Dalits, 129-30, 142-44
Dasgupta, B., 148, 155
Data collection, 195
Decentralization, 23
Decision-making arrangement, 33
Deforestation, 139

Degraded forest area, 35
Degraded land, 253-54
Demolition of temples, 48
Demonstration, 13, 50-51
Developing countries, 207
Development programmes, implementation of, 27-29
Dharma (religion), 13, 21
Dharma-Tantra, 220
Dharmayuga, 246
Dispersed type villages, 31
Distinction between Being and Becoming, 12
Division of labour, 154-55
Diwakar, D.M., 23, 53
Domestic animals, 168
Domestic corporate sectors, 71
Dominant castes, 152
Dow, Alexander, 208
Duffy, Alexander, 210

East India Company, 57
Eco-development programmes, 34
Economic exchange, 155
Economic exploitation, 20-21
Economic parameters, 160
Economic prosperity, 186
Emerging relations, 75-76
Employment, 69-70
  growth of, 256
  opportunity, 253
Endangered languages, 238-42
English education, 212, 222
Ethnologue, 238
European intelligentia, 209
Exogamous units, 42, 45

Factionalism, 144, 186
Farm revenue system, 65
Farmer's suicide, 255
Female illiteracy, 163, 179-80
Festivals, 139-42
First War of Independence, caste and clans in, 49-52
Five Year Plans, 83
Fixed produce tenancy, 67
Food for-work programmes, 134
Foodgrian production, 73-75
Forest Development and Conservation, 34-36
Forest reservation laws, 131
Forest Valley, 29
Fragmentation, 213
Free grants lands, 65
Fuller, C.J., 152-53
5-Point scale, agreement of, 90

Ganga river, 47, 99
Gauntia, economic condition of, 126
Geertz, Clifford, 53
Ghar Jamai, 44
Ghose, Sagarika, 245
Gift of furtune, 46
Gini coefficient, 64
Globalization, 25, 231-36
Gods and Goddesses, 142
Gram Panchayats, 192, 254-55
Gramya Sadak Yojana, 137
Gram Vriddha, 149
Green Agro Pack, 71
Green revolution, 57, 75, 138
Gujar clans, 44-46

Habitation areas, 31, 36
Hamleted villages, 32
Hastinapur, 48
Hierarchical ordering, 203
High Yielding Varieties (HYV), 72
Hinduization, 143
Holi-Milan Samaroh, 115
Holwell, John, 208
Homogenization, 21-22, 105, 201, 235, 249
Horticulture, 31
Households, agricultural landholding, 166-68
  castes and income, 164-65
  drinking water facilities for, 175
  productive assets of, 168-69
  residential landholdings of, 165-66

Huzoor (Tehsil land), 65
Hybrid paddies, 137
Hybridity, 235

Illiteracy, 179-80
Imperialism, 232
Indian caste hierarchy, 99
Indian villages, characterisation of, 185-86
 classification of, 200
 rethinking of, 223-25
Indira Awaas Yojana (IAY), 126
Individual connectedness, 90-91, 156
Indophobia, 209-10
Industrialization, 18, 55, 183, 249
Information technology, 241-42
Infrastructure facilities, 72
Input sharing, 69-70
Integrated Watershed Development Programme, 254
Inter-caste relations, 50, 151
International Clearing House, 238
International languages, 246
International migration, 237, 242
Irrigation facilities, 131, 254-55
 intensity, 70-71
 management system, 28, 34
Isolated homestead village, 30

Jaer, Oyvind, 155
Jagir, 45
Jail Bharo Andolan, 50
Jajmani system, 150-51, 154
James Mill, 209, 210
Janapada (human settlement), 149
Japan, 22
Jat clans, 46, 49-51
Jat *Zamindars*, 49
Jazia, taxation of, 48
Jawaharlal Nehru University, 129
Jharkhand, 87
Joint families, 42
Joint Forest Management (JFM), 34
 implementation of, 35
Judeo-Christian chronology, 209

Kalahandi, 119, 122-24, 130-33, 144-45
 advasi community in, 123-24, 133
 land rights in, 123-24
Kalahandi-Bolangir and Koraput Project, 134
Kama (desire), 13
Kamachar, 219
Kaplan, Robert, 248, 249
Karnataka, 35
Kashmiri Muslims, 151
Kashmiri Pandits, 151
Khalsa (crown land), 65
Khandan, 42
Kharwar community, 81-82, 86-87, 93-94
 economy of, 86-88
Khubars, 43
Kinship pattern, 185
 terminology, 42, 186
Kisan Union, 50
Kolkata, 158-59
Kolenda, Pauline, 42
Koshal movement, 141
Krauss, Michael, 238
Kripa Shankar, 26

Lambert, Helen, 151
Land distribution, 62-63
 inequality of, 155-56
Land resources, 31-32
Land reforms, 63, 76-78
Land settlement, types of, 203-04
Land tenure system, 65-66
Land-holdings, fragmentation of, 63
Landlord capitalism, 54
Languages, 91-93, 141-42, 207-10, 238-40
Lessees, 69-70
Liberalization, 120, 130-32, 234
Liberalization, Privatization and Globalization (LPG), 145
Linear villages, 30
Linkage between education and development, 187
Linton, Ralph, 231

Literacy rate, 193
Loans to farmers, 256

Madan, T.N., 151, 186
Madhya Pradesh, 35
Mahalbari, 57
Mahatma Gandhi, 20, 21, 219
Majumdar, Bhaskar, 25, 148, 183
Management system, 28, 34-35
Manifestation, 157, 205, 223
Mapping cultures, 24-25, 98-116
Marginalization, 84, 93-95
Marriage alliances, 43, 140
Marriott, M., 186
Marx, K., 16, 55
Mass Communication, 243
Massive cluster, 37
Matsyanyaya, 202
Max Muller, 209
Mayer, Adrain, 42
Medicinal herbs and plants, 7, 131
Meerut, 46
  birth and death rates, 193-94
  population of, 192
Microcosm, 214-15
Microcosmic villages, 53
Migration, 131, 184
  sources of, 242
Mishra, G.P., 63
Mishra, R.C., 24, 81, 84, 85
Modern capital goods, utilisation of, 58
Modern technological improvement, 75, 234
Modern World View, 15, 18
Modernization, 98, 99, 137, 139, 184, 224, 236, 241-42
  traditions of, 82
Moksha (release), 13
Moral obligations, 42
Moral sensibilities, 202
Mosaic system, 209
Multicultural societies, 94
Multiculturalism, 237
Multinational companies, 60, 71
Murdoch, Iris, 224
Muslim rule, 221
Mutiny of 1857, 49

National afforestation programmes, 34
Natural resources, 28
  management programmes, 34-38
Naugarh region, villages of, 81-90
Nehru, Jawaharlal, 132, 225
Net Sown Area, (NSA), 71
New economic policy, 135
New technology, 57
Non-food crops, growth rates, 74-75
Non-Government Organizations (NGOs), 125

Objects of labour, 56
Objective changes, 86
Obligations, 43-44
Occupational structure, 183-84
Old Testament, 208
Operational holdings, distribution of, 63-64
Orientalism, 207, 213
Ornaments of women, 103-05
Ostrom, F., 33
Oudh, land tenure system, 65
Outdated technology, 54
Output sharing, 69-70
Oxfam-centad, 71

Pahalwan Baba, 109-10
Panchayati Raj Institutions (PRIs), 29, 39, 189
Pande, G.C., 217, 218
Pandey, Amitabha, 13, 27
Parochialization, 53
Participatory Rural Appraisal (PRA), 39
Pastoral community, 30
Patnaik, U., 57, 58, 60, 75
Patron-clint relationship, 150
Peasant capitalism, 54
Permanent settlement, 57, 65, 123
Plato, 12, 16, 17, 215

Pollution, 150
Post-green revolution, 71
Poverty, 249-50
Powell, Badan, 43
Power hierarchy, 221
Power structure, 186
Prithvi Raj, 47
Private agricultural land, 28
Private educational institutions, 194
Pross of change, trends and debates of, 54-57
Production, strategy of, 55-56, 168-69
Protecting against inequalities, 30
Psychological acculturation, 82
Public distribution system, 161, 175-76
Pulses cultivation, 130
  variables of, 138-39
Punjab agriculture, 58
Purda system, 128
Purushartha, 13, 219, 220
Push and pull factors, 159

Raj Kumar, 24, 118
Rajasthan, 36, 45-48
Raja Bhoj, 47
Rajput clans, 45-48
Rajiv Gandhi, 135
Ram temple movement, 143
Ramachandran, H., 150, 156
Rangarajan, L.R., 149
Ration cards, 175
Rebirth cycle, 13
Reservation of seats, 50-52
Residential houses, 170-71,
  fuel and cooking in, 174-75
Residential land ownership, 165-66
Resource management schemes, 27
Rethinking, process of, 23
Rethinking villages, 199-220, 223-25
Revenue farming, 57
Revenue villages, 29
Reverse tenancy, 67
Revolutionary continuity, 225
Rig Veda, 14, 16
Ritual obligations, 44
Rousseau, 19
Roy, Ramashray, 25, 199
Rudra, A., 57, 58
Rural development, define villages, 32-33, 37-38
  programmes, 27
Rural employment programmes, 254
Ryotbari, 57
Ryotwari Act, 123

Saharanpur, 46-48
Said, Edward, 207, 208
Saman-chittata, 217
Sandwich Cultures, 242
Sanskaras, 217
Sanskritization, 157-58
Scheler, Max, 201, 202, 216
Scheduled caste and Scheduled tribes, 83
School education, beneficiaries of, 127-29
Second World War, 20, 208, 247
Segregation, 84
Selfish motivation, 224
Self-Help Groups (SHGs), 36
Sen Committee Report, 62
Sen, Keshabchandra, 211
Settled people, living condition of, 161
Settlement pattern, 121-22
Shahabpur village, 24-25, 99-116
  castes of, 99-100
  cultural performance, 111-15
  dresses of, 101-02
  festival celebrating, 115-16
  housing : then and now, 107-08
  male ornaments, 106-07
  mapping culture of, 99-116
  musicial instruments of, 108-09
  village community in, 24-25
Shankar, Kripa, 252
Sharecropping, 66-69
Shifting cultivation, 37
Social interaction, 41
Socio-political system, 16
Solomon, Robert, 11, 19, 205
Spiritual dimensions, 14
Spiritual realism, 201, 203
Srinivas, M.N., 118, 150, 152, 155

Srivastava, R., 64, 65, 74, 75
Stakeholders, 37
Star Channels, 243
Sub-urban areas, 160
Swaminathan Committee, 256
SWOT analysis, variables of, 191-92

Tagore Rabindranath, 21, 222
Taluqdari, tenurial system, 65
Tenancy Reforms, 65-66
Tenancy relations, new forms of, 70-71
Tenurial system, type of, 66-67
Terms of tenancy, 66
Thapar, Romila, 43
Tikait, Mahindra Singh, 50
Tiwari, B.N., 24, 25, 98
Totemism, 142
Tourism, 241
Tractorisation, 71
Traditional cultures, 13-15, 45-46, 232
Traditional marriages, 186
Traditions-beliefs-custom immobility, 153
Transcandental egoism, 205-06
Transparency, 26, 257

Umran, 123
Unemployment, 249, 253
Universal ego, 11, 19, 205
Universalization, 53
Unorganised employment, 256
Urban migration, 153
Urbanization, 137, 139
Urbanised societies, 22
User Group, 36
Uttar Pradesh, 41
  administrative regions in, 187
  agrarian structure in, 62-63
  agriculture NSDP of, 73, 78
  emerging relations, 75-76
  land redistribution of, 64-65
  sample villages, 68
Utilitarians, 210-11

Vana Sanrakshana Samiti (VSS), 36
Variables, 189-90
Vegetables, varieties, 138
Viceroy Northbrooke, 211
Vidyarthi, L.P., 32
Village acculturation scale, 88-92
Village classification, 32-33
Village Council, 152
Village Forest Development Committee (VFDC), 35
Village life, characterization of, 200
Village Panchayat, 257
Village projected programmes, 27
Village selection, investigation of, 188-89
Village social accommodation, 156
Villagers, dress patterns of, 140
Vitoria Fransisco, 205
Vivekananda, 212
Voegetin, Eric, 20, 215

Watershed development, 254
  programmes of, 34-36
Water resources, 28
Water supply programmes, 34
Western health system, 9
Westernization, 18-21
Whiteman's Burden, 11, 20, 205, 206
Widow remarriages, 44
William, Raymond, 136
Wolf, Eric, 53
Work participation rate, 194
World revolution, 20
World Wide Fund for Nature, 2

Xynon, 217, 218

Yadav castes, 121-22
Yadava Gauntia, 124
Yajna (sacrifice), 220
Yamuna river, 47
Yatharthala, 220
Yuga-Shakti Gayatri, 143

Zamindars, 57, 65
Zamindari Abolition Act (ZAA), 66
Zamindari system, 122-25
  abolition of, 57, 62
Zoo, 232